# LOSS OF CONFIDENCE

Issues in Policy History
General Editor: Donald T. Critchlow

# LOSS OF
# CONFIDENCE

Politics and Policy
in the 1970s

Edited by
David Brian Robertson

The Pennsylvania State University Press
University Park, Pennsylvania

This work was originally published as a special issue of *Journal of Policy History* (vol. 10, no. 1, 1998). This is its first separate paperback publication.

Production of this volume was cosponsored by the Division of United States Studies, Woodrow Wilson International Center for Scholars.

Library of Congress Cataloging-in-Publication Data

Loss of confidence : politics and policy in the 1970s
    / edited by David Brian Robertson
          p.       cm.
    Includes bibliographical references (p.      ).
    ISBN 0-271-01845-3 (pbk. : alk. paper)
    1. Policy sciences—United States—History.   2. United States
—Politics and government—1969-1974.   3. United States —Politics and
government—1974-1977.   4. United States—Politics and government—
1977-1981.   I. Robertson, David Brian, 1951-.   II. Series
H97.L67 1998
320.973'09'047—dc21

                                                98-26747
                                                CIP

Published by The Pennsylvania State University Press,
University Park, PA   16802-1003

# Contents

# Editor's Note

The decade of the 1970s, as David Robertson aptly observes in his introduction to this volume, offered profound disillusionment within the polity accompanied by significant policy change. The loss of confidence in American political and economic institutions became increasingly apparent as the nation experienced political scandal in the White House, unabated inflation and high unemployment, oil shortages, and a sense that the nation had lost its moral bearings. Although Richard Nixon easily won reelection in 1972, he was forced to resign from office following the Watergate scandal. His successors to the presidency, Gerald Ford and Jimmy Carter, failed to win public confidence. By 1980 many Americans believed that the "American century"—the promise of continued American prosperity and international leadership—had ended in dismal failure.

Nonetheless, even in the midst of this disappointment, important policy changes occurred that revealed the vitality of American democracy. Minorities, women, environmentalists, and consumers gained new access to power both in national politics and the private sector. Proposals for economic deregulation, welfare reform, controlling budget deficits, military downsizing, and returning power to state governments gained in currency and provided the foundation for subsequent policy changes that occurred in the subsequent two decades of the 1980s and 1990s.

This volume captures this seeming paradox of a nation's confidence at loss, even as the nation underwent important political and structural reform that strengthened democratic governance. Furthermore, contributors to this volume reveal another set of apparent paradoxes: administrative hierarchy recast as an "agent for democracy," conservative intellectuals reshaped as "populists," welfare reformed by eliminating the welfare system, and economy managed by rejecting macroeconomic management. As the decade drew to a close, the world of policy had appeared to have been indeed turned on its head. The election of Ronald Reagan in 1980 only confirmed this shift in public policy and political thought.

This volume should be read as an accompaniment to Brian Balogh's, *Integrating the Sixties: Origins, Structures, and Legacy of Public Policy in a Turbulent Decade.*

The continuity between the two decades, while by no means consistent, is apparent in the movement toward democratization of political structures, the emphasis on individual and group rights, rejection of past policy prescriptions and practices, the breakdown of hierarchical authority and tradition, and increased ideological polarization. Yet it was from this period of flux and even chaos, that America's confidence in its political and economic institutions would be restored, albeit with wariness and at high cost.

Donald T. Critchlow
General Editor

# DAVID BRIAN ROBERTSON

# Introduction: Loss of Confidence and Policy Change in the 1970s

The 1970s had at least as powerful an impact on the course of American public policy as the decade that preceded it. Polls showed that confidence in large institutions—including government—was wearing down under the burden of crisis, complexity, scandal, and doubt. Inflation, economic stagnation, and severe oil shortages directly disrupted individual lives. Faith in the future of the nation, its economy, its institutions, and its government eroded.

This erosion of confidence corresponded with a redirection of the American policy-making process. Minorities, women, environmentalists, and consumer advocates forced policy subsystems to come to terms with new interests and new perspectives. Political and policy information became more accessible. At the same time, the ability of the political system to solve problems seemed to evaporate. Parties weakened. Interest groups proliferated. Public and private hierarchies lost authority. Vietnam, Watergate, and the perceived weaknesses of Presidents Ford and Carter undermined the belief in the strong presidency widely shared since the 1940s. Congress reasserted its influence, but centrifugal forces made decisive congressional action even more difficult.

By the end of the 1970s, American policy making had become much more tentative and conditional. The consensus on Keynesian economics—and the active government it implied—unraveled. A sense of pervasive gridlock gripped policymakers and policy analysts. Alternative diagnoses and cures for America's maladies, particularly those promoted by advocates of free markets, gained currency.

These developments marked a fundamental turn in American public policy. Federal spending, taxes, and regulations were advancing steadily in the 1960s and early 1970s. When the nation elected Ronald Reagan president in 1980, however, these trends already had reversed. Tax-cutting fever was sweeping east from California, several industries were being deregulated, and a leading conservative headed the Federal Reserve Board.

This special issue offers six interpretations of various aspects of these changes by leading scholars of politics. Three of these scholars are professional historians, and the other three are political scientists. This volume is not, nor could it be, a comprehensive treatment of American public policy in these years. Together, however, these essays reveal the fundamental change of course driven in part by the national loss of confidence in its leaders. In this introductory essay I set the stage for these interpretations by touching on the changing social context in the 1970s, changes in the policy-making system, and changes in public policy during these years.

## The Erosion of Confidence

Despite tumultuous disagreements over issues such as Vietnam and civil rights, Americans in 1970 still expected that public leaders could and should alleviate social problems. The Democratic party, though divided over foreign policy and cultural issues, was united around government responsibility for economic management and income security for the middle class. Presidents Kennedy and Johnson had helped forge a wide consensus that government could use Keynesian principles of demand management to fine-tune economic performance.

The Democrats' faith in government activism remained popular with the electorate at the outset of the decade. A plurality of voters believed that the Democrats were more capable of maintaining prosperity than the Republicans. The party's electoral coalition seemed formidable. From 1932 through 1968, Democratic presidents had occupied the White House for twenty-eight of thirty-six years. Democrats held majorities in both the U.S. House and Senate in eighteen out of twenty Congresses from 1932 through 1972. Even when they held power, Republicans such as Dwight Eisenhower implicitly conceded that the federal government would not shrink to its pre-New Deal size.[1]

By 1970, then, American policy debate turned on the efficiency, speed, and centralization of government responsibility. Voices that posed fundamental questions about government's role in the market or its capacity to govern had only a small audience.

The authors of the following articles illustrate how Richard Nixon's first administration reflected this consensus on active government. Paul Quirk and Joseph Hinchliffe show that the Social Security amendments in 1972 substantially expanded federal obligations to the elderly by raising benefits and providing for automatic inflation adjustments. David Hoeveler reminds us that Richard Nixon endorsed a progressive income tax bill in 1969. Alice O'Connor explains how the Nixon administration came to endorse a far-reaching welfare-reform proposal, the Family Assistance Plan. During Nixon's first term, the food stamp program expanded and became more generous, job training expanded, and the Emergency Employment Act created public jobs for the unemployed. As John Woolley documents, the Nixon administration assumed an active role in economic management and imposed federal controls on wages and prices. The desegregation of southern schools proceeded rapidly from the late 1960s to the early 1970s; only about one-third of black students attended schools with whites in 1968–69, while about seven out of eight black students did so by 1972–73. He ordered the creation of the Environmental Protection Agency and expressed support for national land-use planning. Amendments to the Clean Air and Clean Water acts established far-reaching national responsibility for regulating pollution. Spending for grants programs, taking inflation into account, more than tripled during the Nixon and Ford years—a faster rate of growth than that of the Kennedy and Johnson administrations. Despite cuts in defense spending, the federal budget increased 30 percent from fiscal year 1968 through fiscal 1972.[2]

By mid-decade, however, profound and deepening pessimism colored Americans' attitudes about the future. The rhetoric of impending disaster became popular. Population growth, economic collapse, limited resources, climatological disaster, and nuclear holocaust all seemed possible, and possibly inevitable. The highly respected economist and political scientist Charles Lindblom, evoked the spirit of these years when he introduced his landmark 1977 book, *Politics and Markets*, with the observation that "relentlessly accumulating evidence suggests that human life on the planet is headed for a catastrophe."[3]

Confidence in American institutions generally and government in particular precipitously declined from the mid-1960s through the 1970s. The percentage of Americans expressing a "great deal of confidence" in the Supreme Court and the executive branch fell to under 30 percent by the end of the decade. By 1980 fewer than one in five Americans expressed a great deal of confidence in Congress, business, unions, or the press. Consumer confidence in the economy, relatively high in the 1950s and 1960s, dropped sharply in the mid-1970s and again at the end of the decade.[4] In 1977, President Carter warned Americans that ignoring the oil crisis would result in an "impending catastrophe." In mid-1979, President Carter spoke to

Americans about the "moral and spiritual" crisis they confronted. This national "crisis of confidence," said Carter, was infused with "growing doubt about the meaning of our lives, institutions and private enterprise, our own families and the very Constitution of the United States" that threatened to "destroy the social and the political fabric of America." The system of government "seems incapable of action," said Carter; "the gap between our citizens and our government has never been so wide."[5]

Popular culture reflected this erosion of institutional faith. Two of the best-selling political books of all time, David Halberstam's *The Best and the Brightest* and Bob Woodward and Carl Berntstein's *All the President's Men*, constituted exposés of the two most disenchanting political events of the 1970s: Vietnam and Watergate. The best-seller list later in the decade reflected interest in previous periods of social collapse (Barbara Tuchman's *A Distant Mirror: The Calamitous Fourteenth Century*, in 1978) and in personal survival (Robert J. Ringer's *Looking Out for #1*, in 1977, Howard J. Ruff, *How to Prosper during the Coming Bad Years*, in 1979, and Douglas R. Casey, *Crisis Investing: Opportunities and Profits During the Coming Great Depression*, in 1980).[6]

Intellectuals of all ideological persuasions fueled this growing skepticism. Among political scientists, for example, Theodore Lowi's *The End of Liberalism* (1969) argued that the moral force of liberalism was dissipating as self-seeking interest groups seized control of policy making (Lowi's book inspired conservatives such as David Stockman, a Michigan congressman who became President Reagan's first budget director).[7] David Mayhew argued that Congress had become an institution that functioned primarily to benefit incumbents. Morris Fiorina described Congress as the keystone of a Washington "establishment" in which special interests and public officials mutually benefited one another. Jeffrey Pressman and Aaron Wildavsky's *Implementation* cast doubt on whether federal policy could be made effective at the local level. Martha Derthick helped popularize the term "uncontrollable spending" in a book about social services grants gone awry. Richard Rose and Guy Peters, examining trends across nations, raised the specter of national government bankruptcy. Public choice analysts such as William Niskanen, James Buchanan, Gordon Tullock, and George Stigler argued that legislators and public administrators, like economic entrepreneurs, were primarily interested in expanding agency budgets and authority, even at the expense of the public. Social critics on the left, such as James O'Connor and Jürgen Habermas, questioned government domestic policy as an effort to subsidize and legitimate capitalism.[8]

## The Changing Economic and Social Context

Sweeping economic and social changes lie at the root of these growing doubts. Economic growth, manufacturing strength, and the nuclear family helped anchor postwar confidence in the American future. Stagflation and deindustrialization created deep doubts about the durability of American prosperity. The concurrent economic shift away from the "frostbelt" states and central cities was undermining the calculus of New Deal politics. The changing workforce and family structure made the reality of the American society seem ever more distant from the idealized nuclear family of the 1950s.

Economic anxiety did the most damage to American self-confidence. The traumatic oil price rises of 1973–74 constituted the most severe shock to the American economy since the early 1930s. The value of the American dollar dropped. The fixed price of gold ceased to anchor the international political economy. Keynesian economic predictions began to falter. Economic growth, which once seemed limitless, seemed increasingly difficult to sustain. Three recessions undercut jobs. Keynesian principles assumed that this sluggish economy would keep prices in check and that budget deficits would stimulate the economy. Consumer prices, however, doubled between 1970 and 1980. The federal budget deficit in 1976 rose to an unprecedented peacetime level, but the economy recovered slowly. Sapped by this stagflation, real wages in private industry rose to a peak in mid-1973 and then declined. In 1973, typical first-time buyers of single-family homes had to pay 22 percent of their average income to purchase a house; by 1982 they had to pay twice as much of their average income. The postwar goal of full employment quietly lost its political force as government seemed less able to steer the economy effectively.[9]

Ballard Campbell points out that these economic threats helped fuel an antigovernment constituency, as they had in the past. The changing economic structure disoriented many Americans and seemed to threaten accepted economic premises. Overseas competitors captured substantial shares of auto and steel manufacturing, two mainstays of the nation's industrial heartland. Other core manufacturing industries also declined, and as they did, manufacturing jobs vanished forever. Labor-union membership continued to decline steadily. In 1970, 30 percent of the nonagricultural workforce was unionized; 23 percent was unionized in 1980.[10] Farm indebtedness increased dramatically.

The geography of economic power shifted. Capital investment flowed disproportionately to southern and western states. The flow of investment to the Sunbelt fueled the flow of jobs, of population, and political power.

These changes exacerbated regional rivalries. Closely contested congressional votes on energy and social policy pitted the Sunbelt against the Frostbelt representatives. Within metropolitan areas, power flowed with investment and population from central cities to the suburbs. In 1970, for the first time, the number of Americans living in suburbs outnumbered those living in central cities.[11]

The idealized nuclear family, with a single, male breadwinner, seemed increasingly distant from the reality of the American family and workplace. The number of households in which individuals lived alone, or in which a female headed the household, grew six times faster than the number of households with a married couple with children under eighteen. Civil rights protections and economic change created new economic opportunities for women and minorities. By the end of the decade, half of all adult females participated in the labor force. Two of every five married women participated in the labor force at the beginning of the decade; by 1980, three of every five married women did so. These economic changes accompanied a decade of massive change in the status of women in America.[12]

All these changes energized some interests to advance new claims. Several of the advocacy groups formed in the 1960s and 1970s matured and became more institutionalized. In environmental policy, for example, these years saw the emergence of the Environmental Defense Fund (1967), Friends of the Earth (1969), the Natural Resources Defense Council (1970), and Greenpeace (1971), as well as the redirection of older environmental groups such as the Sierra Club. These public interest groups, according to Sidney Milkis, fought successfully for access to policy-making institutions.

Business and conservatives also mobilized in the 1970s. Building on forms developed during the previous decade, business much more actively conducted political activity through trade associations, grassroots lobbying, and cross-industry coalitions. Chief executives of General Motors, DuPont, General Electric, and other large industrial corporations formed the Business Roundtable in 1974. The number of corporate offices in Washington and the number of corporate PACs multiplied.[13]

As J. David Hoeveler argues, a populist brand of conservatism matured under these circumstances. The Heritage Foundation (1973) and the Cato Institute (1977) added intellectual ammunition to the conservatives' arsenal of libertarian ideas. The battle against the Equal Rights Amendment and abortion helped Phyllis Schlafly and other leaders to mobilize formidable conservative organizations at the grassroots level. This populist brand of conservatism naturally gravitated to the presidential candidacy of Ronald Reagan.

## The New Conditions Placed on Policy-making Authority

These new uncertainties and pressures placed new constraints on the exercise of policy-making authority. Power had flowed to presidents, policy experts, and congressional committee chairs during the cold war prosperity. Now, growing anxiety and shrinking institutional confidence undercut the ability of policymakers to defend themselves against challenges to their policy power. At the same time, changing circumstances and public concerns allowed new political claimants successfully to insist on new conditions for American policy making. Policy information and access became more widely available. As power became more dispersed and its exercise more conditional, the policy process became more tentative. The very conditions placed on the exercise of political power, then, contributed to a sense of gridlock that further undermined confidence in government's problem-solving capacity.

Milkis shows how profoundly these changes affected the role of the presidency and its relationship to other governmental institutions. From the 1940s to the 1970s, the president had come to embody policy energy and leadership. The most spectacular conditions placed on policy making in the 1970s, then, were placed on the president. Inflated expectations of the president, warned critics, had invited the abuse of presidential power. Lyndon Johnson and Richard Nixon had accepted that invitation, presidential critics argued, and Vietnam and Watergate were the inevitable result. The office of the presidency by 1974 seemed a threat to American democracy itself. The institution had to be reined in. [14]

The reassessment of presidential power, however, constituted only part of a much broader erosion of established policy authority.[15] The credibility of the military fell as the Vietnam conflict persisted. Exposés of policy making in Indochina created the impression of error and deception in the nation's most tortuous foreign policy issue. The political manipulations of Robert Moses, J. Edgar Hoover, and other unallocated public officials became more widely recognized. Environmentalists challenged the objectivity and competence of scientists and engineers. Public interest groups questioned the claims of automobile, oil, and tobacco companies about the impact of regulations. The autonomy of professionals eroded.[16]

Tight alliances (or "iron triangles") of specialized interest groups, public agencies, and congressional committees or subcommittees had dominated water projects, nuclear power, agriculture, and other policy areas in the 1950s and 1960s. Beginning in the late 1960s, environmental, consumer, civil rights, and other groups pried open the boundaries of many of these tight alliances, forcing themselves and their perspectives into policy deliberation. Under concerted assault from these new participants and their allies, farmers and chemical companies were compelled to accept limits on the use of DDT and other pesticides. The Army Corps of Engineers was forced to account for the environmental impact of the locks, dams, and levees they built. Highway interests had to answer charges that they ignored the social and economic side effects of superhighways. The trucking and airline industries began to lose control of their regulatory subsystems as outsiders questioned regulations that protected existing enterprises at the cost of economic efficiency. By the late 1970s, many policy areas seemed to be dominated not by iron triangles but by "issue networks," which were looser, larger, and more diverse than the tight policy alliances of the 1950s and 1960s.[17]

Alice O'Connor and John Woolley show the policy consequences of this erosion of expert authority over the course of the decade. The Nixon administration's welfare-reform plan of the early 1970s reflected the values of welfare policy experts much more than the administration's antiwelfare rhetoric suggested. By the end of the decade, however, policy experts had much less influence on welfare policy; instead, the welfare debate became determinedly ideological. Academic economists heavily influenced the economic policy of the first Nixon term, but by 1980 the most influential economic ideas were coming from George Gilder and Jude Wanniski, two advocates of supply-side economics whose ideas were widely criticized by economic experts.

Across the policy system, reforms aimed especially to break existing monopolies of information. Public interest groups insisted that the government make available new information about the impact of policy. Environmental Impact Statements, for example, armed environmental groups with legal ammunition against agencies. As Quirk and Hinchliffe explain, Congress responded to the public's demand for "government in the sunshine" far more in the 1970s than it ever had before. Amendments in 1974 to the Freedom of Information Act (FOIA) made it possible for citizens to gain access to federal administrative records to improve their political and legal leverage vis-à-vis authorities. Open meetings and public hearings became conventional elements of policy making. More congressional meetings were televised. Campaign contributors and recipients were required to make their actions public. Investigations of public officials began to escalate, as did indictment and convictions. By no means did this expanded access to information always disadvantage powerful interests, however. According to a 1981 estimate, about 85 percent of the FOIA requests filed with the Food and Drug administration came from companies it regulated. These companies sought information for court cases against government, or information about competitors' activities.[18]

Milkis argues that new policy changes aimed to recast administrative power as an "agent of democracy." For example, new federal statutes provided funds to permit public interest groups to sue not only corporations but also public administrators. These efforts, as well as the expansion of regulation and grants-in-aid, placed federal administrators on the defensive. Hugh Heclo concluded at the end of the decade that "the executive establishment in Washington tends to get the worst of both worlds—blamed for poor delivery by its customers and besieged with bills from its middlemen."[19]

Congress reasserted its power as Watergate debilitated the president. The War Powers Act of 1973 attempted to place conditions on the president's power to commit troops overseas. The Congressional Budget Control and Impoundment Act of 1974 limited the president's budgetary discretion. The budget act also established a Congressional Budget Office as a source of information to countervail the president's Office of Management and Budget. Congress made laws increasingly detailed and specific to limit administrative discretion. New laws increasingly included the "legislative veto," which gave Congress more direct power over policy administration. The celebrity enjoyed by the Senate Watergate Committee encouraged the expansion of congressional oversight of the executive branch. In 1973, House committees spent one-ninth of their time engaged in oversight; by 1979, they spent 40 percent of their time doing so. The 1978 Ethics in Government Act provided for the appointment of special prosecutors to investigate wrongdoing in the executive branch. This law in effect armed Congress for protracted offensives against the president and his appointees, elevating the investigation and prosecution of wrongdoing to a form of "politics by other means" in the 1980s.[20]

Power within Congress became more diffuse and conditional even as Congress placed new conditions on the president. Internal reforms substantially weakened the seniority system and the power of the committee chairs who had dominated politics in the House of Representatives for decades. The House in 1975 ousted three of the most autocratic committee chairs. This "revolt" chastened other committee chairs and made them more responsive to subcommittees and individual members. Committee and subcommittee positions became more widely available among the members, a development that further fragmented policy power. Similar developments occurred in the Senate. On both sides of the capitol, staff continued to increase, strengthening the independence of individual members.[21]

The courts expanded their role as policy arbiters and condition makers. The Supreme Court reinforced its image as an independent and powerful policy actor more forcefully in *U.S. v. Nixon* than in any other case since *Brown v. Board of Education*. As Milkis discusses, courts assumed a greater role in administration as reformers defined policy in terms of rights. Civil rights laws, civil liberties issues, and new social regulations invited independent judicial participation in policy disputes. The courts responded to this invitation positively. More federal, state, and local laws were struck down as unconstitutional than in any other decade in the nation's history. Included in this list were state abortion and death penalty laws. Judicial decisions during the 1970s established most of the gender protections that proponents of the Equal Rights Amendment sought.[22]

Election reforms imposed new conditions on the competition for public office, rewarding candidate independence and weakening the traditional strengths of political parties. The rapid spread of primary elections and new campaign finance reforms weakened the links between presidential candidates and their party. Primaries played a relatively minor role in presidential campaigns before 1968. In that year, less than half of the delegates to the Democratic and Republican national conventions were chosen in primaries. Four years later, two-thirds of the Democratic delegates (and four-sevenths of the Republicans) emerged from primaries. More than 70 percent of convention delegates were chosen in primaries four years later. Relatively independent insurgent candidates, such as George McGovern and Jimmy Carter, quickly took advantage of the new nominating system. In the Republican party, Ronald Reagan very nearly did the same in 1976 before succeeding four years later.

At the same time, campaign finance reforms set new conditions on campaign expenditure. Campaign finance reforms in 1972 and 1974 created public financing for presidential elections. After the Supreme Court removed some of the law's provisions, these reforms effectively encouraged the growth of political action committees (PACs) for funding elections. The number of PACs had increased from 608 in 1974 to 2,000 by the end of 1979. PACs increased the direct organizational stake in election finance. Republican National Committee chair William Brock helped revolutionize fund raising through direct-mail solicitations. Campaign spending by winning candidates for the House and Senate doubled from the 1975–76 cycle to 1979–80.[23]

Technological changes encouraged both candidate independence and accelerated fund raising. Television continued its ascendance as a primary and trusted source of public news for American citizens. The dominance of network news had the effect of simplifying, nationalizing, and individualizing

American policy discourse. The time constraints of news broadcasts, and the need to capture and hold viewer attention, biased news coverage of politics toward personal (and visual) conflicts, investigative reporting, campaign strategy, election "horse races," and political scandal. Nationally televised political news focused on the federal government and especially on the White House, at the expense of less photogenic policy-making institutions at the national, state, and local levels. Television news also focused on individual personalities. This individual focus made it more possible for individual candidates to "go it alone," winning nominations and elections without the endorsement of political party leaders (and sometimes despite their opposition).[24] In mid-decade, satellite communications made it practical to deliver television to more specialized audiences. Cable TV subscriptions multiplied in the 1970s, creating the critical mass for live coverage of congressional debate (launched in March 1979), closed-circuit political meetings, and the Cable News Network, among others.[25]

Increasingly limited in their control over candidates, campaign finance, and the conduct of political campaigns, political parties found that their ability to organize political conflict was eroding. Voters and members of Congress became less attached to their parties. Split-ticket voting increased. Unified party control of Congress and the White House, which had been common from 1932 through 1968, became exceptional. For all but half a dozen of the years from 1968 through 1998, the parties have divided control of the presidency and at least one house of Congress. Within Congress, party members became even less inclined to vote in the same way as other members of their party. Political appointees in the executive branch increasingly were experts, recommended by other experts rather than by party leaders. By the end of the 1970s, then, American political parties were widely viewed as being in decline.[26]

The century-old tie between southerners and the Democratic party reached the breaking point. Southern Democrats drifted toward the Republicans during Richard Nixon's reelection campaign. It has been argued that Watergate delayed a massive realignment of southerners from the Democratic to the Republican party in 1972—a realignment finally realized in congressional and state-level southern elections in the 1990s.[27]

## The New Path of American Public Policy

As public confidence eroded and conditions on policy making multiplied, it became increasingly difficult to exercise national policy authority actively to address pressing public problems. Under these pressures, the path of American public policy became altered. A scaled-back national agenda was gaining broader political acceptance. Monetary and fiscal discipline superseded Keynesian demand management.

John Woolley demonstrates that economic conservatism was supplanting Keynesianism as a prescription for the unprecedented economic problems that plagued the nation. Monetarists had argued that government should retreat from using fiscal operations to direct markets and focus instead on ensuring a stable currency. The monetarists argued that Keynesian fiscal policy became self-defeating as citizens anticipated its expected effects and took inflation for granted. As Keynesian predictions became more inconsistent with economic performance in the 1970s, the monetarist diagnosis and cure became more persuasive. Milton Friedman, the best-known American proponent of monetarism, won the Nobel Prize for economics in 1976. Three years later, Jimmy Carter, a Democratic president, essentially repudiated the fiscal activism implied by the Humphrey-Hawkins full employment act of 1978. After his "crisis of confidence" speech in mid-1979, Carter appointed a leading economic conservative, Paul Volker, to head the Federal Reserve Board.[28]

As support for Keynsianism drained away, the issue of government spending and taxing inevitably reemerged at the center of national politics. Startling budget deficits revitalized interest in disciplining federal spending. Budget control already had motivated both presidential impoundment and congressional budget reform by the mid-1970s. Federal spending reached $200 billion for the first time in the 1970s, and then passed $300, $400, and $500 billion. Economic stagnation lowered revenues while countercyclical programs and the expansion of entitlements broadened spending automatically. The concept of "uncontrollable spending" became more commonly used after mid-decade. By 1980, thirty states had called for a constitutional amendment requiring a balanced federal budget. California Governor Jerry Brown called for such an amendment in early 1979.[29]

In his analysis of the genesis of the tax revolts of the late 1970s, Ballard Campbell reveals that the tax issue made it politically feasible to challenge government activism directly. Taxes crept upward, creating increasing pressure on households. As late as 1974, Republican president Ford proposed an income tax surcharge to balance the budget. Inflation, however, was increasing the burden on wage-earners by pushing incomes into higher tax brackets and increasing the taxable value of their property. Tax increases became politically even more difficult to support. Supply-side theorists such as Arthur Laffer and Jude Wanniski argued that tax cuts could result in higher revenues by redirecting the nation's wealth to more productive enter-

prises. Hoeveler points out that taxes were central to the conservative populists' message well before Reagan's election in 1981. Finally, payroll taxes for
Social Security increased in 1977. In the same year, the Republican National
Committee endorsed the 30 percent income tax cut proposed by Jack Kemp
and William Roth (Democratic senators Sam Nunn and Lloyd Bensten also
supported the Kemp-Roth bill).[30] The property tax revolt of the following
year added momentum to the drive against taxes.

Rising concern about the budget eclipsed the rest of the domestic policy
agenda. State and local beneficiaries of grants were among the first to feel
the effects. The urban coalition of the 1950s and 1960s perceptibly weakened as the suburbs and Sunbelt gained political and economic power. Media stories and congressional attention to urban problems declined rapidly
after 1972. President Gerald Ford initially refused to provide federal help
for New York City during its 1975 fiscal crisis (though he reversed that position later). After 1978, local governments began to reduce their dependence
on federal grants-in-aid. Cities seemed to be becoming ungovernable. A presidential panel on national goals, created after Jimmy Carter's "crisis of confidence" speech, concluded that, rather than invest in rebuilding the nation's
central cities, the federal government should encourage the relocation of
their citizens to the suburbs and the Sunbelt.[31]

Liberal issues with bright prospects in the early and mid-1970s faded by
the decade's final years. Welfare reform no longer meant eliminating poverty, but now meant cuts in welfare spending, as Alice O'Connor points
out. Aggressive environmental laws such as the Clean Air, Clean Water, and
Endangered Species Acts were not implemented as envisioned. Required
emissions cuts for automobiles were delayed. Thirty states quickly ratified
the Equal Rights Amendment after Congress approved it in 1972, but its
momentum faded after 1973 and no state ratified after 1977. Many policy
makers believed that national health insurance was inevitable when President Carter took office, but by the end of his term few thought it was possible. No Consumer Protection Agency emerged. Federal Trade Commission plans to regulate funeral directors and used-car dealers foundered.[32]

The quest for an "energy policy" epitomized the effects of the loss of
confidence and the rise of conditional authority on the American policy
agenda. Congress defended controls on the price of crude oil, heating oil,
and gasoline that the Nixon administration had established. The Ford
administration's Energy and Policy Conservation Act of 1975 did not constitute an energy "policy" in any comprehensive sense and created few incentives to conserve energy. Early in his administration, President Carter proclaimed the energy crisis the "moral equivalent of war" and developed a

comprehensive energy plan entirely within the White House. The Carter administration insisted that Congress consider the bill's 113 provisions in a single package. The leaders of the House of Representatives tried to comply with the Carter administration request. Carter's aspiration for a comprehensive energy policy could not survive the centrifugal force of the Senate, however, where fragmented committees and subcommittees carved out individual components. As hope for a comprehensive federal energy plan faded, it seemed increasingly practical to simply relinquish government regulation of energy and permit market forces to work more freely. Ronald Reagan immediately abolished controls on crude oil prices—a move that reduced the role of government in the market while benefiting the oil state constituency that was helping to reshape the Republican party.[33]

## The Policy Legacy of the 1970s

"It seemed like nothing happened," wrote one author in describing common perceptions of the 1970s,[34] but as the contributors to our special issue demonstrate, American public policy changed fundamentally in this decade. The 1970s left a huge legacy of political and policy change, a legacy that affects all aspects of American government today.

Perhaps no part of the legacy of the 1970s is more important than the fundamental questions about public policy that it placed on our agenda. One question, put most eloquently by Charles Lindblom, concerns the appropriate role of government and of markets. What activities should government administer, and what functions should be left to markets? The rise of tax revolts and populist conservatism raised fundamental questions about the role of government that had been taken for granted for nearly two generations.

A second question concerns the appropriate role of the mass public in policy making. Should citizens shape public policy as directly as possible, or have we swung too far away from a system of representation in which officials exercise substantial policy-making discretion?

A third question concerns the appropriate level of governing authority. The drive to decentralize public policy remains popular, despite its modest success since the "New Federalism" announced during Richard Nixon's first term. How much authority—and specifically, what activities—should the national government exercise? How much should be devolved to state and local governments?

The 1970s made these questions central to public policy debate across the board in the United States. All three of these questions remain central to American policy debate as the century ends.

## Acknowledgments

The Woodrow Wilson International Center for Scholars contributed enormously to making this volume possible. Under the auspices of the Wilson Center, we convened a planning conference that permitted the authors to exchange views on the period and determine which direction the volume should take. The Wilson Center also provided a venue for a public conference in which we could engage our ideas with a lively and informed audience. We especially thank Mike Lacey for his intellectual contribution and practical leadership. The indefatigable George Wagner showed uncommon skill in coordinating these Wilson Center activities.

I want to thank each of the authors for their stimulating contributions to this volume and to my introductory essay. Conversations with and comments from Alice O'Connor, John Woolley, Sid Milkis, and Cathie Robertson were especially helpful. Don Critchlow also deserves thanks for making this special issue possible, and for countless conversations about the development of American public policy in the 1970s (among other decades).

*University of Missouri, St. Louis*

## Notes

1. Harold W. Stanley and Richard G. Niemi, *Vital Statistics on American Politics*, 4th ed. (Washington, D.C., 1994), 122-25, 158. On the Democratic coalition, see Thomas Byrne Edsall, *Chain Reaction: The Impact of Race, Rights, and Taxes on American Politics* (New York, 1992); John P. Frendreis and Raymond Tatalovich, *The Modern Presidency and Economic Policy* (Itasca, Ill., 1994), 240; James L. Sundquist, *Politics and Policy: The Eisenhower, Kennedy, and Johnson Years* (Washington, D.C., 1968); A. James Reichley, *Conservatives in an Age of Change: The Nixon and Ford Administrations* (Washington, D.C., 1981).

2. Charles S. Bullock and Charles S. Lamb, *Implementation of Civil Rights Policy* (Monterey, Calif., 1984), 65; Ballard C. Campbell, *The Growth of American Government: Governance from the Cleveland Era to the Present* (Bloomington, Ind., 1995), passim; David Brian Robertson and Dennis R. Judd, *The Development of American Public Policy: The Structure of Policy Restraint* (Glenview, 1989), 141, 149-50; Congressional Budget Office, *The Economic and Budget Out-*

look: *Fiscal Years 1998-2007* (Washington, D.C., 1997), 105-15; Malcolm Forbes Baldwin, "The Federal Government's Role in the Management of Private Land," in Michael J. Lacey, ed., *Government and Environmental Politics: Essays on Historical Developments Since World War Two* (Washington, D.C., 1989), 195.

3. Charles E. Lindblom, *Politics and Markets: The World's Political Economic Systems* (New York, 1977), 3.

4. Stanley and Niemi, *Vital Statistics on American Politics,* 169, 434; Seymour Martin Lipset and William Schneider, *The Confidence Gap: Business, Labor, and Government in the Public Mind* (New York, 1983).

5. Jimmy Carter, "The Energy Problem: An Address to the Nation," in *Public Papers of the Presidents of the United States: Jimmy Carter, 1977,* Book I (Washington, D.C., 1977), 656-62, and "Energy and National Goals," in ibid., *1979,* Book II (Washington, D.C., 1980), 1235-40.

6. Michael Wines, "Successful Political Books Are Less Sober, More Pop," *New York Times,* February 17, 1996, 25; *The Bowker Annual of Library and Book Trade Information* (New York, 1970-81).

7. Theodore J. Lowi, *The End of Liberalism: The Second Republic of the United States* (New York, 1969); David Stockman, *The Triumph of Politics: The Inside Story of the Reagan Revolution* (New York, 1986), 37-38.

8. Richard Rose and B. Guy Peters, *Can Government Go Bankrupt?* (New York, 1978).

9. U.S. Bureau of Labor Statistics, data on National Employment, Hours, and Earnings, Total Private Average Hourly Earnings, 1982 Dollars, Seasonally Adjusted, 1947-1997, <http:/ / stats.bls.gov:80/cgi-bin/surveymost> (13 May 1997); Derek Bok, *The State of the Nation* (Cambridge, Mass., 1996), 99; Peter Gourevitch, *Politics in Hard Times: Comparative Responses to International Economic Crises* (Ithaca, N.Y., 1986); Margaret Weir, *Politics and Jobs: The Boundaries of Employment Policy in the United States* (Princeton, 1992).

10. Barry Bluestone and Bennett Harrison, *The Deindustrialization of America: Plant Closings, Community Abandonment, and the Dismantling of Basic Industry* (New York, 1982); Stanley and Niemi, *Vital Statistics on American Politics,* 190.

11. Richard Franklin Bensel, *Sectionalism and American Political Development, 1880-1980* (Madison, Wis., 1984); Philip L. Rones, "Moving Toward the Sun: Regional Job Growth, 1968-1978," *Monthly Labor Review* 103 (March 1980): 12-19; G. Calvin Mackenzie, *The Irony of Reform: The Roots of American Political Disenchantment* (Boulder, Colo., 1996), 18.

12. U.S. Census Bureau, *Statistical Abstract of the United States, 1996* (Washington, D.C., 1996), 399; Steve Rawlings and Arlene Saluter, *Household and Family Characteristics: March 1994,* U.S. Census Bureau, Current Population Reports, P20-483 (Washington, D.C., 1995), vii; Suzanne Levine and Harriet Lyons, *The Decade of Women: A Ms. History of the Seventies in Words and Pictures* (New York, 1980); Joyce Gelb and Marian Leif Palley, *Women and Public Policies* (Princeton, 1982); William G. Mayer, *The Changing American Mind: How and Why American Public Opinion Changed between 1960 and 1988* (Ann Arbor, Mich., 1992), 121.

13. Cathie Jo Martin, "Business and the New Economic Activism: The Growth of Corporate Lobbies in the Sixties," *Polity* 27 (Fall 1994): 49-76; Kim McQuaid, *Uneasy Partners: Big Business in American Politics, 1945-1990* (Baltimore, 1994); David Vogel, *Fluctuating Fortunes: The Political Power of Business in America* (New York, 1989).

14. Arthur M. Schlesinger Jr., *The Imperial Presidency* (Boston, 1973); George E. Reedy, *The Twilight of the Presidency: From Johnson to Reagan,* rev. ed. (New York, 1987).

15. Aaron Wildavsky, "A World of Difference: The Public Philosophies and Political Behaviors of Rival American Cultures," in Anthony King, ed., *The New American Political System,* 2d ed. (Washington, D.C., 1990), 263-86.

16. Walter A. Rosenbaum, *Environmental Policy and Politics,* 3d ed. (Washington, D.C., 1995), 36; James A. Morone discusses the erosion of professional autonomy in medicine in *The Democratic Wish: Popular Participation and the Limits of American Government* (New York, 1990), 253-85.

17. Christopher J. Bosso, *Pesticides and Politics: The Life Cycle of a Public Issue* (Pittsburgh, 1987); Martha Derthick and Paul J. Quirk, *The Politics of Deregulation* (Washington, D.C., 1985); Hugh Heclo, "Issue Networks and the Executive Establishment," in Anthony King, ed., *The New American Political System* (Washington, D.C., 1978), 87-124; Frank R. Baumgartner and Bryan D. Jones, *Agendas and Instability in American Politics* (Chicago, 1993), 45; Gary Mucciaroni, *Reversals of Fortune: Public Policy and Private Interests* (Washington, D.C., 1995); John P. Heinz, Edward O. Laumann, Robert L. Nelson, and Robert H. Salisbury, *The Hollow Core: Private Interests in National Policy Making* (Cambridge, Mass., 1993). Grant McConnell discusses the preceding period of close relationships between interests and public officials in *Private Power and American Democracy* (New York, 1966).

18. Rosenbaum, *Environmental Policy and Politics*, 30; Roger H. Davidson, *The Postreform Congress* (New York, 1992); Benjamin Ginsberg and Martin Shefter, *Politics by Other Means: The Decline of Elections in America* (New York, 1990), 6; William M. Lunch, *The Nationalization of American Politics* (Berkeley and Los Angeles, 1987), 193.

19. Heclo, "Issue Networks and the Executive Establishment," 93.

20. James L. Sundquist, *The Decline and Resurgence of Congress* (Washington, D.C., 1981); Ginsberg and Shefter, *Politics by Other Means*.

21. Sundquist, *The Decline and Resurgence of Congress*, 367-414; Davidson, *The Postreform Congress*.

22. Ginsberg and Shefter, *Politics by Other Means*, 149-50; Mackenzie, *The Irony of Reform*; Stanley and Niemi, *Vital Statistics on American Politics*, 308; Rosenbaum, *Environmental Policy and Politics*, 30; Jane J. Mansbridge, *Why We Lost the ERA* (Chicago, 1986).

23. James W. Caesar, "Political Parties—Declining, Stabilizing, or Resurging?" in King, ed., *The New American Political System*, 87-138; Stanley and Niemi, *Vital Statistics on American Politics*, 175, 212; A. James Reichley, "The Rise of National Parties," in John E. Chubb and Paul E. Peterson, eds., *The New Direction in American Politics* (Washington, D.C., 1985), 175-200; Frank J. Sorauf, *Inside Campaign Finance: Myths and Realities* (New Haven, 1992).

24. Austin Ranney, "Broadcasting, Narrowcasting, and Politics," in King, ed., *The New American Political System*, 175-202.

25. Merrill Brown, "A Boom Industry Free to Call Its Shots," *Washington Post*, January 12, 1981, 1; Michael Wines, "The FCC and Its Critics Are at Odds on How to Control the Video Explosion," *National Journal* 14 (August 14, 1982): 1408.

26. Stanley and Niemi, *Vital Statistics on American Politics*, 146, 213-14; Sundquist, *The Decline and Resurgence of Congress*, 397; Heclo, "Issue Networks," 112; William Crotty and Gary Jacobson, *American Parties in Decline* (Boston, 1980).

27. Kevin P. Phillips, *The Emerging Republican Majority* (New Rochelle, N.Y., 1969) and *Post-Conservative America: People, Politics, and Ideology in a Time of Crisis* (New York, 1982); Thomas E. Cavanagh and James L. Sundquist, "The New Two Party System," in John E. Chubb and Paul E. Peterson, eds., *The New Direction in American Politics* (Washington, D.C., 1985), 33-67.

28. Herbert Stein, *Presidential Economics: The Making of Economic Policy from Roosevelt to Clinton*, 3d rev. ed. (Washington, D.C., 1994), 140-43, 225-31; Marc Allen Eisner, *The State in the American Political Economy: Public Policy and the Evolution of State-Economy Relations* (Englewood Cliffs, N.J., 1995), 260-83.

29. Juan Cameron, "Carter Takes on the Budget Monster," *Fortune*, January 1977, 82; "Federal Spending Restraint in Vogue," *National Journal* 11:51-52 (December 22, 1979): 2150; Lou Cannon, "Gov. Brown Seeks Balanced Budget Amendment," *Washington Post*, 8 January 1979, 1.

30. Frendreis and Tatalovich, *The Modern Presidency and Economic Policy*, 276; Stein, *Presidential Economics*, 246; Jude Wanniski, *The Way the World Works* (New York, 1978).

31. Baumgartner and Jones, *Agendas and Instability in American Politics*, 142-44; John Robert Greene, *The Presidency of Gerald R. Ford* (Lawrence, Kan., 1995), 90-95; Stanley and Niemi, *Vital*

*Statistics on American Politics*, 324; Douglas Yates, *The Ungovernable City: The Politics of Urban Problems and Policy-Making* (Cambridge, Mass., 1980); Robert Pear, "Panel on National Goals Proposes U.S. Aid for Migration to Sun Belt," *New York Times*, 27 December 1980, 1.

32. Mansbridge, *Why We Lost the ERA*, 12–13; John Kingdon, *Agendas, Alternatives, and Public Policies*, 2d ed. (New York, 1995); Susan J. Tolchin and Martin Tolchin, *Dismantling America: The Rush to Deregulate* (New York, 1983); Richard A. Harris and Sidney M. Milkis, *The Politics of Regulatory Change: A Tale of Two Agencies*, 2d ed. (New York, 1996)

33. David Howard Davis, *Energy Politics*, 4th ed. (New York, 1993), 109–13, 116; Greene, *The Presidency of Gerald R. Ford*, 78–79; Erwin C. Hargrove, *Jimmy Carter as President: Leadership and the Politics of the Public Good* (Baton Rouge, La., 1988).

34. Peter N. Carroll, *It Seemed Like Nothing Happened: The Tragedy and Promise of America in the 1970s* (New York, 1982).

PAUL J. QUIRK
and
JOSEPH HINCHLIFFE

# The Rising Hegemony
# of Mass Opinion

The Founding Fathers warned about the dangers of an "excess of democracy" and designed the Constitution in large part with a view toward preventing it. Judging from most commentary on American politics, with respect to most of the intervening two hundred years, they needn't have worried: The mass public has only occasionally been a dominant force in national policy making. Elites, although often responding to broad public concerns, have usually defined the specific directions of policy change.

Indeed, by most accounts, the principal weakness of the American political system has been just the opposite: a tendency toward domination by organized interest groups, business, and the privileged classes. Few commentators on American politics have echoed the Founders' fears about demagogues and unruly mobs. Indeed, most have heartily approved of mass political movements—from Populism and Progressivism to the civil rights movement, Vietnam War resistance, consumerism, environmentalism, and feminism.[1]

In recent years, however, appreciation of the Founders' concerns about mass politics has been on the increase.[2] Scholars have written critically about the rise of a "plebiscitary presidency," thoroughly dependent upon immediate public approval, and the increasing tendency for presidents to exercise leadership largely through direct appeals for public support.[3] Some have argued that Congress cannot legislate effectively because of the extreme openness of its decision processes and the relentless efforts of its members to please the voters.[4] Others have criticized the dramatic growth of policy making by initiative and referendum—forms of direct democracy—in many states.[5]

In our view, the hazards of overly direct and compelling mass influence seem apparent in a variety of major policy developments of the past two decades. These include the large budget deficits of the 1980s and 1990s, especially the difficulty of achieving either tax increases or reductions in middle-class entitlement programs to reduce the deficit; the huge costs and limited benefits of some regulations concerning health, safety, and environmental protection; the failure of the United States in the early 1990s to offer substantial economic aid to support the transition to democracy in Russia; the emphasis on demonstrably unsuccessful interdiction and law-enforcement strategies, rather than prevention and treatment, for dealing with drug abuse; and a reform of the welfare system that overlooked serious issues of workability and potential harm. In all these cases, we believe, uninformed prejudices of the mass public and leaders' appeals to those prejudices played a critical role in shaping policy.

In this article we examine the recent arrival of democratic excess in American politics. We argue that in the late twentieth century mass opinion has emerged as a hegemonic political force, the dominant influence in policy making. To a great extent, the relative availability of effective popular rhetoric to support various positions has become the main determinant of policy outcomes. Other forces, such as expert opinion and interest-group demands, remain important, and sometimes determine outcomes, but generally they play a smaller role than in the past. To account for the expanded influence of mass opinion, we point to very broad changes, first noticeable in the 1960s, in how citizens connect with the political world—that is, in the kinds of information they receive and how they use it. In brief, more citizens are making judgments on more policy issues and using those judgments more often in their political decisions, including their choices of parties and candidates.

The effects of this change in the nature of mass politics, we argue, began to emerge in the politics of policy making in the 1970s. To illustrate and provide some modest empirical support for this claim, we offer brief descriptions of several major episodes of policy making from the 1970s and early 1980s. Our cases cover a wide range of subject matter—from environmental regulation to Social Security, and from energy pricing to taxes and the budget, among others. In various ways, they all represent new landmarks for the influence of mass opinion.

The cases also suggest that rising mass influence cuts two ways with respect to the performance of government. On the one hand, it can help to overcome the organized interest groups and other narrow forces that have often dominated American politics. On the other hand, with the increased risks of demagoguery and greater deference to even biased or uninformed public opinion, an increasingly powerful mass opinion also can lead to policies that are reckless, irresponsible, or ill-suited to their purposes.

## Citizens, Information, and Policy Making

A variety of theoretical and historical arguments are available to account for a substantial increase in the influence of mass opinion in national policy making in recent decades. One view suggests that the increased influence has resulted from changes in public mood or ideology. Another attributes it to developments in institutional rules or structures. We will argue, however, that only a more fundamental change in ordinary citizens' awareness of and responses to policy conflict can provide a satisfactory account.

### Institutions, Ideology, and Information

Some scholars, such as Samuel Huntington[6] and Sidney Milkis and Richard Harris[7], have attributed populist tendencies in policy making to the rise of a participatory, anti-authoritarian ideology in the 1960s and early 1970s. In Huntington's analysis, this mood was an instance of the "creedal passion," or renewed and intensified commitment to the nation's democratic values, that appears cyclically in American history. And it produced a "crisis of governability"—with the public's demands leading to an explosion of costly or impractical benefits and claimed rights along with the consistent budget deficits of the late 1960s and early 1970s. In Milkis and Harris's similar view, a participatory, anticapitalist ideology influenced by the New Left led to the development of the "public-lobby regime" of the 1970s.

From a more recent perspective, however, we can see that an ideological account of rising mass influence largely fails. It cannot explain why the enhanced influence of mass opinion has survived the shift toward conservatism that began in the late 1970s and has endured into the mid-1990s. The democratic creedal passion and postmaterialist participatory values of the 1970s have subsided, but plebiscitary policy making has not.

Another group of scholars, finding support in the political thought of the Founding Fathers, stresses the role of political institutions in determining the influence of mass opinion.[8] In this view, the danger of "democratic excess" is an essential feature of representative government. To avoid unjust or destructive policies, representative government must subdue the effect of public opinion. It may do so through institutional arrangements such as indirect election, lengthy and varying terms of office, checks and balances, and restrictions on publicity.

Unfortunately, in these commentators' view, institutional protections against democratic excess have eroded over the course of American history and especially in recent decades. Indirect election has been eliminated for senators, formally, and for presidents, as a practical matter. Beginning with Theodore Roosevelt and Woodrow Wilson, presidents have abandoned a nineteenth-century norm that prohibited their appealing to the public to seek support for specific policies.[9] In the 1970s, Congress made several changes in rules and procedure, such as permitting television coverage of floor proceedings, that have undermined its ability to resist public pressure and deliberate independently.[10] But this account has problems too. It does not explain why we find an apparent rise in mass influence by the early 1970s, prior to the main institutional changes of the decade, or why those institutional changes themselves were adopted.

In contrast, we do not trace the increase in mass influence to ideology, political attitudes, or institutional structures. Our primary focus, rather, is on broad changes in how citizens use information and make judgments about politics.

## Competing Forces in Policy Making

Fundamentally, we may consider that policymakers weigh the preferences or recommendations of three main categories of actors: special-interest groups, policy experts oriented toward broad interests, and ordinary citizens or public opinion. Roughly speaking, policy experts (as here defined) and public opinion are concerned with the same widely shared interests. But they define those interests differently. Experts define them, somewhat autonomously, on the basis of careful reasoning and specialized knowledge. The public defines its interests more casually, using whatever beliefs, hunches, or prejudices it happens to have. To a considerable extent, as researchers have shown, citizens take their cues from political leaders.[11] But, we would add, they are likely to listen mainly to those leaders whose messages comport with their own predispositions—those who say what they want to hear or, at least, can readily accept. On certain issues, public officials are an independent source of policy preferences, with interests of their own in governmental growth, autonomy in decision making, or security in office, among other things.[12]

## Information and Mass Influence

The relative influence of mass opinion is not a fixed feature of the political system. It will vary, in particular, with changes in how ordinary citizens connect with the political world. The central factors are how many voters respond to issues in making choices between parties or candidates and how many issues they respond to. Those quantities may vary over time.

In the 1950s, at the outset of survey research on mass political behavior, mass politics was largely devoid of specific policy issues. Most citizens had little awareness of issues or ideologies. In voting, such citizens did not choose between parties or candidates on the basis of their liberalism or conservatism; they did not even understand those terms. Nor did most citizens use particular issues to make choices. Instead, they chose between candidates primarily on the basis of personal qualities or party labels; and they chose between parties on the basis of the parties' broad appeals to social groups or their apparent success in producing peace and prosperity. Accordingly, parties and candidates emphasized group appeals and symbolic themes in their campaigns.[13]

With most citizens so detached from debates over policy, we would not expect public opinion to be a dominant force in policy making. In such circumstances, the voters, by holding elected officials accountable for the conspicuous results of their decisions, should have considerable influence over the general direction and priorities of government: whether government is more active or less, whether it makes new efforts to reduce crime, and the like. But they should give policy experts little competition in shaping specific strategies and measures. Policy should pursue specific strategies, and meet criteria of workability, that are largely defined by elite opinion. As V. O. Key wrote in 1964, "The articulation between government and mass opinion is so loose that politicians enjoy a considerable range of discretion within which to exercise prudence and good sense.[14]

Special interests in such circumstances, by contrast, should have influence over narrower, less consequential issues, but with less constraint from elite opinion. Facing only a modest risk of an effective negative public response, policymakers should be highly responsive to special-interest demands. Elite criticism should prevent special-interest policies that would have readily noticeable harmful effects—for example, to require a tax increase or reduce economic growth perceptibly. But subsidies, anticompetitive regulations, or other special-interest policies that impose small, invisible costs on taxpayers or consumers should be relatively easy to adopt and sustain.

## The New Electorate

By the late-1960s, however, the public was becoming more aware of issues. To an extent, the change reflected secular increases in levels of education and access to media. The proportion of voters with at least some college education had been rising substantially in the post–World War II era. The proportion of the adult population with at least some college education increased between 1960 and 1970 from 16.5 percent to 21.2 percent. This 28 percent increase in the number of college-educated adults came at a time of rapid growth in sources of information. The number of book titles and new editions offered for sale more than doubled, and the numbers of commercial television stations and AM radio stations each increased by around one-quarter. Although newspaper circulation increased more slowly, the electorate of the 1970s was better educated and had access to more information than any previous generation.[15] An increased awareness of political issues was also stimulated by the social unrest and divisive policy conflicts of the 1960s—especially the sharp ideological cleavage between the two candidates, Democrat Lyndon Johnson and Republican Barry Goldwater, in the 1964 presidential election.

Political scientists by the mid-1970s were beginning to describe a "changing American voter."[16] Compared with the 1950s, voters in the late 1960s and early 1970s had become more cognizant of the basic terms of political debate. They were more ideological in their judgments about issues and more issue-oriented in their judgments of candidates. Nie, Verba, and Petrocik reported responses of citizens who were asked to mention things they liked or disliked about presidential candidates.[17] Between 1952 and 1972, the proportion of respondents making reference to party had declined from 46 percent to 24 percent. The proportion making reference to issues climbed from 49 percent to 67 percent. Over roughly the same period, ideological thinking, as measured by an index of attitude consistency, became more prevalent. From 1956 to 1973, the percentage of the population with consistent attitudes rose from 26 percent to 44 percent. The proportion of respondents with well-defined liberal or conservative views rose from 25 percent to 44 percent.[18]

Although critics challenged some of these findings on methodological grounds,[19] they have largely held up in subsequent research. Indeed, Russell Dalton has reviewed extensive research documenting the trend toward a more sophisticated, issue-oriented electorate not only in the United States but also in France, Great Britain, and West Germany.[20]

Students of mass behavior mostly have welcomed the new and seemingly improved post-1964 electorate. Dalton, indeed, applauds it:

As modern electorates have become more sophisticated and politically interested, and as the availability of political information has expanded, many citizens are now better able to reach their own voting decisions without relying on broad external cues. . . . In short, citizens now possess the political resources to follow the complexities of politics; they have the potential to act as the independent voters described in classic democratic theory but seldom observed in practice. [21]

In one respect, overlooked in most discussions of citizen competence, however, no such gains have been registered—a point that makes Dalton's celebration premature. As Delli-Carpini and Keeter[22] show in their analysis of a half-century's survey evidence, Americans in the 1990s have essentially the same level of factual information about government and public policy that they had fifty years earlier. Despite dramatic advances in income, formal education, and access to media, the proportion of people who can, for example, give the name of the vice president or identify the purpose of a major domestic program has hardly changed. Nor can we suppose, therefore, that voters have acquired any greater ability to make informed judgments about the issues in politics. In short, the post-1964 electorate knows where the parties and candidates stand on a number of issues; but it may know little else about those issues.

## The Response of Policymakers

As citizens have become more prone to judge politicians on the basis of policies, politicians have become more assiduous in figuring out what policies citizens want. As Jacobs and Shapiro point out, White House polling operations first achieved state-of-the-art sophistication during Nixon's presidency.[23] President Jimmy Carter's pollster, Patrick Caddell, was the first public-opinion analyst to join the president's inner circle of policy advisers.[24] The scale of White House survey research has increased rapidly in the 1980s and 1990s. Although with fewer resources at their disposal, politicians outside the White House are undoubtedly following suit. Moreover, election campaigns of the past two decades have focused less on party labels and more on issues and ideology. Issue-oriented appeals, although often negative and almost always highly superficial, have become the principal currency of campaign politics.[25]

With citizens far more oriented to policy debate than they were in the 1950s, we would expect public opinion to be a far more important, if not dominant, force in policy making. The voters not only hold elected officials accountable for results; they choose them and often throw them out for their positions on issues. In such circumstances, special interests should lose a good deal of their influence. Policymakers who defer to special-interest demands are at considerable risk of coming under attack and losing support at the next election.

With the public making more specific demands, policy experts should also lose some of their influence. In the face of powerful pressures from public opinion, policymakers will no longer treat experts' judgments about the workability of policies as a decisive consideration in choosing them. In fact, the integrity of expert advice will also suffer. If the pressures of public opinion make policymakers less willing to listen to experts, some experts will slant their advice to cater to policymakers' inclinations, and indeed, therefore, to public opinion.

## Public Opinion and Policy Making in the 1970s

Public opinion has always had an important role in policy making in American government. In this section, we offer evidence that this role had grown significantly by the 1970s. We look very briefly at six major cases of policy making that, in our view, provide such evidence. Though not chosen randomly, the cases cover a wide range of policy areas and span the decade. They are: the Clean Air Act of 1970; government-in-the-sunshine reforms of Congress; the 1972 Social Security benefit increase; the regulation of petroleum pricing; the deregulation of the trucking industry; and the Reagan tax cut of 1981.

The cases differ in many respects. Naturally, each one was shaped by a variety of forces, from economic trends to ideological changes, among others; we are not advocating a single-factor theory of politics. Some were salient to the general public; some were not. But each case demonstrated a distinctively fulsome response to the wishes or concerns of ordinary citizens. By prior standards for each given area or type of policy, each was a monument to public opinion. Like monuments that commemorate military victories, they also represented defeats. In at least one case (deregulation) and arguably a second (congressional reform), public opinion helped defeat powerful organized interest groups and vindicate a conception of the public interest. In the other four, however, it drove policymakers to overlook serious concerns, advanced by credible experts, about the workability of their proposals. The defeat was for careful thinking about public policy.

## Clean Air

The Clean Air Act of 1970, widely considered the most costly regulatory measure in American history, was a massive expansion of federal regulation of air pollution. It was largely a response to an unprecedented mobilization of public concern about the environment, highlighted by Earth Day. Although few would argue that prior federal legislation on air pollution had been remotely adequate to address the issue, most commentators agree that the 1970 act seriously neglected considerations of efficiency, technological feasibility, and cost.

Federal legislation in this area began with the Air Pollution Control Act of 1955 and continued with several amendments in the 1960s.[26] In 1967, Congress gave the Department of Health, Education, and Welfare (HEW) modest authority to work with states to establish air pollution control districts and automobile emission standards.

By 1970, however, when the Clean Air Act of 1967 was scheduled for reauthorization, the public wanted tougher action. In one of the more dramatic developments in public opinion on record, concern about the environment, already quite high throughout the 1960s, went through the roof in the late 1960s and early 1970s. The number of people believing that air pollution was a very or somewhat serious problem jumped from 28 percent in May 1965 to 69 percent in June 1970. For big-city residents, that percentage jumped from 52 percent to 93 percent.[27] Perhaps more important, many people became actively mobilized about the environment. In September 1969, Senator Gaylord Nelson (D-Wis.) proposed a national environmental "teach-in." This event became Earth Day with coordinated activities at more than 700 colleges and 1,400 high schools. The media covered Earth Day heavily, starting with the preparations more than two months before the event.[28] Earth Day and other mobilization efforts generated significant new public interest in the environment. For example, state hearings on clean-air standards drew overflowing, often vociferous crowds. Said one environmentalist in 1970, "We've got citizens beating on the doors of the control agencies."[29]

The public fervor over the environment touched off a bout of institution-building in Washington. In 1969, President Richard Nixon created the Cabinet Committee on the Environment and "restructured" the Citizens Advisory Committee on Environmental Quality. In 1970, he signed separate bills creating a Council on Environmental Quality and an Office of Environmental Quality.[30] And rejecting a proposal to assign the environmental mission to the Interior Department, Nixon established the

Environmental Protection Agency.[31]   As a reporter observed, "environment" was a "trigger word" in Washington.[32]

In making his initial proposal for the 1970 clean air reauthorization bill, Nixon sought to emphasize that the fight against pollution "is not a search for villains."[33]   To strengthen the federal role, Nixon called for authority to establish national air-quality standards and to enforce them in both inter- and intrastate cases. He also sought continued authority to set automobile emissions standards and new authority to regulate gasoline additives.[34]   The House of Representatives largely accepted the administration's suggestions, producing a bill that expanded existing authority incrementally. Approved by the Commerce Committee unanimously, the bill was passed by the House on a vote of 374–1.[35]

The House floor debate, however, had shown signs of popular pressure for more extreme measures. Environmentalist members argued that the bill did not go far enough. They claimed that air pollution caused by vehicles could be virtually eliminated by the mid-1970s, chastising the committee for not adopting this objective. They charged that the bill "appears to bend over backward to accommodate the auto and oil industries."[36]   Led by Leonard Farbstein (D-N.Y.), the critics unsuccessfully pressed several amendments to toughen the bill. One would have allowed states to set vehicle emission standards higher than those of the federal government's. A more ambitious amendment would have phased out the internal combustion engine. Partly in awareness of the popular demand for more radical steps, industry generally endorsed the House bill's expansion of the federal role. National Steel Corporation, for example, complained that state hearings on air-quality standards were dominated by "highly emotional, overzealous, and sometime uninformed citizens."[37]

With avid support from Senator Edmund Muskie (D-Me.) and his Public Works Subcommittee on Air and Water Pollution, the demands for stronger measures won out in the Senate. Muskie's response is widely attributed to a sharp attack on his environmental record in a report by a Ralph Nader study group.[38]   Released amid the committee's proceedings, the report charged:

> Senator Muskie has failed the nation in the field of air pollution control legislation. . . . [Muskie] is the chief architect of the disastrous Air Quality Act of 1967. That fact alone would warrant his being stripped of his title as "Mr. Pollution Control." But the Senator's passivity since 1967 in the face of an ever worsening air pollution crisis compounds his earlier failure.[39]

Muskie, considered a leading contender for the 1972 Democratic presidential nomination, responded by reporting a bill with air-pollution standards that were a quantum leap beyond those that had been advocated by the administration or adopted by the House.

The Muskie bill provided for EPA approval of state emission limitations and federal enforcement of air pollution standards in civil and criminal proceedings. More important, where earlier law had provided for the establishment of "feasible" emission standards for new vehicles by administrative action, the bill mandated specific, highly ambitious reductions in automobile emissions: By 1975, vehicle exhaust emissions had to be reduced by 90 percent of their 1970 levels. To ensure compliance, new cars and new car designs were subjected to a government-run certification and testing procedure.[40]

In fashioning the bill, Muskie and the subcommittee essentially set aside economic and technological considerations as irrelevant.[41] Affected industries pleaded for more time to consider the proposals.[42] Some said bluntly that the new standards would be impossible to meet. The Ford Motor Company asserted that the prescribed automobile emission levels "are lower than any we know how to meet . . . [and] would not permit us to continue to produce cars after January 1, 1975."[43] Nevertheless, the subcommittee held few hearings and did not debate the "technology forcing" required by the bill. Indeed, it conceded that the act might cause economic disruption—including, specifically, that it might require a reduction of 75 percent in automobile traffic around urban areas and the closing down of entire industries unable to comply with the new law.[44]

In the Senate floor debate, Muskie acknowledged that his committee had neither explored the technological feasibility of the bill's stringent requirements nor tried to assess their economic consequences.[45] The committee's rationale for the bill played to the public's concern about health effects of pollution and even used some of the villain-blaming that Nixon had recommended against. The new law, the committee argued, "would establish that the air is a public resource, and that those who would use that resource must protect it from abuse, to assure the protection of the health of every American."[46]

With the Senate holding the rhetorical upper hand, both the House and the Nixon administration gave up pursuit of a moderate approach, and the Clean Air Act of 1970 became law largely as Muskie had drafted it. To be sure, the law has improved air quality. But the costs and inefficiencies of the measure, according to analysts, have been vast.[47] Undoing mistakes of the Clean Air Act has been a major theme of regulatory reform efforts for more than two decades.

### "Sunshine" Reform in Congress

The 1970s saw some of the most significant changes that have ever occurred in the structures and procedures of Congress.[48] The main reforms increased the power of party leaders and individual members while reducing that of committee chairs; they reflected conflicts within Congress and the majority Democratic party, not responses to public opinion. An additional aspect of the reforms, however, largely reflected public sentiment: By adopting measures to record and publish more of its votes and to televise more of its proceedings, Congress exposed itself more fully to public scrutiny.

A preference for "government-in-the-sunshine" has been a permanent feature of American public opinion, part of the nation's democratic political culture. Yet, in this period Congress responded to that preference far more than ever before, even though issues of congressional process were far from being from highly salient. To simplify our account, we will focus on the debates and decisions in the House of Representatives, although the Senate response was closely parallel.

Before 1970, the House of Representatives voted on many issues, including amendments, by unrecorded teller votes in the Committee of the Whole. In such votes, members voted by passing before either the aye or the nay teller, who recorded only the respective numbers of votes. Because no record was made of individual votes, members could not be held accountable on these issues. The House of Commons had adopted anonymous teller voting in the Committee of the Whole, in 1641, to protect members from retaliation by the king. It had abolished the practice as part of a broader democratization of government in 1832. But the House, which had copied the Parliament's rules during the First Congress, ignored the democratic objections and kept anonymous voting for almost an additional 140 years.[49]

Committee voting was even less open. Most committees were not required to meet in public; votes were often unrecorded; and even that a vote had occurred could remain secret. In 1969, 43 percent of all House committee meetings were closed to the public, including all meetings of the Appropriations Committee.[50] There had been calls for reform of the House, led by the Democratic Study Group (DSG), since the 1950s. But until 1970 reform efforts were stymied by the leadership.[51]

The Legislative Reorganization Act of 1970 opened House voting to public view. On an amendment sponsored by future Speaker Thomas P. (Tip) O'Neill Jr. (D-Mass.) with 183 co-sponsors, the House agreed to record the members' votes in the Committee of the Whole on the request of 20 members. The act also required that members' votes on all committee roll calls be recorded and made public in the committee reports.[52]  In part, these measures were meant to favor liberal causes. "If the people at home knew how we actually voted," O'Neill said, "I believe that we would probably have passed more pieces of legislation." [53]  The AFL-CIO, the National Education Association, and the National Farmers Union all urged an end to "secrecy" in the conduct of House business. But a populist attack on secrecy also had bipartisan appeal. "Secrecy undermines the democratic process and saps public confidence in the House as a responsive and effective legislative body," said Rep. Barber Conable (R-N.Y.), who, along with Rep. Sam Gibbons (D-Fla.), led a bipartisan group promoting open processes in the House.[54]

The main opponents of greater publicity were committee chairs and senior members, including some liberals. Rep. Emanuel Celler (D-N.Y.), the long-serving liberal chairman of the Judiciary Committee, said the reforms would make legislating like working in a "goldfish globe." He added, "I do not think the public should be admitted to and should know every detail . . . of the debate when [a] bill is being written up." The weakness in Celler's argument was that few citizens shared his aversion to treating members like goldfish. Business lobbying groups, which might have opposed reform for the same reason that liberal groups supported it, declined to associate themselves with the defense of secrecy. The Chamber of Commerce called legislative reform "strictly an 'in-house' matter."[55]

The main strategy of the reformers was to keep the debate from being seen that way, using a media campaign to draw as much public attention to it as possible. Rep. Donald Frasier (D-Minn.), chairman of the DSG wrote about the reforms to more than six hundred newspaper editors. A bipartisan group of twenty-two members, both liberals and conservatives, wrote to more than two thousand editors. And the media were naturally eager to carry their message. Endorsing the reforms, Robert M. White II of the American Society of Newspaper Editors argued that "the more the public knows about Congress, the better the Congress."[56]

In reviewing this strategy, one reformer captured both the limited salience of congressional procedures and the reformers' advantage in appealing for public support.

> We were extremely eager that the stakes be seen as being larger than merely a housekeeping matter of small concern to the public. The way this was done was to package our moves as "an anti-secrecy drive." Since the press hates secrecy in all its forms, this proved to be a highly productive technique.[57]

In the end, the recording of roll-call votes was adopted both for committee and for floor votes without significant opposition.[58]

Congress during the 1970s also opened itself up for public inspection in another way, by expanding television coverage of its proceedings. Widespread criticism of televised hearings on communist subversion and organized crime in the late 1940s and early 1950s and a ruling by Speaker Sam Rayburn (D-Tex.) that the rules of the House did not permit televised coverage of its proceedings killed off interest in broadcasting congressional proceedings for almost two decades.[59] Support for such broadcasts reemerged in the late 1960s, however, and grew rapidly through the 1970s. The Legislative Reorganization Act of 1970 authorized broadcasts of congressional hearings. In 1974, a Joint Committee on Congressional Operations recommended gavel-to-gavel television coverage. And in 1977, members' demands forced a reluctant Speaker O'Neill to run a ninety-day experiment with television broadcasting of floor debate. After the experiment was widely deemed a success, the House voted 342–44 to make gavel-to-gavel broadcast permanent.[60]

The impetus for expanded television coverage partly reflected Congress' rivalry with the president. President Nixon pre-empted network television eleven times in 1969 and 1970 to explain his policy on Vietnam.[61] Senator George McGovern (D-S.D.) and thirteen other senators requested free air time to reply to Nixon; but they were permitted only to purchase time, only on one network, only once. Congress needed improved communication with the public, said Sen. Lee Metcalf (D-Mont.), chair of the Joint Committee, because "a Congress only able to whisper . . . cannot check and balance the power of the Executive."[62]   That television could enable Congress to do more than whisper, in its struggles with the Executive, was underlined in 1974 when the televised Senate and House committee proceedings in the Watergate scandal culminated in Nixon's resignation.

The House leadership resisted televising floor debate on the grounds that it would interfere with the orderly conduct of business and reduce the quality of deliberation. A few members voiced concern that broadcasting floor proceedings would change the House "from a forum to a theater."[63]

But the popular appeal of a measure to increase openness gave the advocates of television coverage a decisive advantage. Reportedly, many members who feared harm to the deliberative process felt uncomfortable expressing that fear.[64] Understandably so: To say that allowing the public to observe floor debate reduces the quality of deliberation does not pay the public a compliment. Broadcasting congressional proceedings was "one of those motherhood issues," a congressional aide observed: "No one wants to come out against it."[65]

Even though the public was at no time much absorbed in debates about congressional reform, the general public sentiment in favor of openness in government helped push congressional procedures to greater openness than they had ever before had—with the recording of nearly all roll-call votes and television broadcast of congressional proceedings. In turn, those measures, adopted in the early and middle 1970s, made the sentiments of ordinary citizens even more powerful in succeeding years.

### Social Security Benefits

The Social Security Amendments of 1972, providing a huge benefit increase for retirees, largely transformed the retirement program from a popular and noncontroversial program into what is often considered the most bloated spending element of the federal budget and the untouchable "third rail of American politics." The adoption of these amendments is a paradigmatic case of the enlarged influence of mass opinion in the 1970s: For no particularly evident reason, a perennially popular policy measure—increasing Social Security benefits—was carried further than ever before. Policy considerations that had traditionally been advanced by experts, especially those of long-term financial soundness, took a back seat.

The Social Security program has always had been popular, in large part because it was designed to be immune to political attack. As Martha Derthick has shown, it was fashioned to give the illusion of insurance.[66] In the program's terminology, benefits are "earned" by "contributions" to an account. In reality, benefits for most individuals have greatly exceeded the proceeds of their contributions and have been heavily subsidized by taxes on current workers. People have enjoyed the illusion of self-reliance along with indulgence of subsidy. As President Franklin D. Roosevelt explained this design privately, retirees would have "a legal, moral and political right to collect their pensions. . . . With those taxes in there, no damn politician can ever scrap [it]."[67]

In fact, the Old Age Program has had almost universal public support. As Skocpol and Ikenberry have noted, middle- and working-class Americans have consistently supported programs like Social Security, whose benefits they consider "earned."[68] From the early 1960s through the early 1980s, very large majorities (80-90 percent) opposed cuts to Social Security, wanted to spend more on it, or believed that the government should do more to improve Social Security benefits.[69] Those who attacked the program—like 1964 Republican presidential candidate Barry Goldwater—or even seemed to trifle with it—like 1972 Democratic presidential candidate George McGovern (who suggested a Social Security-backed minimum benefit of $1,000 for all Americans)—have paid the price that Roosevelt would have predicted. For more than three decades prior to 1972, Social Security grew incrementally. Adopting carefully modulated benefit increases or expansions of program coverage was a time-honored tactic of reelection-seeking in national politics.

What changed in the 1970s was the magnitude of policymakers' response to this incentive. The 1972 Amendments provided a 20 percent boost in benefits, which came on top of a 15 percent increase in 1969 and a 10 percent increase in 1971.[70] Although the inflation of the period knocked the total increase down to about 23 percent in real terms,[71] the Amendments also locked in the new boost by indexing benefit levels to the cost of living. In important respects, the 1972 Amendments abandoned the conservative actuarial and economic assumptions that had provided assurance of the Old Age program's financial soundness since the 1930s. It switched funding from a "partial reserve basis" to a "pay-as-you-go" system (with reserves, on average, only equal to annual payments), although that change largely represented formal recognition of existing practice. More important, it adopted "dynamic earnings" assumptions—the expectation of rising wage levels—for long-term revenue forecasts. Finally, it did not impose a tax increase to pay for the new benefits. Instead, it allowed reserves to fall in the short term to only 80 percent of annual payments, near the bottom of the planned range.[72]

Experts from the Social Security Administration (SSA) endorsed these decisions. But as Derthick suggests, with the recent departure of long-time Chief Actuary Robert J. Myers and the arrival of experts selected by an expansion-minded commissioner, Robert Ball, the SSA staff had lost some of the nonpartisan independence it had exercised in the past.[73] In sharp contrast to the past practice of keeping a margin for error, therefore, the 1972 Amendments used an optimistic scenario and pushed the benefits it would allow to the limit.

In some degree, the new style in Social Security policy resulted from a transformation in the priorities of Rep. Wilbur Mills (D-Ark.), the influential chairman of the House Ways and Means Committee. For a generation Mills had built the reputation of a conservative who had unmatched knowledge of the committee's legislation and who exercised "the utmost caution, responsibility, and prudence" in policy development.[74] A careful guardian of Social Security, he had opposed earlier proposals for indexing.[75] The classic congressional insider as well, Mills surprised almost everyone in Washington by announcing his candidacy for the 1972 Democratic presidential nomination, and surprised them again, shortly before the New Hampshire primary, by calling for a Social Security benefit increase of 20 percent.

But more important than the change in Mills was that his surprising proposal did not encounter much resistance. Senator Frank Church (D-Ida.), working with the senior-citizens' lobby, recruited forty-eight Senate co-sponsors for the 20 percent benefit increase. On the House floor, Republicans tried to limit the increase to 10 percent. But on Mills's assurances, the House defeated that effort.[76] The Nixon White House initially had dismissed Mills's proposal as "a political ploy."[77] But with the election approaching, Nixon too fell in line and signed into law the largest increase in the nation's largest social program.

Writing in the late 1970s, Derthick expressed some puzzlement about the 1972 Amendments and took note of two seemingly conflicting interpretations. Her reference point was the domination of Social Security policy making by elites—program administrators, analytic experts, and specialists in Congress—from the 1940s to the early 1970s. On one view, she suggested, the 1972 act represented the "old system of policymaking carried to a perverted pathological extreme. . . . [A] quantum increase in benefit levels was enacted on the authority of experts that it was the thing to do." On another view, however, the act's adoption may be "a transitional event," and may lead to "a new system that would be more accessible to nonspecialists."[78]

From the standpoint of our general argument, we find the two views compatible, and we endorse both. We certainly agree that the 1972 Social Security Amendments was a transitional event leading to a greater role for nonspecialists; it was one of several major policy decisions that demonstrated the increased influence of mass opinion in the 1970s. Yet we are not surprised that the process of decision still seemed dominated by experts and specialists. We argue that policy making had generally become more deferential to mass opinion, compared with the past, no matter who was directly conducting it. Because elected officials were dealing with a more issue-oriented mass public, even program specialists in the belly of the bureaucracy were more responsive to mass opinion.

## Petroleum Price Policy

In the early and middle 1970s, the United States developed and implemented a massively complex and intrusive regulatory regime to control energy pricing and distribution. The creation of this regime was largely a response to mass opinion. In this case, the popular demands were specific, salient, and new: The public was experiencing economic distress from inflation and, in particular, dramatic price increases for gasoline, fuel oil, and natural gas. Encouraged by congressional Democrats, the public resisted realistic, though painful, market-oriented strategies for dealing with shortages, credited conspiracy theories of the energy crisis, and demanded protection from higher prices. Policymakers rejected the advice of most economists and vigorous protests from the energy industries and put in place a hugely inefficient regulatory regime.

From the late 1950s to the early 1970s, U.S. intervention in petroleum markets was designed not to protect consumers but, if anything, to raise prices and profits for the petroleum industry. For the ostensible purpose of protecting national security, a system of import quotas kept U.S. oil prices well above world levels.[79] By the late 1960s, this system was coming under attack. A Nixon administration cabinet task force, led by Secretary of Labor George Schultz, recommended eliminating import quotas in favor of a less intrusive tariff.[80]

But instead of ending government intervention in the oil market, Nixon reversed the goal of intervention. In August 1971, responding to rising public anxieties about inflation, Nixon ordered a ninety-day freeze on all wages and prices, including petroleum prices. Then, responding further to the public's more specific anxieties about prices for gasoline and heating oil, he extended controls on petroleum prices as the general freeze was ended. Over the next year and a half, however, price increases resumed as controls were relaxed, with wholesale petroleum prices rising at an annual rate of 20 percent during the first half of 1973. Nixon imposed another wage-and-price freeze. And shortages of petroleum became manifest."[81] By late 1973, summer gasoline lines, escalating world prices, and the Arab Oil Boycott had made petroleum prices a major issue.

The issue of regulating petroleum prices was highly partisan—with Democrats demanding tough controls to protect consumers and Republicans defending the oil industry and the virtues of free markets. But Republicans, who had the less popular cause, had less taste for the battle. Nixon gave up without a fight—seeking and obtaining, in the Emergency Petroleum Allocation Act of 1973, temporary governmental authority to stabilize oil prices, allocate crude oil to refineries, and make preparations for gasoline rationing. President Ford initially tried to deregulate oil prices administratively.[82] And he resisted the efforts of congressional Democrats' efforts to legislate long-term controls. But in the end he reluctantly signed the Energy Policy and Conservation Act of 1975, which imposed a "long-term, all inclusive regulatory regime,"[83] with authority for presidential rationing of petroleum and a pricing formula for domestic oil.[84]

Democrats had the upper hand on petroleum policy because they had the superior strategy from the standpoint of popular rhetoric—blaming the industry for high prices. Senator John O. Pastore (D-R.I.), chairman of a Democratic Party panel on energy, stated the liberal Democrats' indictment of the oil companies in 1975: "All they're doing is socking it on, socking it on, socking it on. And by the time they get through, the American public is going to freeze to death. I say shame on the oil industry. They own the oil, they own the gas . . . and pretty soon they're going to own the country."[85] A liberal Republican joined in, calling the oil-industry lobby "the biggest and slickest and richest of them all."[86]

Attacks on the oil industry had a receptive audience. As a January 1974 poll showed, more than 80 percent of the public blamed the administration, Congress, or both for the energy crisis—a defensible view, considering the actual contribution of import quotas and price controls. But a massive 87 percent of the public blamed the oil companies—with a majority, 56 percent, assigning them "major" blame.[87] The General Accounting Office observed that federal officials generally agreed on the reliability of oil-industry reports about petroleum availability. But "much of the public believes the present energy shortages have been contrived by the industry for the purpose of raising prices and increasing profits."[88] Such opinion militated against permitting the oil companies to raise prices.[89]

The preoccupation with consumer sensibilities and public opinion distorted the debate on petroleum policy in Congress. Substantively, as Nivola points out, the most certain benefit of price decontrol was to induce conservation and reduce demand, the inevitable effect of higher prices.[90] That such prices would also increase supplies was more debatable: Estimates of effects on supply depended on assumptions about the availability of undiscovered oil.[91]

Politically, however, the relative value of the two arguments was just the reverse. Democrats dismissed the expectation that higher prices would reduce the demand for oil significantly as "economic idiocy." And Republicans rarely bothered to challenge the point. Not even advocates of decontrol were willing to push the benefits of conservation—and tell voters, in effect, they would be forced to turn down their thermostats. Said House Minority Leader John J. Rhodes (R-Ariz.), "The name of the game, as far as energy is concerned, is supply." Because the notion of using prices to induce conservation would not sit well with ordinary citizens, the most important economic consideration favoring decontrol was mostly left out of the congressional debate.[92]

Although criticizing the measure, President Ford signed the Energy Policy and Conservation Act late in 1975 to remove the issue of petroleum pricing from the 1976 election campaign.[93] As a result, a massive scheme of regulation discouraged conservation, suppressed the growth of supplies, and allocated crude oil and petroleum products arbitrarily for the remainder of the decade. Summing up the debate on petroleum pricing, Wildavsky and Tenenbaum opine that energy may have been "the worst-handled policy problem of the century."[94]

## Trucking Deregulation

A central policy development of the 1970s and early 1980s was the deregulation of several major industries that had long enjoyed regulatory protection from competition—including stock brokerage, banking, savings-and-loans, telecommunications, airlines, railroads, and, our main focus in this section, trucking—that had long enjoyed regulatory protection from competition. Such regulation prohibited price cuts, excluded potential competitors, and restricted services, among other things, largely for the producers' benefit. The sweeping reduction of such regulation was a major change in American economic policy. Despite mixed results in some cases, deregulation has been credited with increasing efficiency and innovation in the affected industries, with benefits for the economy generally.

The deregulation of the trucking industry in 1980 was not primarily a response to public opinion. Nevertheless, mass politics played an important role in the outcome. We argue that the anticipation of diffuse public support for reform balanced off the intense organized opposition and made action on expert advice a plausible proposition in political terms. In contrast with the other cases we have discussed, the relevant public attitudes were quite distinct from the liberalism of the 1960s and early 1970s.

An ideologically neutral "good government" reform, trucking deregulation was sponsored by leaders of both political parties and both branches of government. On the advice of his Domestic Council Review Group on

Regulatory Reform, President Gerald Ford endorsed trucking deregulation, indicating that he was not moved by the opposition: "[I]f the Teamsters and truckers are against it," he reportedly told his aides, "it must be a pretty good bill."[95] Although Jimmy Carter did not campaign on deregulation in 1976, he also endorsed it after assuming the presidency. The main congressional advocate was Senator Edward Kennedy (D-Mass.), who began investigating trucking and pushing for a deregulation bill upon passage of the Airline Deregulation Act in 1978.[96]

The enactment of such a bill was facilitated by the Interstate Commerce Commission (ICC) which adopted increasingly aggressive deregulatory measures administratively in 1979 and 1980. To keep the ICC from undoing regulation piecemeal, the trucking industry demanded a resolution of the issues from Congress. Congress gave the industry a resolution, but not the one it wanted: The Motor Carrier Act of 1980 ratified nearly all of the ICC's actions and largely abolished regulatory protection for the trucking industry.

Deregulation was strongly and essentially unanimously endorsed by economists. Along with the ICC, the executive departments most concerned with the issue—Transportation, Justice, and Agriculture—all supported deregulation. Presidential staff agencies—the Council of Economic Advisors and the Council on Wage and Price Stability—also expressed strong support. Moreover, two respected, nonpartisan congressional agencies—the Congressional Budget Office and the General Accounting Office—joined in the chorus of support. Government opinion was seconded by academic experts across the ideological spectrum. Economists from the two leading Washington think tanks—the Brookings Institution and the American Enterprise Institute—and from various universities gave authoritative testimony favoring reform. In contrast, opponents of trucking deregulation had a striking lack of credible expert support. For supposed expert testimony, they were reduced to relying on hired consultants to the trucking industry.

Notwithstanding the weakness of their case on the merits, the most active organized interest groups vehemently opposed deregulation. A number of business groups, including the National Association of Manufacturers and the National Federation of Independent Business, supported deregulation, but no such groups mounted a major effort on its behalf. Only the American Trucking Association (ATA) and the Teamsters Union cared deeply about the issue and devoted substantial resources to fighting about it. They pulled out all the stops. The ATA spent more than $2 million in a publicity campaign, a hefty amount in the late 1970s. The ATA and the Teamsters each brought hundreds of members to Washington to lobby

Congress at crucial junctures. Both stressed that trucking deregulation was the major issue they would use to distinguish friends and enemies. In short, therefore, the most compelling interest-group pressures facing Congress on the issue opposed reform.[97]

Importantly, however, anticipated public support helped balance the political scales in some degree. Trucking deregulation was far from salient to the general public. A trucking industry survey found that few people even knew that the industry was subject to economic regulation. Newspapers reported developments on the trucking bill mainly in the business section. Nevertheless, there were grounds for expecting a generally favorable public response. Reform advocates were able to link deregulation to two widespread public concerns—inflation and big government—and they stressed these links in their rhetoric. With help from Common Cause, the White House pushed these themes to stimulate newspaper editorials endorsing deregulation.[98] In opening the Senate floor debate on the bill, Senate Commerce Committee Chair Howard Cannon (D-Nev.) called it a "rare opportunity . . . for the Senate to be able to do something more than merely pay lip service to reducing government regulation."[99] Confirming the political value of these appeals, several pro-reform senators who ran for reelection in 1980 used the inflation and big-government appeals to claim credit for trucking deregulation in their campaigns.[100]

These appeals to mass opinion were critical to the outcome. In the end most observers judged that the electoral politics of the trucking issue, on balance, opposed reform for most members of Congress. In electoral terms, the truckers and Teamsters were the main forces. Accordingly, senators of each party were more supportive of deregulation the further they were from their next election.[101] Nevertheless, the relatively effective public appeals helped overcome the interest-group pressures. They made a judgment on the balance of electorally relevant forces in some degree "a close call" for many members, as one reform advocate said.[102] Certainly, we would not expect a congressional majority to override massive, one-sided pressures against reform merely to follow the advice of economists. That popular appeals were able to play an important role in defeating powerful, intensely concerned interest groups—even on an issue of modest salience— was yet another indication of the growing power of public opinion.

## The Reagan Tax Cut

The Reagan tax cut of 1981 was the culmination of the rising influence of mass opinion in the 1970s and early 1980s. To an extraordinary degree, the measure had origins in and was shaped by the rhetorical needs of election campaigns. Premised on economic claims with virtually no support among professional economists, it was also an extraordinary rejection of conventional expertise. In a word, the tax cut was a paradigmatic case of policy driven by mass opinion. The consequences, moreover, were vast: Accompanied by only modest cuts in domestic spending and by increased spending for defense, the tax cut produced huge federal budget deficits and led to an era of conflict and frustration over deficit reduction.

Ronald Reagan ran for president in 1980 on the arresting promise that he would cut income tax rates 30 percent, increase defense spending substantially, and nevertheless balance the budget.[103] This platform repeated the tax proposals that many congressional Republicans, led by Representative Jack Kemp (R-N.Y.) and Senator William Roth (R-Del.), had supported and campaigned on in 1978 in an effort to set aside the political burden of the party's traditional fiscal austerity.

Reagan's promises were designed to indulge the conflicting demands of mass opinion on taxes and spending. Between 1976 and 1980, around two-thirds of the public felt that taxes were too high.[104] Indeed, California voters' approval of Proposition 13 in 1979 signaled the arrival of a "tax revolt." Many citizens, especially Republicans, supported more spending on national defense.[105] And nearly everyone wanted a balanced budget: More than three-quarters of the public favored a constitutional amendment to require such balance. On the other hand, although about 40 percent of the public saw excessive domestic spending as the cause of inflation, few wanted to cut any particular domestic programs.[106]

To support his projection of a balanced budget, Reagan made the remarkable claim that his proposed reduction in tax rates would stimulate so much economic growth that the revenues collected, instead of decreasing, would actually increase. The claim appealed to the doctrine of "supply-side economics," which was advocated mainly by an otherwise obscure economist, Arthur Laffer, and an editor of the *Wall Street Journal*, Jude Wanniski. It would be hard to overstate the lack of support for the supply-side claims in professional economics. Commenting on the Kemp-Roth bill in 1978, former chairman of the Council of Economic Advisors Gardner Ackley called it "the most irresponsible policy proposal—seriously advanced by people who should know better—that I can recall . . . I am ashamed of my profession for the fact that a handful of its members have suggested or endorsed this policy."[107] Arthur Okun of the Brookings Institution warned that the adoption of Kemp-Roth would be "the most irresponsible and ill-conceived fiscal action . . . [in] the history of this Nation."[108] Nobel laureate James Tobin called the bill an "irresponsible and dangerous proposal," and added that "the extravagant claims [made] on its behalf are wholly speculative, without analytical or empirical foundation."[109]

Even the prominent Republican economist Herbert Stein, a former advisor to Presidents Nixon and Ford, flatly rejected the supply-side claims: "There is no present evidence to support the opinion that a large tax cut . . . would increase . . . revenue." To the contrary, he warned that it might reduce revenue "substantially."[110] Along with other conservative economists, Stein stressed that any large tax cut should be matched by comparable reductions in federal expenditures.[111] Capturing the attitude of mainstream economists in his rival campaign for the Republican nomination, George Bush ridiculed Reagan's plan as "voodoo economics."

After his landslide victory in the general election, President Reagan proceeded vigorously to enact the voodoo. In the candid view of Budget Director David Stockman, the administration's budget was riddled with internal contradictions.[112] But Reagan succeeded in selling it to the public. In three nationally televised speeches, Reagan warned of "an economic calamity of tremendous proportions" if his economic plan were not enacted. Without the tax cut, he said, "a growing tax burden will put an end to everything we believe in and to our dreams for the future."[113]

The White House staff made sure that Reagan's message was disseminated widely. It gave special briefings for television networks, wire services, and major newspapers. Reagan loyalists outside the White House hired a public relations firm to create television commercials and organize a grassroots letter-writing campaign in support of the proposals.[114] By taking his case to the public, as Kernell argues,[115] Reagan managed to generate powerful pressures on members of Congress to go along.

With even Republican leaders of Congress expressing serious doubts, Congress passed the Reagan tax cut and most of his budget. Instead of the promised boom, a recession followed, and the budget deficit soared above $200 billion, more than three times higher than had ever before been experienced during peacetime. As Anthony Campagna dryly concludes, after reviewing the episode, "The supply-side estimates of the revenue effects of the tax cuts were simply overly optimistic. . . . The tax cuts were not self financing."[116]

Significant for our broader argument, the Reagan tax cut marked the abandonment of the liberalism of the 1960s and early 1970s. Unlike some of our other cases, therefore, this policy change cannot be attributed to a passion for participation connected with the liberal mood of that period: That mood had long since passed. It does, however, fit our interpretation.

In our view, the heightened responsiveness to mass opinion that produced reckless, overambitious liberal policies in the early 1970s—like the Clean Air Act of 1970 and the Social Security Amendments of 1972—also produced a conservative policy that was even more reckless and overambitious, the Reagan tax cut, a decade later.

## Conclusion

We have suggested the sweeping proposition that public opinion has become the dominant force in American politics. We have not, however, provided correspondingly broad support for that claim. Rather, we have identified causes of this development in changes in mass political behavior in the 1960s and succeeding decades. And we have pointed to manifestations of the public's dominant role in several of the leading policy conflicts of the 1970s and early 1980s.

As students of mass behavior have demonstrated, the American public changed considerably in the decades after the 1950s, essentially the starting point for modern survey research on political behavior. By the late 1960s or early 1970s, the public had become more educated, more ideological, and, most important for our purposes, more concerned about specific issues of public policy. Put simply, more citizens were expressing opinions or acting politically on more issues than in prior periods of American history.

This increasing issue-engagement of the mass public, we have argued, has had effects on the politics of policy. It has increased the influence of ordinary citizens' beliefs and concerns and that of rhetoric designed for their consumption. Conversely, it has diminished the power of organized interest groups. It has deprived public officials of some autonomy. And because most people do not follow policy debate in detail, it has sometimes reduced the influence of experts and specialists and, therefore, of careful thinking about policy problems.

Our six brief case studies suggest that such effects became apparent, shortly after the changes in mass politics, in major policy developments of the 1970s and early 1980s. To be sure, it is very difficult to make comparisons of the influence of public opinion over time. And our evidence is not conclusive. But it is suggestive. We have shown that several of the preeminent policy developments of this period have a common feature: They reflect a distinctively strong policy response, compared with previous responses on the same issues, to the preferences of ordinary citizens. Crudely stated, on clean air, government-in-the-sunshine, Social Security benefits, petroleum prices, deregulation of trucking and other protected industries, and reduced taxation, the public got far more of what it has generally wanted in these areas than ever before. In a sense, we infer a broad change in performance—a rising influence of public opinion—from the observation of remarkable deference to such opinion, by previous standards, in a wide range of specific areas.

We do not suggest that all policy making has become "high politics," with the president, party leaders, or other major figures struggling to win the hearts and minds of an attentive public. Rather, the visibility of the decisions and the specificity of public opinion varied. In some cases, such as those of clean air, petroleum pricing, and the Reagan tax cut, the mass public had strong, directly pertinent sentiments, and was highly attentive. In others, such as congressional reform and trucking deregulation, the public was largely unaware of the dispute. Policymakers responded to more general public attitudes, such as a preference for open procedures or hostility toward big government, that indicated potential reactions to such issues. With an electorate more open to issue-based appeals at election times, policymakers will attempt to weigh public opinion, actual or anticipated, even when issues are only moderately important and are decided without attracting wide notice.

Considered as a set, these decisions did not reflect a particular ideology or public mood. The responsiveness to mass opinion that produced major liberal victories in the early 1970s later produced an ideologically neutral, "good-government" reform, trucking deregulation, and a huge conservative victory, the Reagan tax cut. We believe that an increased role of mass opinion has remained apparent in major policy developments of the 1980s and 1990s: the successful tax reform of 1986, the perpetual frustrations of reforming entitlements and reducing budget deficits throughout this entire period, and the simplistic and often extreme measures dealing with crime and welfare in the 1990s, among others. The duration of this tendency and the variety of its policy effects point to origins, not in any ideological shift or transitory enthusiasm for participation, but rather in a general and lasting change in the role of issues in mass politics.

Finally, the consequences of this change for the performance of government are mixed. Public opinion is an increasingly effective weapon for policy advocates of many stripes. More than ever, the winners in policy conflict are those who enjoy the advantage of more effective appeals to mass opinion. As a result, policy making is better protected from narrow groups seeking private gain. Special-interest benefits are easy targets for popular rhetoric. But there is an important downside: Policy making is also more vulnerable to popular leaders advancing dubious claims of entitlement, offering emotional release, or promoting fantasy.

## Acknowledgment

We are grateful to Stella Herriges Quirk for helpful criticism of an earlier draft.

*University of Illinois at Urbana–Champaign*

## Notes

1. There is a significant literature, largely inspired by McCarthyism and the "radical right," that criticizes mass movements, however. For a discussion and critique, see Michael Paul Rogin, *The Intellectuals and McCarthy: The Radical Specter* (Cambridge, 1967).

2. Joseph Bessette, *The Mild Voice of Reason: Deliberative Democracy and American National Government* (Chicago, 1994); Anthony King, *Running Scared: Why America's Politicians Campaign Too Much and Govern Too Little* (New York, 1997).

3. Theodore J. Lowi, *The Personal President: Power Invested, Promise Unfulfilled* (Ithaca, 1985); Samuel Kernell, *Going Public: New Strategies of Presidential Leadership* (Washington, D.C., 1993); Paul Brace and Barbara Hinckley, *Follow the Leader: Opinion Polls and the Modern Presidents* (New York, 1992).

4. Bessette, *Mild Voice of Reason*, 220–28; Thomas E. Mann, "Renewing Congress: A Report from the Front Lines," in James A. Thurber and Roger H. Davidson, eds., *Remaking Congress: Change and Stability in the 1990s* (Washington, D.C., 1995), 174–85.

5. Thomas E. Cronin, *Direct Democracy: The Politics of Initiative, Referendum, and Recall* (Cambridge, 1989); Mickey Kaus, "Why California Hates Politics," *Washington Monthly* 17 (February 1985): 25–31.

6. Samuel P. Huntington, "The United States," in Michael Crozier, *The Crisis of Democracy: Report on Governability of Democracies to the Trilateral Commission* (New York, 1975); Samuel P. Huntington, *American Politics: The Promise of Disharmony* (Cambridge, Mass., 1981).

7. Richard A. Harris and Sidney M. Milkis, *The Politics of Regulatory Change: A Tale of Two Agencies*, 2d ed. (New York, 1996).

8. For a discussion of these views, see Jeffrey K. Tulis, "The Two Constitutional Presidencies," in Michael Nelson, *The Presidency and the Political System*, 3d ed. (Washington, D.C., 1990), 85–115.

9. Tulis, "Two Constitutional Presidencies"; Kernell, *Going Public*.

10. Bessette, *The Mild Voice of Reason*, 1994.

11. John Zaller, *The Nature and Origins of Mass Opinion* (New York, 1992).

12. On many issues, one or more of the sources of demand are relatively coherent: Mass opinion has a clear predominant tendency; most general-interest-oriented experts agree; or the most concerned interest groups are one side of a dispute. For example, the public favors the income-tax deduction for mortgage interest; so does the real estate

industry; but most economists are critical of it. On other issues, such as abortion or the progressivity of the tax code, all of the sources are thoroughly divided.

Most other influences on policy making (party platforms, ideological doctrines, agency testimony, and so on) are derivations or combinations of these kinds of demands.

13. Angus Campbell, Philip E. Converse, Warren E. Miller, and Donald E. Stokes, *The American Voter* (New York, 1960); For a summary of this literature, see Norman H. Nie, Sidney Verba, and John R. Petrocik, *The Changing American Voter* (Cambridge, Mass., 1979).

14. V. O. Key, *Public Opinion and American Democracy* (New York, 1964), 557-58.

15. Bureau of the Census, *Statistical Abstract of the United States: 1975* (Washington, D.C., 1975): 118 Table 199, "Years of School Completed, By Race and Sex: 1960 to 1974"; 525 Table 873, "New Books and New Editions Published, By Subject 1960 to 1974"; 517 Table 855, "Commercial Broadcast Stations, Number and Revenues: 1950-1973."

16. Nie, Verba, and Petrocik, *Changing American Voter.*

17. Ibid.

18. Nie, Verba, and Petrocik, *Changing American Voter,* 167, fig. 10.6, "Frequency of Evaluation of Candidates in Terms of Party Ties, Personal Attributes, and Issue Position"; 142, fig. 8.4, "The Rise of Political Consistency: Percent of Population with Consistent Attitudes, 1956-1973"; 143, fig. 8.5, "Distribution of Population on Political Beliefs."

19. For a response, see Bruce E. Keith et al., *The Myth of the Independent Voter* (Berkeley and Los Angeles, 1992); James L. Sullivan, James E. Parisian, and George E. Marcus, "Ideological Constraint in the Mass Public: A Methodological Critique and Some New Findings," *American Journal of Political Science* 22 (May 1978): 323-49; George F. Bishop, Alfred J. Tuchfarber, and Robert W. Oldendick, "Change in the Structure of American Political Attitudes: The Nagging Question of Question Wording," *American Journal of Political Science* 22 (May 1978): 250-69. Norman H. Nie and James E. Rabjohn, "Revisiting Mass Belief Systems Revisited: Or, Doing Research Is Like Watching a Tennis Match." *American Journal of Political Science* 23 (February 1979): 139-75.

20. Russell J. Dalton, *Citizen Politics in Western Democracies: Public Opinion and Political Parties in the United States, Great Britain, West Germany, and France* (Chatham, N.J., 1988), 192-200.

21. Ibid., 200.

22. Michael X. Delli Carpini and Scott Keeter, *What Americans Know About Politics and Why It Matters* (New Haven, 1996).

23. Lawrence R. Jacobs and Robert Y. Shapiro, "The Rise of Presidential Polling: The Nixon White House in Historical Perspective," *Public Opinion Quarterly* 59 (Summer 1995): 163-95.

24. Michael Barone, "The Power of the President's Pollsters," *Public Opinion* 11 (September-October 1988): 2-4.

25. Kathleen Jamieson Hall, *Dirty Politics: Deception, Distraction, and Democracy* (New York, 1992).

26. Gary C. Bryner, *Blue Skies Green Politics: The Clean Air Act of 1990 and Its Implementation* (Washington, D.C., 1995), 107.

27. Hazel Erskine, "The Polls: Pollution and Its Costs," *Public Opinion Quarterly* 36 (Spring 1972): 120-35.

28. James R. Wagner, "Washington Pressures/Environmental Teach-In," *National Journal* 2 (21 February 1970): 408-11.

29. Richard Corrigan, "Tough Local Actions on Air Quality Boost Nixon's National Standards Plan," *National Journal* 2 (9 May 1970): 968-70.

30. James R. Wagner, "Environment Report/Cautious New Council Makes Presence Felt in Government," *National Journal* 2 (5 September 1970): 1916-22.

31. Daniel J. Fiorino, *Making Environmental Policy* (Berkeley and Los Angeles, 1995), 37.

32. Richard Corrigan, "Nixon, Democrats, Agencies Rush to Take up New Environmental Cause," *National Journal* 2 (31 January 1970): 206-10.

33. Richard Corrigan, "Nixon's Antipollution Plan Seeks Federal Standards, Enforcement," *National Journal* 2 (14 February 1970): 326-28.

34. Richard Corrigan, "Environment Report: Air Pollution Bill May Force Cities to Curb Use of Automobiles," *National Journal* 2 (15 August 1970): 1756-58.

35. Charles O. Jones, *Clean Air: The Policies and Politics of Pollution Control* (Pittsburgh, 1975), 186-91.

36. "Clean Air Act Amendments," *Congressional Quarterly Weekly Report* 28 (19 June 1970): 1576-77.

37. Corrigan, "Tough Local Action," 969-70.

38. R. Shep Melnik, *Regulation and the Courts: The Case of the Clean Air Act* (Washington, D.C., 1983), 26-27; Jones, *Clean Air*, 191-95; Corrigan, "Environment Report," 1758.

39. Jones, *Clean Air*, 196.

40. "Senate Passes Stringent Anti-Pollution Bill, 73-0," *Congressional Quarterly Weekly Report* 28 (25 September 1970): 2315-20.

41. Alfred Marcus, "The Environmental Protection Agency," in James Q. Wilson, ed., *The Politics of Regulation* (New York, 1980), 273.

42. Jones, *Clean Air*, 197.

43. Ibid.

44. Ibid., 198.

45. Ibid., 201.

46. "Senate Passes Stringent Anti-Pollution Bill," 2316.

47. See, for example, Robert W. Crandall, *Controlling Air Pollution: The Economics and Politics of Clean Air* (Washington, D.C., 1983); Lawrence J. White, *The Regulation of Air Pollution Emissions* (Washington, D.C., 1982).

48. Roger H. Davidson and Walter J. Oleszek, *Congress Against Itself* (Bloomington, Ind., 1977), 270.

49. "Members Vote in Anonymity on Many Crucial Issues," *Congressional Quarterly Almanac, 91st Congress, 2nd Session, 1970* (Washington, D.C. 1971), 454.

50. "First Congressional Reform Bill Enacted Since 1946," *Congressional Quarterly Almanac, 91st Congress, 2d Session, 1970* (Washington, D.C., 1971), 447-57.

51. Michael J. Malbin, "Congress Report/New Democratic Procedures Affect Distribution of Power," *National Journal* 6 (14 December 1974): 1881-83.

52. "First Congressional Reform," 448, 453.

53. Ibid., 453.

54. Andrew J. Glass, "Congressional Report/Legislative Reform Effort Builds New Alliances among House Members," *National Journal* 2 (25 July 1970): 1607-14.

55. Ibid., 1611-12.

56. Ibid., 1612.

57. Ibid.

58. "First Congressional Reform," 453.

59. Ronald Garay, *Congressional Television: A Legislative History* (Westport, Conn., 1984), 35-65.

60. Ibid., 57-84, 87-94, 97-103.

61. Ibid., 64-69.

62. Ibid., 79.

63. "House Gets Set to Televise Sessions with Its Own Hand on the Camera," *Congressional Quarterly Weekly Report* 35 (17 December 1977): 2605–8.

64. "House Leadership Opposes Broadcast Plan," *Congressional Quarterly Weekly Report* 34 (20 March 1976): 623.

65. "Congress on TV: Who Will Control the Camera?" *Congressional Quarterly Weekly Report* 33 (26 April 1975): 866–70.

66. Martha Derthick, *Policymaking for Social Security* (Washington, D.C., 1979), 228–51.

67. Ibid., 230.

68. G. John Ikenberry and Theda Skocpol, "Expanding Social Benefits: The Role of Social Security," *Political Science Quarterly* 102 (Fall 1987): 389–416.

69. Benjamin I. Page and Robert Y. Shapiro, *The Rational Public: Fifty Years of Trends in Americans' Policy Preferences* (Chicago, 1992), 119.

70. John Myles, "Postwar Capitalism and the Extension of Social Security into a Retirement Wage," in Margaret Weir, Ann Shola Orloff, and Theda Skocpol, *The Politics of Social Policy in the United States* (Princeton, 1988), 274.

71. Derthick, *Policymaking*, 346.

72. Robert J. Myers, *Social Security* (Philadelphia, 1993), 388–89, 396–97, 432–33.

73. Derthick, *Policymaking*, 367.

74. Richard F. Fenno Jr., *Congressman in Committees* (Boston, 1973), 54.

75. Derthick, *Policymaking*, 350.

76. Carolyn L. Weaver, *The Crisis in Social Security, Economic and Political Origins* (Durham, N.C., 1982), 166.

77. Derthick, *Policymaking*, 360; "Mills Proposes 20% Benefit Rise in Social Security," *Wall Street Journal*, 24 February 1972, 2:2; "Nixon Aides, Others Puzzled by Mills Plan to Boost Social Security Benefits by 20%," *Wall Street Journal*, 29 February 1972, 3:2.

78. Derthick, *Policymaking*, 367, 368.

79. Edward W. Chester, *United States Oil Policy and Diplomacy: A Twentieth-Century Overview* (Westport, Conn., 1983), 30–36.

80. Ibid., 45; "Oil Import Review Nears End; Substantial Changes May Ensue," *National Journal* 1 (8 November 1969): 82–83; "Oil Import Policy," *Congressional Quarterly Almanac, 91st Congress, 2nd Session 1970,* 26 (1971): 895–99.

81. David Glasner, *Politics, Prices, and Petroleum: The Political Economy of Energy* (San Francisco, 1985), 93–103.

82. Richard Corrigan, "Energy Report/Federal Energy Office Fuel Priorities Spell Trouble for American Motorists," *National Journal* 5 (29 December 1973): 1950–51; "Mandatory Fuel Allocation Program Approved," *Congressional Quarterly Almanac, 93rd Congress, 1st Session 1973,* 29 (1974): 523–631; Elder Witt, "Energy and Environment," *Congressional Quarterly Almanac, 94th Congress, 1st Session, 1975,* 31 (1976): 173–76.

83. Pietro S. Nivola, *The Politics of Energy Conservation* (Washington, D.C., 1986), 23.

84. Richard Corrigan, "Energy Report/'Compromise' Oil Bill Ends up Pleasing Few," *National Journal* 7 (27 December 1975): 1735.

85. Richard Corrigan, "Energy Report/Ford, Congress Struggle over Petroleum Policy." *National Journal* 7 (1 March 1975): 318–23.

86. Richard Corrigan, "Tower Seeks Bloc of Oil, Gas States," *National Journal* 7 (15 March 1975): 402. The member quoted was Representative Silvio Conte (R-Mass.).

87. Barbara C. Farhar, "The Polls—Poll Trends: Public Opinion about Energy," *Public Opinion Quarterly* 58 (Winter 1994): 603–32.

88. Aaron Wildavsky and Ellen Tenenbaum, *The Politics of Mistrust: Estimating American Oil and Gas Reserves* (Beverly Hills, 1981), 121–22. (Italics in original.)

89. Nivola argues, very differently, that public opinion was ambivalent toward energy regulation and did not fundamentally constrain policymakers. His interpretation, however, is based on responses to nuanced, conditional questions in opinion polls. He writes:

> Polls revealed that majorities objected to deregulation if its main consequence was higher prices, but that they approved of it if the likely result was a larger oil supply. When samples were told that the probable outcome would be a little of both—fewer shortages but higher prices—opinion was fairly bifurcated between those who favored continued price controls and those who either disagreed or were undecided. (256)

This interpretation has two weaknesses: First, it finds ambivalence by grouping the undecided arbitrarily with the opponents of price controls. Second, and more important, it presumes that nuanced, conditional questions are the relevant predictors of citizens' responses at the next election. A more natural reading of the poll evidence would suggest that an elected official who supported decontrol of oil prices would have had much to fear in the voters' response.

90. Nivola, *The Politics of Energy Conservation*, 52-67.

91. Ibid., 57-60; Wildavsky and Tenenbaum, *Politics of Mistrust*.

92. Nivola, *The Politics of Energy Conservation*, 57, 63.

93. Ibid., 27.

94. Wildavsky and Tenenbaum, *Politics of Mistrust*, 9.

95. Derthick and Quirk, 46.

96. Ibid., 45-50.

97. Ibid., 100-101; 120-25; 164-74.

98. Ibid., n. 48.

99. Ibid., 131.

100. Ibid., 132 n. 66.

101. Ibid., 134.

102. Ibid., 132-33.

103. Anthony C. Campagna, *The Economy in the Reagan Years: The Economic Consequences of the Reagan Administration* (Westport, Conn., 1994), 32-34.

104. Page and Shapiro, *The Rational Public*, 160, fig. 4.16: "Taxes, 1947-1990."

105. During this period, the percentage of the public believing that "too little" was spent for defense rose from 22 percent to 51 percent. William G. Mayer, *The Changing American Mind: How and Why American Public Opinion Changed between 1960 and 1988* (Ann Arbor, Mich., 1993), 414.

106. Ibid., 93, 454-57, 468. About half of the public felt that the country was spending "too little" on "improving and protecting the environment," "improving and protecting the nation's health," and "improving the nation's education system." Somewhat smaller numbers of people felt that "too little" was being spent on "improving public transportation" (about 40-50 percent); "solving the problems of the big cities" (about 40 percent); and "improving the conditions of blacks" (about 25 percent).

107. Committee on Ways and Means, U.S. House of Representatives, *Tax Reductions: Economists' Comments on H.R. 8333 and S. 1860 (The Kemp-Roth Bills) Bills to Provide for Permanent Tax Rate Reductions for Individuals and Businesses* (Washington, D.C., 1978), 17.

108. Ibid., 71.

109. Ibid., 92.

110. Ibid., 89.

111. Ibid., 86-91.

112. Stockman revealed his opinion a few months after the debate was over in a notorious magazine interview: William Greider, "The Education of David Stockman," *The Atlantic Monthly* 248, December 1981, 27–54.

113. Gail Gregg, "'Let Us Act Together' Reagan Exhorts Congress," *Congressional Quarterly Weekly Report* 39 (21 February 1981): 331–37.

114. Ibid., 333.

115. Kernell, *Going Public*, 121–55.

116. Campagna, *The Economy in the Reagan Years*, 79.

# SIDNEY M. MILKIS

# Remaking Government Institutions in the 1970s: Participatory Democracy and the Triumph of Administrative Politics

## Introduction: The Quest for Democratic Administration

Interpreting the 1970s is a difficult business. On the one hand, reformers struggled earnestly and effectively to codify the exalted vision of a good society that was celebrated during the 1960s. And yet in doing so, they appeared to routinize rather than resolve the virulent conflicts of the previous decade. Scholars tend to agree that the reforms of the 1960s and 1970s marked a transformation of political life no less important than the Progressive Era and the New Deal. Unlike these earlier reform periods, however, the 1960s and 1970s did not embrace national administrative power as an agent of social and economic justice. Instead, reformers of the 1960s and 1970s championed "participatory democracy" and viewed the very concept of national governmental authority with deep suspicion. Indeed, Hugh Heclo characterizes the reform legacy of the 1960s and 1970s as one of intractable fractiousness, as a "postmodern" assault on the modern state forged on the anvil of reforms carried out during the Progressive and New Deal eras. "In the end, it appears that a great deal of postmodern policymaking is not really concerned with 'making policy' in the sense of finding a settled course of public action that people can live with," he writes. "It is aimed at crusading for a cause by confronting power with power."[1]

Still, the institutional reforms of the 1970s are miscast as the second phase of an antinomian attack on government authority. To be sure, there was a large element of hostility to centralized administrative power evident in the politics of the New Left reformers who played an important part in the civil rights and antiwar movements of the 1960s; moreover, the reform politics of these movements, championing community action and grassroots participation, inspired the self-styled "public interest" advocates of the 1970s who advanced policies that increased the national government's responsibilities to ameliorate racial and sexual discrimination and to enhance consumer rights and environmental protection. Notwithstanding their antiestablishment rhetoric and profound suspicion of centralized power, however, reform activists of the 1970s were intrepid liberals who sought to remake rather than to dismantle government institutions. As Jeffrey Berry has written, "Leaders of the new [public interest groups] wanted to transcend 'movement politics' with organizations that could survive beyond periods of intense emotion."[2] In truth, the public interest movement sought to harness the revolutionary fervor of the civil rights and antiwar movements as an agent for change within the system.

In seeking a departure from the progressive reforms of the past, public interest advocates targeted the modern presidency. Committed to strengthening national administrative power in the service of economic security, Franklin Roosevelt and his New Deal allies advanced political reforms that established the president, rather than Congress or the party organizations, as the principal agent of popular rule. Beginning with the Great Society, however, a new phase of liberalism was launched, emphasizing "quality of life" concerns. Lyndon Johnson first gave voice to this new philosophy in a commencement address at the University of Michigan on May 22, 1964. Those remarks, drawing on some of the principles championed by the New Left, boldly set forth Johnson's hopes for the Great Society. The new phase of liberalism "demanded an end of poverty and racial injustice," the President told the students and their families, "but that was just the beginning." Challenging his audience to embrace more ambitious goals for America, LBJ described his vision of a good society as one "where the city of man serves not only the needs of the body and the demands of commerce but the desire for beauty and hunger for community."[3]

Like FDR, Johnson was a presidentialist: The thrust of his institutional approach was to strengthen the managerial tools of the presidency with a view to enhancing the programmatic vision and energy of executive agencies. Yet the vision of the Great Society presupposed a "hunger for community" that suggested the limits of presidential government. Implicit in this philosophy of liberalism that emerged during the 1960s was the view that the problems afflicting the well-to-do and the poor could not be solved by centralized administration and federal largesse alone, but required a more creative intervention of the state that would address the underlying causes of social and political discontent: alienation, powerlessness, and the decline of community. It is not surprising, therefore, that one of the outside task forces established by the Johnson presidency to identify and seek solutions to social problems recommended that community action be made an integral part of the war on poverty. In pursuance of this proposal, the Community Action Programs, governed by federal guidelines requiring "maximum feasible participation of residents of the areas and the groups served," were established to administer antipoverty policy.[4]

Such programs actually played a limited part in the Johnson administration, which in an unprecedented fashion relied on presidential politics. But the Community Action Program was an important and revealing prelude to the emergence of participatory democracy as a leading principle of the reformers who gained influence with the demise of the modern presidency. Hoping to reconcile national authority with the New Left's dedication to participatory democracy, reformers of the late 1960s and 1970s rejected the New Deal practice of delegating power to the executive branch. These public interest advocates championed statutes and judicial rulings that would reduce the discretionary power of presidents and administrative agencies. Just as significant, reform activists played the principal part in revamping administrative law during the 1970s, so that liberal provisions were established for public participation. Taking account of these changes, Samuel Beer noted at the end of the 1970s that "it would be difficult today to find a program involving regulation or delivery of services in such fields as health education, welfare, and the environment that does not provide for 'community input.'"[5]

In part, the effort of reformers to circumscribe executive administration can be attributed to the emergence of "divided government" as a regular feature of political life in the United States. Richard Nixon's election in 1968 marked the beginning of an increased tendency for voters to place the presidency in Republican hands and Congress under the control of Democrats; this pattern of ticket splitting would endure for the better part of two decades. New Deal reforms were conceived with the view that the modern presidency would be an ally of programmatic reform; in contrast, the liberalism of the 1970s was born of institutional confrontation between a conservative Republican president and a reform-minded Democratic Congress. Greatly suspicious of, if not avowedly hostile to, presidential power, reformers of the 1970s and their allies on the Hill were determined to protect liberal programs from unfriendly executive administration.

The battles that Democrats and Republicans waged for control of departments and agencies transcended narrow partisanship, however. As the unhappy term of Jimmy Carter revealed, one-party control of the White House and Congress did not assure institutional harmony. In fact, the restraints imposed on presidential power during the late 1960s and 1970s, reflecting a strong suspicion of centralized power, marked an impressive effort to ameliorate what Alexis de Tocqueville called the "puerilities of administrative tyranny."[6] As such, the reforms of the 1970s attempted to make national administrative power more legitimate by appealing to the antistatism that was so deeply rooted in the principles and historical traditions of political life in the United States.

Paradoxically, however, the reforms of the 1970s fixed the business of government more on administration. In their efforts to enhance the representative character of government action, reformers did not seek to retrain administrative power, but rather attempted to recast it as an agent of democracy. This required that Congress, the courts, and public interest groups become more involved in the details of administration. Thus, the reforms of the 1970s circumscribed the administrative power of the president but at the cost of making other government and political institutions more bureaucratic in their organization and activities. As a result, the expansion of liberalism during the 1970s resulted in the enervation, rather than the surge, of popular rule.

More penetratingly, public interest liberals were not always in harmony with the public they purported to represent. Although advocating a participatory democracy, public lobby groups articulated an ethos that indirectly expressed grave reservations about the core principles and standard procedures of political life in the United States. As Michael McCann has argued, whereas traditional, narrowly focused interest groups had often been celebrated for moderating deep social and economic divisions in the United States, public interest advocates "sought to promote a fundamental ideological debate over the very purposes and standards of public authority . . . by pitting quality against quantity, people against profits, and health against wealth."[7] Thus, in seeking to depart from the New Deal's emphasis on economic security, contemporary social reformers were alienated from the values and institutions that earlier progressives accepted as an inherent part of American life. It is not surprising, then, that public interest advocacy tended to focus on administrative and legal channels that were somewhat insulated from the more political institutions in American politics. Tragically, the public rights advocacy of the 1970s provided participatory opportunities for only a small circle of public lobbyists, while corroding the link between citizens and their government.

## Richard Nixon and the New Congress

In a generally sympathetic biography, Steven Ambrose attributes the fall of Richard Nixon to his lack of virtue. "In a free, open, and democratic society, politics is above all an education process," Ambrose observes. "The leader leads through persuasion and consent. Nixon tried to lead through surprise and manipulation."[8] The ugly events of Watergate were not simply the result of Nixon's character flaws, however; in part, they grew out of his determination to uphold the modern presidency in the face of growing doubts about it.

In the first instance, the administrative actions of the Nixon presidency were a logical extension of the practices of the Franklin Roosevelt and Lyndon Johnson. The centralization of authority in the White House and the reduction of the regular Republican organization to perfunctory status during the Nixon years was hardly new. The complete autonomy of the Committee for the Re-Election of the President (CREEP) from the Republican organization in the 1972 campaign was but the final stage of a long process of White House preemption of the national committee's political responsibilities. And the administrative reform program that was pursued after Nixon's reelection, in which executive authority was concentrated in the hands of White House operatives and four cabinet "supersecretaries," was the culmination of a long-standing tendency in the modern presidency to reconstitute the executive branch as a formidable and independent instrument of government.

Indeed, the strategy of pursuing policy goals through the administrative capacities that had been created for the most part by Democratic presidents was considered especially suitable by a minority Republican president who faced a hostile Congress and bureaucracy intent on preserving those presidents' programs. Nixon actually surpassed previous modern presidents in viewing the party system as an obstacle to effective governance. Yet, mainly because of the Watergate scandal, Nixon's presidency had the effect of strengthening opposition to the unilateral use of president power, even as it further attenuated the bonds that linked presidents to the party system.[9]

In the final analysis, Nixon's downfall grew out of his bitter relations with Congress. The sequence of events that defined the Watergate affair was the principal cause of Nixon's having the unhappy distinction to be the first president in American history to resign his office. Nixon's impeachment was assured by the Supreme Court action in *United States v.*

*Nixon*, which rejected the president's sweeping claims of executive privilege and forced release of tapes that showed the president had known all along of the cover-up.[10] But the willingness of Congress to take the extraordinary step of removing a president was in part a response to Nixon's repeated attempts to circumvent the legislature.[11] Certainly, Congress's resolve was strengthened by the ideological and partisan struggles that marked the relations between the president and Congress. Just as important, Congress had undergone important changes during the 1960s that prepared it to undertake an assault not only on Nixon but also on the authority of the executive office.

The reconstruction of Congress began in 1958 with the significant gains Democrats made outside the South that year in congressional elections. Liberals, in fact, now made up a majority of the House Democratic party. Frustrated by the advantage that the seniority rule continued to accord conservatives from the noncompetitive South in obtaining powerful committee chairs, liberal Democrats created the House Democratic Study Group (DSG) in 1958. This group of liberals within the House Democratic caucus focused their efforts on lessening the power of the conservative committee chairs and spreading that power more widely among all Democrats, particularly the liberal majority.[12]

Nevertheless, the conservative coalition—the alliance forged between Southern Democrats and Republicans during Roosevelt's second term—continued to thwart liberal legislation through the Kennedy presidency. Johnson's mastery of legislative matters enabled him to overcome the opposition of Southern Democrats in the enactment of the 1964 Civil Rights Act, and the landslide victory achieved soon thereafter brought enough Northern liberal Democrats into Congress to wrest power in the House and Senate from the "conservative coalition." With the passage of the 1965 Civil Rights Act, moreover, Johnson ensured the transformation of Southern Democracy that eluded his illustrious predecessor. The weakening of the conservative coalition and the concomitant rise of the DSG combined to cause the transformation of the legislative branch, culminating in the procedural changes of the early 1970s that dramatically altered the congressional power structure.

The reconstructed Congress was not content to protect programmatic liberalism from an indifferent or hostile presidency. Rather, it pursued an ambitious liberal agenda that sought dramatically to extend the boundaries of FDR's economic constitutional order. The problem of hunger, for example, was "discovered" in America just as LBJ was cutting back on the War on Poverty to make room in his budget for the military build-up in

Vietnam. This was no accident—it was the result of efforts by a few senators, notably Robert Kennedy, George McGovern, and Joseph Clark, and their allies in the labor movement (especially Walter Reuther), foundations (such as the Ford and Field Foundations), newly formed "citizen" groups, and media to make the problem of hunger apparent to the American people, and thus to revitalize the flagging War on Poverty. As a result, the politics of food stamps changed suddenly and dramatically toward the end of the Johnson era. The coterie of food stamp reformers, dedicated to the creation of a right to a "nutritionally adequate diet," had previously seen the president and the Department of Agriculture as their primary allies in the fight against the conservative coalition in Congress. They now turned on Lyndon Johnson and his Secretary of Agriculture, Orville Freeman—a member in good standing of the Minnesota Farm Labor Party—whom they accused of being callously cautious. Liberal democrats in Congress, using the Senate Select Committee on Human Needs as a forum, worked with the press and a small but skilled group of "hunger lobbyists" to force Johnson's hand and to write legislation requiring program expansion.[13]

The hunger issue was part of a broader endeavor that reshaped liberalism during the late 1960s and 1970s. As noted, the expansion of the liberal agenda included commitments not just to programmatic advances in the war against poverty, but also to new issues such as community control and "participatory democracy" that led liberal activists to challenge New Deal institutions. Once Nixon sat in the White House, partisan politics sharpened the reformers attacks on the executive branch. Although Nixon's attack on the liberal state was modest by contemporary standards—indeed, his administration proposed and implemented the largest expansion of the food stamp program in history—he was constantly scorned by food stamp advocates. Before long, however, the enemy had become not just the Nixon administration, in particular, but the modern presidency in general.

In his battles with the liberal establishment, Nixon relied on what Benjamin Ginsberg and Martin Shefter call "institutional combat," a form of political warfare befitting an era of political decline and electoral stalemate. With the advent of divided government, they have written, "The Democrats and Republicans continue to contest elections. But rather than pin all its hopes on defeating its foes in the electoral arena, each party has begun to strengthen the institutions it commands and to use them to weaken its foes' governmental and political base.[14] Thus, the "new" politics of the 1960s and 1970s was gradually developing into a form of party politics centered on government rather than the electorate. Furthermore, this partisan and institutional combat revolved around the task of controlling the administrative levers of powers, thus further eroding and making unlikely the renewal of partisan attachments in the electorate. Indeed, the Liberal response to Watergate emphasized the need to tame rather than win back the modern presidency. The legislation passed during the 1970s designed to accomplish this task, such as the War Powers Resolution, should be viewed only in part as an attempt to revive Congress's constitutional prerogative; just as surely, such measures were intended to facilitate an ambitious expansion of welfare and regulatory programs. Similarly, the passage of the Budget Control Act of 1974, which was designed to give Congress control over the executive budget, was intended to protect social reform from the sort of fiscal assault on social welfare programs Nixon sought to carry out after his 1972 reelection.

These laws in and of themselves would have only a marginal effect on presidential power. But their enactment was associated with a determination of the "new' Congress to reestablish itself as an equal partner, indeed, the dominant force in the government and nation. It was this determination that gave rise to the procedural reforms of the early 1970s that remade the legislative power structure—the result was a decentralized yet aggressive legislature that was well equipped to participate in the details of administration. The most important reforms were those that increased the number, power, autonomy, and staff of congressional subcommittees. A decentralized institution since the rebellion against Speaker Joseph Cannon during the Progressive Era, Congress became even more so; in effect, the power of standing committees devolved into subcommittees. But this time the legislative rebellion was carried out by insurgents whose target was as much the president as their more stolid and conservative adversaries in Congress. As R. Shep Melnick has written about this administrative reform:

> Using subcommittee resources, members initiated new programs and revised old ones, challenging the president for the title of "chief legislator." No longer would Congress respond to calls for action by passing vague legislation telling the executive to do something. Now Congress was writing detailed statutes that not infrequently deviated from the president's program. Subcommittees were also using oversight hearings to make sure that administrators paid heed not just to the letter of legislation, but to its spirit as well.[15]

It is important to realize, however, that the reform assault on the modern presidency was not simply a pragmatic adjustment of institutional arrangements to ensure a more strident and consistent commitment to Liberal programs. In fact, the restraints imposed on the presidential power during the late 1960s and 1970s reflected a strong suspicion of administrative power that was not open to public participation. In important respects, such a suspicion was a logical outgrowth of the reform vision of the Great Society. Just as the Community Action Program represented more than a substitute for substantive benefits during the Johnson era, so the procedural niceties in statutes enacted during the 1970s were not simply intended by Congress to be an ersatz government benefit; nor were congressionally created procedural rights merely a method for avoiding issues on which legislators received conflicting pressures. There was a strong antibureaucratic, anti-institutional ethos in the "new" Congress; in fact, those legislators who had revolted against the seniority system claimed to support "participatory democracy" within Congress. Republican control of the presidency made liberal Democratic legislators even more enthusiastic about guaranteeing public interest groups and "average" citizens, most of whom were adversaries of the Nixon administration, an active role in the administration of government programs. Consequently, by one count, there were approximately 226 citizen participation programs mandated by federal statutes by 1977, and the courts were vigilant in making sure that state and federal agencies adhered to the letter and spirit of these participation requirements.[16] The assault on the prerogatives of the modern presidency, then, was associated with institutional changes that expanded the national government's administrative power but tied the use of such power to procedural safeguards designed to reconcile centralized administration and participatory democracy.

## Public Participation and the Reform of Administrative Politics

The effort to enhance the representative character of the administrative state was most closely associated with the expansion of regulatory programs during the late 1960s and 1970s. Most significant, ambitious new undertakings were launched in the area of "social" regulation, leading to the creation of new administrative agencies and the redirection of certain existing ones to address issues such as employment discrimination against minorities and women, environmentalism, consumer protection, and health and safety. The rise of social regulation began with the 1964 Civil Rights Act, which created the first of the new social regulatory agencies: the Equal Employment Opportunity Commission, charged with administering Title VII (concerned primarily with employment discrimination) of the landmark civil rights statute. During the late 1960s and 1970s, a vast array of new federal laws and new federal agencies were enacted that looked well beyond civil rights, thus giving concrete expression to the "quality of life" concerns that most clearly distinguished the New Deal and Great Society.[17]

In part, this new social regulation constituted a change in the political economy that required unprecedented centralization of the national government's administrative power. Business found the new social regulation especially disturbing because it empowered executive agencies to intrude into broad problem areas with detailed prescriptions for the manufacture and sale of products. As Bernard Falk of the National Electrical Manufacturers' Association noted about the expansion of the government's regulatory role in the 1970s, "In the past going back ten or fifteen years, you didn't have a consumer movement. The manufacturer controlled the make-up of his own product, and Washington could be ignored. Now we all have a new partner, the federal government."[18]

Yet, paradoxically, this centralization of power went hand in hand with changes in administrative law that reflected strong suspicion of administrative power. As such, the institutional initiatives that were linked with the social reforms of the 1970s were motivated by concerns to recast the concept of citizenship in American politics to conform with the expansion of national administrative power. These changes reflected the view, first articulated by the carriers of the new politics during the 1960s, that the New Deal, while bringing valued reforms, had devolved into an impersonal, bureaucratic, centralized form of governance that was dehumanizing American society. Moreover, reformers during the late 1960s and 1970s believed that the procedures by which decisions were made in the administrative state were controlled by large business interests that were inattentive to public values—the prominent social problems that dominated the political agenda of the 1970s, such as the despoliation of the environment and the manipulation of consumers, were depicted by reformers as a byproduct of the capture of the public sector by corporate interests.

The apparent tension between national administrative power and democratic citizenship created a real dilemma within the American political system. On the one hand, local government and community control remain at the heart of the American idea of democracy. On the other hand, since the New Deal, Americans had come to accept as just and inevitable the development of a strong national government, deemed necessary to provide for economic security, protect freedom from foreign threats, limit the power of corporations, and guarantee equal protection of the law.

The public interest advocates who had such a strong influence on public policy during the 1970s were committed to expanding the programmatic responsibilities of the national government, and, therefore, were not predisposed to reduce the prerogatives of the executive departments and agencies per se. Consequently, the task in large part was to establish new agencies, such as the Environmental Protection Agency, and refurbish existing ones, such as the Federal Trade Commission, thereby creating new centers of administrative power that would not become as inefficient and unresponsive as regulatory agencies typically had in the past. As Ralph Nader urged, regulatory bodies were not to be delegated responsibility to act for the public, but to be governed instead by the administrative mechanisms providing liberal provision for public participation, "so that agency lethargy or inefficiency could be checked by interested citizen activity."[19] The achievement of civil rights, consumer, and environmental regulations was deemed worthless so long as the administrative process was not opened up to direct citizen action.

The commitment to public participation required an ongoing presence of public interest groups in administrative decisionmaking. Hence the culmination of liberalism was associated not with the renewal of party politics, but with the rise of public interest groups tailored to facilitate the direct participation of citizen activists in the administrative process. To be sure, many regulatory reform groups that arose in the 1970s resembled the organizations that became part of the New Deal coalition. For example, labor and civil rights groups, which became major constituencies of the New Deal coalition, often worked with but did not formally become part of the Democratic party. This represented a new form of presidential coalition that both converted independents to Democratic allegiance and made conventional, partisan participation less important. But public interest activists, lacking the well-defined popular support labor unions and civil rights groups could draw upon, largely abstained from partisan strategies of grassroots mobilization and electoral alliance as a means of developing effective political influence. Although conceding that the goal of expanding popular electoral participation may be valuable in itself, public interest liberals found such a strategy largely irrelevant in the face of the New Deal institutional legacy—unrelated to the task of rendering either the bureaucratic state or corporate elites accountable to the public.[20] As Richard Ayres, then senior attorney for the National Resources Defense Council (NRDC), noted with respect to the creation of this environmental group:

> The motivating or animating idea of the NRDC was the realization that in the twentieth century and especially since the New Deal the

executive branch is the most powerful of the three and the interests of the public get lost for lack of expertise and knowledge of the administrative process. In the past environmental or other citizen groups won victories in the legislative branch only to lose in the executive branch. It is clear that the administrative process is where the action is. . . . It is interesting that Labor which clearly challenged the political-economic establishment never learned how important the administrative arena was. . . .They haven't got for all their legal expertise, an organization like the NRDC. They are involved in Congress and party politics which matter less and less.[21]

In little more than a decade, as Walter Rosenbaum noted toward the end of the 1970s, the attempt to marry administration and democracy had led to a "radical redefinition of public rights in the federal administrative process." Beginning with a few precarious innovations in the 1960s, the "new" public involvement "now threatened to become a cliché as a multitude of statutory mandates and agency regulations . . . prescribed citizen involvement in agency affairs vastly exceeding the standard once considered appropriate."[22] One of the earliest of these new programs could be found in the Federal Water Pollution Control Act Amendments of 1972. As Section 101(e) of the statute read: "Public Participation in the development, revision and enforcement of any regulation, standard, effluent limitation, plan or program established by the Administrator, or any State under this Act shall be provided for, encouraged and assisted by the Administrator and the states."[23] Beginning in 1975, Congress intensified its efforts to foster public participation and began to legislate provisions explicitly authorizing direct financial aid for participation of citizen groups in specific regulatory actions of certain agencies, most notably the Federal Trade Commission, the Consumer Product Safety Commission, and the Environmental Protection Agency.[24]

The first, pathbreaking enactment of legislative authorization for financial assistance came in the Federal Trade Commission Improvement Act of 1975: the Magnuson-Moss Act. This legislation created an "intervener funding program," which authorized the FTC to pay attorney fees and expert witness costs and other expenses of participation by parties otherwise unable to represent their interests in rule-making proceedings.[25] These funds overwhelmingly went to public interest groups supportive of the ambitious pro-consumer policies that were increasingly pursued by the FTC after 1975.[26] It is rather ironic that these "public" participation funds were concentrated among a relatively few organizations and law firms that came to comprise a specialized "pro-consumer FTC bar." Yet consumer activists claimed that the failure to foster genuine "grass roots" participation was symptomatic of the great difficulty involved in striking a balance between the technical competence demanded by the administrative state and "partipatory" democracy. Those groups that were part of the privileged "public" asserted that without the continuity of representation achieved by a few organizations receiving federal support to participate in several regulatory proceedings, the consumer activists could not achieve equality with business and trade-group respondents.[27]

The attempt to reconcile centralized administration and participatory democracy through funding a rather limited universe of "public" interest groups was troublesome; no less problematic was the development of the judiciary during the 1960s and 1970s as a critical channel for public participation in administrative rule-making procedures. The judiciary did not intervene in the details of FTC proceedings because this agency was created during the Progressive Era as an independent regulatory commission, and is thus entitled to act as a court of equity in defining and enforcing values. Yet many other agencies, particularly those created at the height of the "participatory revolution," were subjected to extensive judicial oversight, which played a significant part in expanding regulatory activities in the areas of civil rights, environmentalism, public health, and safety. This expansion went hand in hand with the courts' recognition of elaborate procedural rights for groups directly affected by government programs, as well as for organizations claiming to speak for the "public."

The alliance forged between citizen action and the Judiciary was a strange one, because the courts are organized within the American constitutional framework to be extensively independent of public views. But the statutes passed during the 1960s and 1970s were often couched in terms of entitlements—as statutory rights—rather than bureaucratic obligations, thereby inviting the federal judiciary to become a forceful and consistent presence in administrative politics.[28] Until the 1960s, the executive was guided by the Administrative Procedures Act, which, reflecting the New Deal commitment to guaranteeing economic security and its faith in "enlightened administration," left departments and agencies considerable autonomy from judicial and legislative interference. With the formulation of a new version of liberalism during the Great Society, there was a great expansion of programmatic rights: the right to be free of discrimination; the so-called "collective" rights associated with consumer and environmental protection; and, significantly, the right of those affected by government programs (and those representing the "Public") to participate in the administration of these programs. As public participation evolved into a procedural right during the 1970s, the courts became vigilant in making sure that federal agencies adhered to the newly recognized procedural requirements. These developments resulted in a de facto, if not de jure, amendment of the Administrative Procedures Act. As Martin Shapiro has written, during the late 1960s and 1970s, "[the courts] invented a host of procedural requirements that turned rulemaking into a multi-party paper trial. They also imposed a rulemaking record requirement that allowed courts to review minutely every aspect of that trial . . . The courts . . . did these things to reduce the independence and discretionary scope of a mistrusted bureaucracy and to subordinate it to more control by the regulated, the beneficiaries of regulation, and the public at large."[29]

The statutory provisions relating to procedural rights reinforced the courts' extensive efforts beginning in the late 1960s to expand participation of those claiming to speak for the poor, racial minorities, consumers, and environmentalists. In particular, lawsuits in the 1960s and 1970s helped to establish the standing of citizen groups to sue federal agencies for law enforcement. Moreover, many statutes, especially environmental laws, lent Congress's support to this development by granting automatic standing to sue and establishing liberal provisions for class actions. Consequently, the lawsuit, once considered the province of the privileged, became the principal tool during the 1970s of opening up the administrative process. As Richard Stewart wrote in the wake of this transformation of administrative law, "Courts have changed the focus of judicial review (in the course of expanding and transforming traditional procedural rights), so that its dominant purpose is no longer the prevention of unauthorized intrusion on private autonomy, but the assurance of fair representation for affected interests in the exercise of legislative power delegated to agencies."[30] As with intervenor funding, however, it was "public" interest groups, rather than the public, that benefited directly from this development.

## Public Participation and the Crisis of the Liberal Order

Although the public interest movement did gain substantial influence on the policy process by building elaborate organizational networks and making effective use of the media, this influence was never really solidified into an enduring political coalition. The emphasis of public interest groups on single-issue advocacy and use of the media was characteristic of what James Q. Wilson refers to as "entrepreneurial politics," that is to say, social regulatory policy was dominated by a small number of Washington-based activists, who served as "vicarious representatives" of diffuse and poorly organized interests.[31] To a point, such advocacy was necessary, for environmental, consumer, and health laws and regulation conferred general benefits on the public at a cost to small, albeit well-organized, segments of society. Since the incentive to organize is relatively weak for beneficiaries but strong for opponents of such policies, it is perhaps necessary for public interest advocates to position themselves as representatives of the public. Nevertheless, the defense of "collective" rights puts public lobbyists in a precarious position: Because as defenders of general rather than specific concerns, they are often without strong political allies.

The public interest movement, then, while capable of eliciting popular support by dramatizing corporate abuse and defending unassailable values such as clean air and consumer rights, was, in fact, built on a fragile institutional foundation. The institutional structure was well suited to harnessing symbolic political campaigns into regulatory programs, yet incapable of establishing deeply rooted political affiliation among the public. As consumer advocate and former chairman of the FTC, Michael Pertschuck admitted:

> It might be said that we represented the late New Deal liberal tradition. . . . We were disproportionately Ivy Leaguers, do-gooders, knee-jerk liberals, occupied with alleviating the hardships of others, fueled by faith in the capacity of government to represent the people against "private greed," so long as the government was peopled or stimulated by us. We defended ourselves against charges of elitism with the strong evidence that the principles we stood for and the causes we enlisted in enjoyed popular, if sometimes passive support. But if we were "for the people," for the most part we were not comfortably "of the people."[32]

The "elitist" character of the public interest movement was reinforced by its emphasis on administrative politics. In the final analysis, the reformers of the 1970s embraced administrative politics, even as they sought to make it more accessible to direct political action. Indeed, the role of the courts and the Congress in the "new" American political system involved less a challenge to administrative government—and the revival of legislation and adjudication per se—than it involved the legislative and judicial branches in the "details of administration." The institutional reforms in the Congress during the 1970s that devolved policy responsibility to subcommittees and increased the number of congressional-support staff members were compatible with the attention being paid by legislators to policy specialization, which increased congressional oversight of the executive while making Congress more administrative in its structure and activities. By the same token, the judiciary's decreasing reliance on constitutional decisions in its rulings affecting the political economy and its emphasis on interpreting statutes to determine the programmatic responsibilities of executive agencies was symptomatic of its new role as the "managing partner of the administrative state."[33]

Thus, whereas the reformers of the 1960s and 1970s rejected the New Deal instrument of progressive government—the modern presidency—as undemocratic, they devolved public authority to a less visible coalition of bureaucratic agencies, courts, congressional subcommittees, and public interest groups that defied meaningful public discourse and broad-based coalitions. Public interest groups did generate large rosters of committed supporters through direct-mail solicitations. But these appeals to the public asked not so much for citizens' votes, time, energy, and ideas as for small contributions to fund campaigns waged by legal experts. Consequently, as Hugh Heclo has pointed out, with the recasting of liberalism in the 1970s, American society further "politicized itself" and at the same time "depoliticized government leadership."[34]

The root of this problem can be attributed to the moral basis of contemporary liberalism. The pursuit of "quality of life" issues resulted in an indifference to, if not a rejection of, the self-interested basis of American politics. Whereas the New Deal emphasis on economic security essentially accepted commercial values as an inherent part of American life, the expressed aims of the Great Society explicitly rejected a view of the individual as most essentially defined by acquisitive desires. The Johnson administration's indictment of material self-interest was for the most part restrained; for all his commitment to reform, Lyndon Johnson was a cautious leader. But such restraint was less evident in the rhetoric and political action of citizen activists, who expressed a far less compromising commitment to addressing problems of the "spirit rather than the flesh." As Ralph Nader wrote in 1971:

> This year the gross national product of the United States will exceed one trillion dollars, while the economy will fail to meet a great many urgent needs ... Indeed, the quality of life is deteriorating in so many ways that the traditional statistical requirements of the "standard of living" according to personal income, housing, ownership of cars and appliances, etc. have come to sound increasingly phony.[35]

It is easy to dismiss such a concern to deflect attention from material progress as mere rhetoric. But the moral principles that animated programmatic liberalism during the 1960s and 1970s resulted in a dramatic transformation of constitutional government in the United States. The American constitutional framework established conditions whereby "ambition would counteract ambition," thus fostering a system of mutual constraints among a diversity of interests. The New Deal altered this free play of self-interest in significant ways, particularly in shifting the locus of decision-making to the executive, but the institutional reforms of the 1970s extensively displaced the pluralistic character of American politics. The institutional arrangements that had emerged by the 1970s subordinated particularistic political ambitions to the programmatic ambitions of reformers, though these programs were usually constructed within discrete issue areas.

The moral basis of the public interest movement required it to maintain an uneasy, paradoxical relationship to the American public. If the frenetic materialism and conspicuous consumption of American society could merely be attributed to the machinations of corporate capitalism, then direct and widespread citizen action might be consistent with the strident criticism of public interest advocates. To the degree that relentless materialism was deeply imbedded in the American way of life, however, "citizen" advocacy was in tension with a commitment to democratic politics. Widespread support could readily be obtained for many of the specific goals of social regulation, yet the principles underlying these specific programs were largely unacceptable in the context of American politics, and, when unchecked, were capable of strong political backlash against the public interest movement. To be sure, these movements were not anticapitalist—there was no vision that conveyed an urgency to eliminate private property or to redistribute wealth. In fact, reformers of the 1970s defended values such as clean air and product safety, that cut across traditional class conflicts, explaining in large part their success in achieving broad, if not deeply rooted, support among the American people. Yet the emphasis on "quality of life" issues, the warning against resource limitations, and the criticism of consumer preference that characterized much public interest advocacy indirectly rejected the foundation of a society dedicated to the pursuit of material satisfaction.

Thus, in seeking to depart from the New Deal's emphasis on economic security, contemporary social reformers were alienated from the values and institutions that earlier progressives accepted as an inherent part of American life. Undoubtedly, reformers of the 1970s were not simply antimaterialistic. Nor is American political culture simply materialistic; the concerns for democratic citizenship and the criticisms of big business that characterized the reform activists of the late 1960s and 1970s have a long tradition in the United States. But the public plainly was simply not willing to reject the materialism that many citizen advocates found unacceptable. It is not surprising, then, that the contemporary liberal reformers focused on administrative and legal channels that were far removed from the more democratic institutions in American politics. Administrative tribunals and the courts were certainly more appropriate forums than the more political institutions for efforts to remake so substantially the character of the American political system. It is ironic and tragic that the resulting triumph of administrative politics, designed to strengthen citizen action, signified a distressing deterioration of representative democracy.

## The Legacy of the 1970s for Politics and Government

The rise of programmatic liberalism as the country's public philosophy during the 1930s weakened but did not eliminate the deeply ingrained distrust of national administrative power in the United States. Indeed, administrative aggrandizement came at the expense of the more decentralizing institutions of constitutional government, such as Congress, local governments, and political parties, that traditionally had been the primary agents of popular rule in the United States. Thus, as Barry Karl has noted, the New Deal "threatened our sense of ourselves as citizens."[36]

Although the reformers of the 1960s and 1970s set out to temper the administrative state and to revitalize self-government in the United States, the changes they brought continued, and even increased, the dominance of political administration in the councils of government. The "institutional partnership" that liberals forged during the 1970s limited the administrative power of the president but involved Congress, the courts, and public interest groups in the details of administration. These institutional developments not only fixed the business of government more on administration but also accelerated the decline of political parties.

Indeed, the McGovern-Fraser reforms carried out in the wake of the 1968 Democratic Convention, which virtually stripped party leaders of their authority to nominate presidential candidates, were the result of the same systemic forces that led to the reform of government during the 1970s. The reformers who took command of the Democratic party after the Chicago debacle followed the progressive tradition of emphasizing the candidate over the party—of desiring the emancipation of the presidency from the constrictive grip of partisan institutions. But they viewed the modern presidency as the *instrument* rather than the *steward* of the public welfare. Failing to address the question of the type of leadership or the type of executive that was desired, party reformers of the 1970s took for granted the general ideas current in the late 1960s and 1970s that presidential politics should be directed by popular movements.[37]

In the wake of these developments, the modern president was relegated to the role of modulating the liberal state; the executive was no longer in command of it. Nixon, Ford, and even the Democrat Jimmy Carter sought to put a lid on "uncontrollable" spending and to moderate the activities of the many regulatory agencies that were refurbished and created by the newly resurgent Congress. Most dramatic were the battles between Republican presidents and the Democratic Congress over spending and deficit levels. But conflict between the president and Congress, especially with respect to budgetary matters, became institutionalized after 1974. Carter, although he was less conservative than his Republican predecessors, tried to hold budget costs down, especially as inflationary pressure mounted during the latter part of his term. He was no more successful than Nixon and Ford, however, in getting the liberal Congress to respond to his call for fiscal restraint.

The most important development of the administrative presidency during the 1970s was Nixon's reorganization of the budget bureau. Just as the subcommittee became the soul of Congress during the 1970s, so the Office of Management and Budget had become the nerve center of the administrative presidency.[38] Not only did the enlarged OMB review spending requests and legislative proposals, as it had prior to the 1970s, but it proposed agency rules as well. The reshaping of liberalism during the 1970s, establishing a loose coalition of bureaucratic agencies, congressional subcommittees and staff, courts, and public advocacy groups, eroded considerably the discretion of presidents and executive officers to shape public policy. These channels posed a direct threat to presidential governance. Moreover, the explosion of regulation and the recasting of administrative institutions coincided with, and to a degree contributed to, increasing public doubt about the expansion of government. Beginning in the early 1970s, therefore, presidents were compelled to undertake the unenviable task of controlling the expanding and increasingly disparate activities of the bureaucracy.[39]

But after the fall of Nixon, Ford and Carter were unable to regain control of the president's domain. The OMB became an important competitor in the administrative process during their presidencies; it did not dominate it. Consequently, federal administrators found themselves whipsawed between the competing demands of subcommittees and the lieutenants of the president in the executive office. The end of the Carter years seemed to mark the triumph of the new institutional partnership that had been built to house liberalism while creating considerable doubt about the viability of the Democratic party as an instrument of government.

Carter's ostensible purpose was to move his party to the center and thus prepare it to compete more effectively at a time when the New Deal and Great Society appeared to be losing support in the country. He said often and earnestly that he intended to cut waste, run things efficiently, and balance the budget. But Carter's presidency marked the culmination of institutional separation between the presidency and the party. His 1976 campaign demonstrated how the new rules that governed the nomination process made it possible for an outsider to win his party's nomination; moreover, Carter's election demonstrated the striking decline of the regular party organization that reformers since Woodrow Wilson had decried as a stain on the American political process. As such, Carter's presidency represented a celebration of what Wilson called the "extraordinary isolation" of the presidency. At the same time, Carter's unsteady command of the nation revealed that this splendid isolation spawned by the New Deal and Great Society was at best a mixed blessing. Presidents and legislators had become independent entrepreneurs, establishing their own constituencies. As a result, they were less likely to view each other as partners in a shared endeavor, dedicated to promoting a party program. "I learned the hard way," Carter noted in his memoirs, "that there was no party loyalty or discipline when a complicated or controversial issue was a stake—none. Each legislator had to be wooed and won independently. It was every member for himself, and the devil take the hindmost!"[40]

Carter never did anything to ameliorate this disarray; in fact, he greatly contributed to it. His relationship to his party was usually aloof, occasionally accommodating, but never purposeful. In matters of public policy, the White House staff reflected the president's desire to be fiercely independent and a scourge to traditional Democratic approaches. But his appointees to the Cabinet were liberal Washington insiders such as Joseph Califano (Health, Education, and Welfare) and Patricia Robert Harris (Housing and Urban Development), thus setting the stage for enervating conflict between the White House and executive departments. Furthermore, acting oftentimes on the recommendations of Ralph Nader, Carter appointed aggressive public interest advocates to many regulatory agencies, such as Pertschuck and Joan Claybrook (National Highway and Transportation Administration), who proceeded to convert strong commitments to social regulation into government policy. The collective impression that Carter's appointees gave was one of an irresolute leader who was eager to accommodate all sides.

Carter never seemed to be in control of events, but his weaknesses were not merely attributable to his personal inadequacies; rather, they were symptomatic of the crisis of the liberal order. As Erwin Hargrove has suggested, Carter was president at a time of transition, after a Democratic period of reform and achievement and before a Republican resurgence. "The Ford and Carter presidencies belong together in this respect," Hargrove concluded, "both providing few possibilities for heroic leadership."[41] Liberals in Congress, prodded by the institutional partners in public interest groups, the courts, and administrative agencies, had imposed severe constraints on the executive since the end of Nixon's reign, reflecting a profound suspicion of the modern presidency. Not surprisingly, they provided a limited audience for decisive leadership that challenged the prevailing pattern of liberal policy demands.

In the notorious denouement of his presidency—his "malaise" speech of July 15, 1979—Carter described the fractiousness of the 1970s as a "fundamental threat to American democracy." In fact, Carter never used the term "malaise"; the press, unaccustomed to the extraordinary spectacle of a president "scolding his fellow citizens . . . like a . . . pastor with a profligate flock," dubbed it so.[42] "This is not a message of happiness or reassurance," Carter announced gravely, "but it is the truth. And it is a warning." Carter's unhappy truth told of a "crisis of confidence":

> We have always believed in something called progress. We have always had a faith that the days of our children would be better than our own. Our people are losing that faith. Not only in government itself, but in their ability as citizens to serve as the ultimate rulers and shapers of our democracy. . . . In a nation that was proud of hard work, strong families, close-knit communities and our faith in God, too many of us now tend to worship self-indulgence and consumption. Human identity is no longer defined by what one does but by what one owns. But we have discovered that owning things and consuming things does not satisfy our longing for meaning.

Like Lyndon Johnson's sermons a decade earlier, Carter sought to summon the American people to a higher calling. But his speech lacked the hopefulness that animated the Great Society; in contrast to LBJ's celebration of government reform, Carter's words bespoke a profound distrust, indeed a "growing disrespect" for government and its leaders. "Looking for a way out of this crisis, our people have turned to the Federal Government and found it isolated from the mainstream of the nation's life," he lamented.[43]

By speaking truth to the fractious politics and public estrangement of America, Carter hoped that he could rally her people to the moral equivalent of war against the energy crisis. But the President's words seemed only to reinforce the country's growing doubts about the Liberal order. Tellingly, Carter's "crisis of confidence" anticipated the Reagan "revolution" that would force him from office. In the final analysis, Carter's unhappy isolation did not give him the presence of a modern-day Isaiah, righteous in his scorn for a profligate nation; instead, the American people tended to view him as the rear-guard of a decrepit Liberalism that had rendered effective presidential leadership an elusive, if not unattainable, prospect.

More significant, Carter's tortured moralism sheds light on the love-hate relationship that Americans have formed with the state —the defining characteristic of contemporary liberalism's legacy for political life in the United States. Even as Liberalism became a discredited doctrine, the Reagan revolution failed to roll back many of its programmatic achievements. Republicans won dramatic electoral victories, most notably in 1980 and 1994, by promising to get government off the backs of the people; and yet, the public's persistent commitment to middle-class entitlements, such as Social Security and Medicare, environmental and consumer protection, and health and safety measures, makes unlikely the renewal of local self-government. In part, the public's ambivalence about the role of government reveals the profound difficulty of combining a modern positive state with the American natural rights tradition. Just as surely, it sheds light on a chronic political disease that threatens to suck the meaning out of representative government in the United States. As Wilson Carey McWilliams has written, "For thirty years or so, liberalism has promoted government responsibility for economic and social life; at the same time, it has defended a panoply of liberties, rights, and entitlements, especially for favored constituencies, that create immunities from politics, reducing government authority." These cross-purposes, McWilliams concludes, "amount to a long-term prescription for frustration and failure."[44]

The uneasy foundation of the Liberal state helps us understand why the continual efforts during the twentieth century to advance democratic administration have been self-defeating; why the culmination of these efforts during the 1970s provided participatory opportunities for only a small circle of program advocates. The decline in turnout in elections, the emergence of the "plebiscitary Presidency," and the vitiation of the legislative process during these years testify to the fact that the noble experiment to combine centralized administration and democratic citizenship has gone badly awry. This is the conundrum, and this is the challenge, that the politics of the 1970s has left us.

*Brandeis University*

# Notes

1. Hugh Heclo, "The Sixties' False Dawn: Awakenings, Movements, and Postmodern Policy-Making," *Journal of Policy History* 8:1 (1996): 56.

2. Jeffrey Berry, *The Interest Group Society* (Boston, 1984), 28.

3. *Public Papers of the President of the United States: Lyndon Baines Johnson*, 1963-64, vol. 1, 704. Richard Goodwin, who drafted the Great Society speech, acknowledges that it was partly inspired by the Port Huron Statement, which was issued in 1962 by the newly formed Students for a Democratic Society. One aspect of that address, in particular, impressed the presidential aide as expressing a yearning that went well beyond the utopian vision of radical fringe groups, and was shared by many Americans: "Some would have us believe that Americans feel contentment amidst prosperity—but might it not better be called a glaze above deeply felt anxieties about their role in the new world? And if these anxieties produce a developed indifference to human affairs, do they not as well produce a yearning to believe there is an alternative to the present, that something can be done to change circumstances in the schools, the workplaces, the bureaucracies, the government? It is to this latter yearning, at once the spark and agent of change, that we direct our present appeal." To be sure, it is not easy to imagine Lyndon Johnson embracing New Left doctrine. But, Goodwin argues, persuasively, that such ideas corresponded "to Lyndon Johnson's own impulses, could help define and fuel the larger purposes he wished to pursue." Students for a Democratic Society, "Port Huron Statement," printed in *The New Left: A Documentary History*, ed. Missimo Teodori (Indianapolis, 1969), 165. See also Richard Goodwin, *Remembering America* (Boston, 1988), 274, 276.

4. Daniel P. Moynihan, *Maximum Feasible Misunderstanding: Community Action in the War on Poverty* (New York, 1970).

5. Samuel Beer, "In Search of a New Public Philosophy," in *The New American Political System*, ed. Anthony King (Washington, D.C., 1979), 27-28.

6. Alexis de Tocqueville, *Democracy in America* (Garden City, N.Y., 1969), 263.

7. Michael W. McCann, "Public Interest Liberalism and the Modern Regulatory State," *Polity* 21 (Winter 1988): 392.

8. Stephen E. Ambrose, *Nixon*, Volume 3: *Ruin and Recovery, 1973-1990* (New York, 1991).

9. On the tension between the modern executive and the party system, see Sidney M. Milkis, *The President and the Parties: The Transformation of the American Party System Since the New Deal* (New York, 1993).

10. *U.S. v. Nixon*, 418 U.S. 683 (1974).

11. Fred I. Greenstein, "Nine Presidents in Search of a Modern Presidency," in Greenstein, ed., *Leadership in the Modern Presidency* (Cambridge, Mass., 1988), 334.

12. On the House Study Group, see Mark F. Ferber, "The Formation of the Democratic Study Group," in *Congressional Behavior*, ed. Nelson W. Polsby (New York, 1971).

13. R. Shep Melnick, *Between the Lines: Interpreting Welfare Rights* (Washington, D.C., 1994), 196-200.

14. Benjamin Ginsberg and Martin Shefter, *Politics by Other Means* (New York, 1990), 16.

15. R. Shep Melnick, "The Politics of Partnership," *Public Administration Review* 45 (November 1985): 653-60.

16. Walter A. Rosenbaum, "Public Involvement as Reform and Ritual: The Political Development of Federal Participation Programs," in *Citizen Participation in America: Essays on the State of the Art*, ed. Stuart Langton (Lexington, Mass., 1978).

17. For a more detailed discussion of the meaning and significance of social regulation, see Richard A. Harris and Sidney M. Milkis, *The Politics of Regulatory Change: A Tale of Two Agencies*, 2d ed. (New York, 1996), especially chapters 1 and 3.

18. Falk cited in Berry, *The Interest Group Society*, 36.

19. Ralph Nader, "The Case for Federal Chartering," in *The Consumer and Corporate Accountability* (New York, 1973), 365.

20. McCann, "Public Interest Liberalism and the Modern Regulatory State," 389, 394.

21. Interview with Richard A. Harris and Sidney M. Milkis, July 11, 1986.

22. Rosenbaum, "Public Involvement as Reform and Ritual," 81.

23. Ibid., 83.

24. Joan B. Aron, "Citizen Participation at Government Expense," *Public Administration Review* 39 (September–October 1979): 477–85.

25. Max D. Peglin and Edgar Shore, "Regulatory Agency Responses to the Development of Public Participation," *Public Administration Review* 37 (March–April 1977): 142.

26. Indeed, the list of grants made under the intervenor funding program looked very much like an honor role of staunch consumer advocates, including Americans for Democratic Action ($177,000 in grants to participate in five separate rule-making proceedings), Action for Children's Television ($84,614 to participate in a children's advertising proceeding), and the Consumers Union ($132,257 to participate in four separate rule-making proceedings). For a list of grants made under the FTC public-intervenor funding program, see Hearings, Subcommittee for Consumers, Committee on Commerce, 96th Cong., 1st sess., "Oversight to Examine the Enforcement and Administrative Authority of the FTC to Regulate Unfair and Deceptive Trade Practices," September 18, 19, 27, 28; October 4, 5, 10, 1979, 158–60.

27. Barry Boyer, "Funding Public Participation in Agency Proceedings: The Federal Trade Commission Experience," *Georgetown Law Journal* 70:1 (1980): 71.

28. On this development, see Melnick, *Between the Lines.*

29. Martin Shapiro, "APA: Past, Present, and Future," *Virginia Law Review* 72 (1986): 461–62.

30. Richard B. Stewart, "The Reformation of American Administrative Law," *Harvard Law Review* 88:8 (June 1975): 1712.

31. James Q. Wilson, "The Politics of Regulation," in James Q. Wilson, ed., *The Politics of Regulation* (New York, 1980), 370–71.

32. Michael Pertschuck, *Revolt Against Regulation: The Rise and Pause of the Consumer Movement* (Berkeley and Los Angeles, 1982), 130.

33. Jeremy Rabkin, "The Judiciary in the Administrative State," *The Public Interest* 71 (Spring 1983): 63.

34. Hugh Heclo, "Issue Networks and the Executive Establishment," in King, ed., *The New American Political System*, 124.

35. Ralph Nader, "A Citizen's Guide to the American Economy," in Nader, ed., *The Consumer and Corporate Accountability*, 4.

36. Barry D. Karl, *The Uneasy State: The United States from 1915 to 1945* (Chicago, 1983), 238.

37. James Ceaser, *Presidential Selection: Theory and Development* (Princeton, 1979), 283.

38. R. Shep Melnick, "The Politics of Partnership: Institutional Coalitions and Statutory Rights," Occasional Paper No. 84–3, Center for American Political Studies, Harvard University, 8.

39. For a review of these institutional developments and how they were modified during the Reagan years, see Harris and Milkis, *The Politics of Regulatory Change*, chapter 4.

40. Jimmy Carter, *Keeping Faith: Memoirs of a President* (New York, 1982), 80.

41. Erwin Hargrove, *Jimmy Carter as President: Leadership and the Politics of the Public Good* (Baton Rouge, La., 1988), 192.

42. "The Scramble Starts," Editorial, *Los Angeles Times*, July 17, 1979, part II, 4; and Robert Shogan, "Carter Returns to Moralistic Themes," ibid., I, 1, 15.

43. Transcript of President Carter's Address to the Country on Energy Problems," *New York Times*, July 16, 1979.

44. W. Carey McWilliams, "Conclusion: The Meaning of the Election," in Gerald Pomper et al., *The Election of 1996: Reports and Interpretations* (Chatham, N.J., 1997), 258–59.

# J. DAVID HOEVELER

# Populism, Politics, and Public Policy: 1970s Conservatism

A quarter century and more has passed since the 1970s made its debut. History, always problematic as an objective undertaking, encourages present-mindedness when proximity to events in question governs our perspectives. This article does not pretend to have avoided this pitfall. Today the animus against government dominates political discourse. "Outsiders" who aspire to office boast of that status; "insiders" obscure theirs. All politicians design to show their commonness, their oneness with the people, the beleaguered people, victims of the socially privileged, of haughty bureaucrats, and the sundry occult forces that sustain their misery. Ours, it has been observed, has become a dominantly "populist" culture, its anti-elitism resounding from local Serb Halls in Milwaukee and elsewhere to the very chambers of the Capitol itself.

The last quarter-century has also witnessed a conservative resurgence. Republicans have dominated the presidency for all but eight years in this time and in 1994 the "Gingrich" revolution restored that party to congressional control for the first time in more than forty years. All but the most committed Democrats seemed reluctant to describe themselves as "liberals." Democratic President Clinton presided over major welfare reform and defied labor unions to see a free-trade policy (NAFTA) through strenuous opposition to congressional endorsement. Thus it would seem that making sense of recent American political history would require some understanding of the coincidence of these phenomenon—the prevailing populist frame of mind and the ascendant conservative political ethos. This correlation having been observed, the focus hereafter will be the 1970s. I will try to show that this decade did produce a significant shift in American conservatism, one that affected attitudes toward government and public policy. I will argue that the 1970s experienced not so much a "loss of faith" as a shift of faith, for the conservative recovery did not challenge the democratic priorities of American liberalism, but sought instead to reclaim them for its own. Conservative populism, to be sure, had earlier roots in American history. But its 1970s flourishing reflected special historical circumstances. It responded to important changes in liberalism. It corresponded to significant demographic shifts. And, perhaps most significant, it made a new departure in the populist tradition itself. Conservatism in the 1970s is a study in ideas, but it is a study in ideas within a very definite social context.[1]

No political movement can long sustain itself against the democratic ethos of the nation. Historically, "European" notions of conservatism, best expressed by Edmund Burke in the late eighteenth century, have seemed to reflect an alien quality here. This conservatism speaks of tradition and the ordered society, with its ranks and privileges. It recoils from mass society and its leveling habits, its coarse and crude mannerisms, and its deference toward the "vulgar" numbers. American conservative thinkers who embrace this way of thinking have done so not through an ideology that rejects democracy but within the larger ideal of an improving democracy. Irving Babbitt, a leader of the traditionalist New Humanists, wrote in 1924: "The only check to the evils of an unlimited democracy will be found to be the recognition in some form of the aristocratic principle."[2] In 1949, when Peter Viereck offered his book *Conservatism Revisited*, he avowed that "democracy . . . is the best government on earth when it tries to make all its citizens aristocrats."[3] These sentiments, which could be readily elaborated,[4] suggest that conservatism ought to approach populist ideals with some hesitancy. How then, one might ask, and on what terms, might conservatism accommodate a populist ideology? Can it do so and yet bear the label of a conservative public philosophy? And what would its policy agenda look like? As it turns out, we have a historical illustration that answers these questions and those answers return us to the 1970s.

Populism means a deference to the ordinary citizen of a given community. It finds in the conventional wisdom of the common people a superior intuitive understanding about things or a basic common sense. It invariably honors such thought above the informed or expert judgments of trained specialists. Populism is suspicious toward the prevalence of this higher opinion in law and government. Anti-intellectualism often flourishes in populism. Coinciding with this suspicion is a mistrust of elites—of almost any kind. In democratic societies especially, populism strives to explain why privileged groups exercise a controlling power, and it often takes on conspiratorial perspectives. It must account for the unfair discrepancy of wealth and power in a society that proclaims egalitarian values. Populism seeks to reclaim the priorities of "the people," and not just in the political arena. It honors folkways and lifestyles expressive of the wide democratic base of the community or nation.

Populism confounds American political ideologies. It does so precisely because it can express both radical and reactionary attitudes. But the confusion is a recent phenomenon in American history. From Andrew Jackson in the nineteenth century into the mid-twentieth century, populism offered various political agendas that expressed an animus against the business community. In the Populists and William Jennings Bryan, in Robert La Follette, in Father Charles Coughlin, the privileged powers of well-connected businesses appeared as the root causes of social injustice and the plight of the common people. What form, then, might a right-wing populism assume? The first answer appeared in the 1950s.

The Cold War laid the foundations for this kind of populism. The rise of the Iron Curtain in Eastern Europe after World War II and the "loss" of China to the Communists in 1949 caused many Americans to wonder how the great victory of the world war left the United States so vulnerable in a faltering international arena. Senator Joseph McCarthy made the case for conspiracy and betrayal. And he located the villains among the "bright young men," often the Ivy College–educated elites, now located in the State Department and other bureaucratic rivulets of the federal government. This class, "born with silver spoons in their mouth," McCarthy said, were "selling this nation out." McCarthy's attacks expressed prejudicial populist rhetoric as he referenced "parlor pinks and parlor punks" and mocked the "phony" British accent of Secretary of State Dean Acheson. McCarthy appealed to "150 million normal Americans" against Acheson, Alger Hiss, and their like. Significantly, McCarthy, the Republican, made an opening to America's white ethnics, soon to be a significant factor in the political party shifts that were about to follow.[5]

McCarthy's campaign occurred just when the conservative intellectual movement began to cohere. William F. Buckley Jr., Yale-educated and the product of a wealthy Catholic family, conveyed erudition and polish in his writing and speaking, but he also anticipated populist conservative themes. He gained notoriety as conservatism's brash young man when he published God and Man at Yale in 1951. Buckley went after his own alma mater, and its professors particularly, in outlining a great betrayal. Yale, Buckley wanted America to know, no longer stood for what most Americans valued—a religious foundation of learning and a free-market economy. Thus, the Yale faculty that Buckley portrayed seemed to be in isolated and conspiratorial revolt against the rest of the country.[6] These judgments located

Buckley in a position of democratic majoritarianism, in which the broad base of Americans stood at odds with its elite intellectual leadership. On these grounds, too, Buckley came to the defense of McCarthy. He and brother-in-law L. Brent Bozell legitimated McCarthy's defense of the anti-Communist feelings of Americans. "It is characteristic of society," the authors wrote, "that it uses its sanctions in support of its own folkways and mores, and that in doing so it urges conformity." Majority sentiments had a higher claim than the rights of individual dissent.[7]

The conservative shift in a populist direction, it is interesting to note, occurred at a time when liberal thinkers began to find reasons for a mistrust of populism. Arthur Schlesinger Jr. published *The Vital Center* in 1949. This manifesto, a major contribution of the anti-Communist liberal wing, located the sources of totalitarianism in the destabilizing effects of industrialism and the mass society it helped create. Mass movements, with their pretense to provide security and place for anonymous and uprooted individuals, made fascism and Bolshevism possible."[8] Through this perspective, mass movements in America, even those of a reformist nature, appeared less sanguine. When Richard Hofstadter studied the Populists in 1955, he found a politics of sentiment and nostalgia, rooted in agrarian "folklore," and a literature of conspiracy laced with ethnocentrism and anti-Semitism.[9] The same year, Daniel Bell edited *The New American Right*. Its seven contributors offered different perspectives on this subject, but collectively the book reflected a growing disaffection of intellectuals with particular trends in American democratic culture, a disaffection that the New Deal years had done much to repair. David Riesman and Nathan Glazer, for example, found that big business and liberal intellectuals stood closer to each other on issues of civil rights and foreign policy than either did with farmers and lower-class groups in the cities.[10]

The liberal suspicions of populist politics opened the way for a new Left to claim that position. It did so, but on new terms. The New Left, in its quest for a radical "participatory democracy," could not round up the usual cast of characters. Sociologist C. Wright Mills presented his book *The Power Elite* in 1962. He wanted to show that the military and the government, but the labor unions, too, all cooperated in a huge complex of industrial capitalism. Wright (before New Leftist theoretician Herbert Marcuse used the term in his 1964 book) described a one-dimensional society, its citizens locked in mental stupor by the media and no oppositional vitality at work within the whole social structure. Only students and intellectuals, Mills believed, might offer some locus of resistance to this controlled society.[11] Under such conditions a populist reform movement would seem to have very dim prospects.

Mills's writings inspired the student New Left. Its manifesto, the Port Huron Statement of 1962, stated the same themes that Mills did. It specifically singled out the loss of radicalism in the American labor movement; captured by bureaucracy, softened by materialism, it lay dormant and stagnant.[12] Marcuse, in turn, could only marvel, and despair, as he observed labor unions working hand in hand with the munitions industry for new contracts from the Pentagon.[13] The New Left's form of populism, then, would find a new base among the urban poor, the truly deprived, but also the constituency most removed from the system. To this end, the New Left did not look to existing government structures or local city machines to run the new antipoverty programs; it looked to the poor themselves to make the decisions that affected them. Ironically, the populist Right would build on a similar loss of faith in liberal government.

The New Left could not be the agency of a politically effective populism. It chose too narrow a base for its politics, and, in its strident rhetoric, denounced the evils brought by the American presence around the world and alienated nearly all segments of the American public. The New Left assaulted the liberal tradition in the United States and made it a factor of racism and an oppressive corporate "fascism."

It remained to be shown, then, how an emerging rightist populism could locate itself with the political party system. The Republican party offered the best opportunity. However, that party's long domination by an Eastern establishment, with its cosmopolitan outlook and internationalist orientation, gave little hope. This Eastern wing, as Mary Brennan has observed, "shared a common background of Ivy League education, exclusive club memberships, and financial success." They controlled the party machinery, purse strings, and policy-making functions.[14] The makings of a challenge, nonetheless, were well under way. Buckley made his case against the moderate and ineffective Republican administrations of Dwight Eisenhower. He charged that Eisenhower failed to see the real seriousness of the Communist challenge, and showed nothing of the existential passion brought to that issue by Buckley's friend Whittaker Chambers. At the same time, Buckley helped prepare for the future "southern strategy" of the Republicans by employing majoritarian democratic principles in behalf of white southerners.[15]

By the late 1950s the Republican party confronted an insurgency in its own ranks. It came from the South and West, supported by business leaders of those regions and joined by Midwesterners, most of whom had supported Robert Taft of Ohio in the 1952 party contests. Barry Goldwater, around whom this insurgency coalesced, spoke of a new populist movement in the party. Goldwater accused Eisenhower, now perceived as spokesman for the Eastern wing, of "dime-store New Dealism." Conservative publications such as *Human Events* also expressed their discontents. The same year, the party faced a decisive turn. Richard Nixon, a product of California, seemed to have solid anti-Communist credentials. But Nixon realized he had to strike an accord with Nelson Rockefeller of New York to fend off a possible challenge from this man whom the conservatives reviled as the new symbol of the Eastern liberal wing. Goldwater blasted the accord and warned that the "Liberal militants" would regret the naked power push to keep control of the party. One heard talk of the "Munich of the Republican party."[16]

The 1964 election revealed significant shifts. First, amid the Republican rout, it could be lost on no one that the conservative Goldwater made a Republican breakthrough in the South, the "solid" Democratic South that had prevailed since the end of the nineteenth century. By the next election, the leading Republican candidate, Richard Nixon, would be talking of the party's "southern" strategy. Another, less noticeable shift also occurred. The divisions in the Republican party reflected a breach in American businesses, between large capital-intensive multinational corporations and smaller labor-intensive firms. The former had always shown greater sympathy to the New Deal reforms and President Kennedy, after 1961, wooed them successfully. Along the way, however, conservative Republicans were becoming the greater recipients of money from the smaller businesses, widely represented by the Southern Rim industries. They formed the new rank-and-file base of the conservative wing in the party, now no longer dependent on corporate money. It was said of this group that "these are men who have built up their own enterprise, who are strong on individual initiative."[17]

The new patterns might have set the party structures for the next several years. The emergence of George Wallace, however, forced both parties to confront a powerful populist expression, first in the South and then elsewhere. Wallace had authentic credentials for the role he created for himself. He came from an Alabama family so poor it could not at one point pay its electric bills. He grew up in a southern county where 85 percent of the schoolchildren had hookworm. He married a poor working-class girl whom he met at the local Kresge's. A pugnacious kid who went on to win boxing championships, intellectual life meant little to him. He could recall from his days at the University of Alabama no memorable book or any professor who influenced his thinking. As a young state politician, he was described by an acquaintance as almost a "New Deal socialist" and he attached his early career to "Big Jim" Folsom, "the little man's friend." Part of a recurring populist politics in Alabama, Wallace identified as his political enemies the

"Big Mules," the upstate industrial interests and Black Belt agribusinesses that usually controlled the Democratic party. Wallace called them "the decent and dignified" elements of the party and showed them no respect. He won the reputation of a dangerous liberal.[18]

Alabama politics in the era of the White Citizens Councils moved Wallace's politics toward racism. Wallace won national attention for his effort to defy the court-ordered desegregation of the University of Alabama. By 1964, furthermore, Wallace had become convinced that the racial question was not simply a southern one. To the dismay of many, he tapped into white working-class sympathy in the North. He attracted overflowing crowds at Serb Hall in Milwaukee. "The whole United States is Southern!" he said. Wallace took his cause into independent party politics in 1968 and moved it into the northern presidential primaries that year. This time he won union endorsement in Michigan. As always, he brought along famous country-and-western singers, identifying with a cultural norm in blue-collar America. Soon Republicans realized that Wallace so threatened to cut into conservative votes that he might deliver the election to Hubert Humphrey and the Democrats. Nixon then moved deliberately to co-opt Wallace on issues of law and order, desegregation, and the liberal courts. He even got his own country-and-western singers.[19]

Wallace sounded the racial fears of working-class whites and others, but his contribution to political change went further. Anticipating an important trend among conservatives, Wallace's populism expressed angry anti-elitist views. It took significantly anti-intellectual form, too, against academics and bureaucrats. In his 1970 effort to regain the Alabama governorship, Wallace warned that should his rival win, the state would fall to a "spotted alliance" of blacks and "sissy britches from Harvard who spend most of their time in a country club drinking tea with their finger stuck up." Wallace mocked the limousine lifestyles of the wealthy Mountain Brook country clubbers and their martini habits. They, the wealthy, he said, speak up for school integration, but they send their own children to private schools. The poor whites could not. Wallace ridiculed experts. He denounced the "briefcase-carrying bureaucrats" who set public policy for the liberals' agenda. "Maybe a fellow ought to advise himself from the seat of his pants, just what his common sense tells him," said Wallace. He posed a radical gap between the "so-called intelligentsia, the intellectual snobs" and the common people.[20]

The opportunities for a new rightist populism came from the Wallace lesson and from another unexpected trend. It took the keen perception of Kevin Phillips to make sense of it and to show the Republicans how to capitalize. His book of 1969, *The Emerging Republican Majority*, became a landmark of political analysis, but his 1975 book, *Mediacracy*, even better illustrates the populist persuasion of Phillips himself. Phillips served the Nixon administration as voting-patterns analyst for the candidate's campaign manager, John Mitchell.

A book full of charts and statistics, *Republican Majority* described a political evolution in the United States, an emerging new party paradigm, "the beginning of a new era in American politics." More than class or economics, it had to do with ethnicity and culture, now the key fault lines in American politics, Phillips believed. It also had to do with geography. In the key areas of the Northeast (New England and the Middle Atlantic states), Phillips located a new liberal Establishment. In place of the industrial and financial Establishment dethroned by the New Deal, Phillips found "a new Establishment—the media, the universities, conglomerate corporations, research and development corporations."[21]

This area, Phillips noted, had once been the bastion of conservatism, but now the "silk-stocking" districts of the big cities, and the suburbs, were trending liberal. Here Goldwater and Wallace fared most poorly. On the other hand, the urban Italian and Irish, rural non-Yankees, new suburban areas (more "ethnic" than the old), lower-income Jews, and milltowners, were trending conservative. And these had once provided bedrock support for the New Deal and the Democratic party. Here, too, said Phillips, one saw the vanguard for a "popular conservatism." When Phillips carried his study to other parts of the country, which he did with much statistical subtlety that defies too easy summary, he nevertheless confirmed the major trend—a conservative, Republican insurgency among white, and especially ethnic white, America in the lower income levels, and the gravitation of other whites—more affluent, located in older suburbs, or in "fashionable" city wards—to the Democrats.[22]

By 1975, Phillips could place his new pattern into a larger theoretical framework. In *Mediacracy*, he identified the political shifts with the emergence of postindustrial America and its sociological effects. By the postindustrial situation Phillips meant the communications revolution, as significant for the late twentieth century, he believed, as the Industrial Revolution had been for the nineteenth. The 1972 presidential election informed much of Phillips's discussion of this subject. Two examples will suffice. First, the Harvard Law School, in a straw poll, backed Democrat George McGovern six to one against Richard Nixon. Second, Mississippi—the country's most impoverished state, the least cultured, the least educated—gave the Democratic candidate the lowest percentage of all the states, and this for the fourth election in a row. Massachusetts—near the top of the states in wealth, education, and culture—was the only state won by George McGovern.

These symbolic facts, Phillips believed, gave clues about postindustrial America. Replacing the old bastions of industrial America were the huge communications empires, the elite universities, the networks of think tanks, the charitable trusts, "and the huge corporate giants of knowledge technology—IBM, Xerox, and so forth." For Phillips, those economic forces most connected to postindustrial change constituted the new liberal elite in America. Neoconservative intellectuals would give this "New Class" a much more monolithic identity than Phillips did, but this point supplied a critical weight to the emerging populist conservatism. The new postindustrial elite, said Phillips, lived far removed from the tangible world of industry and manufacturing and commerce. It trafficked in and thrived in a marketplace of ideas and information, where newness and change provided its sustaining milieu. Wrote Phillips: "Instead of having a vested interest in stability, as did previous conservative business establishments, the knowledge sector has a vested interest in change—in the unmooring of convention, in socioeconomic experiments, in the ongoing consumption of new ideas." Furthermore, Phillips believed, the communications industry had a definitive connection to the liberal adversary culture. He cited magazines such as *Time* and *Newsweek*, and Eastern city papers such as the *New York Times*, the *Washington Post*, the *Boston Globe*, and the *Baltimore Sun*.[23]

Phillips not only discovered the new basis for a populist politics; he spoke for it too. By the mid-1970s, furthermore, this redirection of strategy and ideology gained a powerful reinforcement from the major conservative intellectual movement of the decade. Neoconservatism emerged in the 1960s. It grew out of liberalism and had radical roots in the 1930s. But it had already learned to locate enemies on the Left, especially among those it believed had not been sufficiently appreciative of the Communist threat.[24] With representatives among the New York intellectuals and Jewish voices prominent in its ranks, neoconservatism struck many as a new conservative expression, to be differentiated from the Old Right. Neoconservatism played two major roles; it spoke to a wide range of policy issues and it prepared the way for Reagan-style populism.

In 1965, Irving Kristol and Daniel Bell introduced their journal *The Public Interest*. This neoconservative publication sought to confront Lyndon Johnson's Great Society programs and the idealistic tendencies of the Left with a thoroughgoing skepticism. *The Public Interest* was sociology for conservatives. It took the measure of liberal policy in a wide variety of its efforts and confronted it with empirical studies. Altogether, its contributors demonstrated the severe limitations, and often the misdirected idealism, of 1960s liberalism. In the ensuing decade it continued to focus on policy issues and it found much to criticize. Among the subjects it addressed, *Public Interest* policy critics made their most severe assessments on federal housing pro-grams,[25] pollution and the environment,[26] national health insurance,[27] energy policy,[28] unemployment,[29] education,[30] immigration,[31] affirmative action,[32] urban programs,[33] and taxation.[34] *The Public Interest* registered academic loss of faith in government.

This aspect of neoconservatism suggested a kind of academic formal-ism—sociology, economics, political science—that at least appeared to bring value-free measure to policy issues. But there was more to this activity than met the eye. For the *Public Interest* was making a full-scale attack on the elite policymakers who inspired the ambitious liberal agenda. From aca-demic advisers whose scholarship and counsel helped formulate the vari-ous programs to the titular officials in the bureaucracies who saw to their implementation, neoconservatives calculated the effects of good intentions, noble ideas, and intellectual theorization gone awry. In that way they brought their severest charges against the progressive Left. Neoconservatives, how-ever, even in their early days on the left, had identified this particular enemy—the elitist as radical, the socially or educationally privileged as the unelected reformer.[35]

This animus dated back to the 1950s and the Alger Hiss case. Many of the eastern intellectual elite defended Hiss. Just as many of the New York intellectuals found him contemptible. Hiss represented to them the inau-thentic radical, the corporate leftist of pinstripe respectability. "The roster of Hiss supporters," wrote William Phillips of *Partisan Review* magazine in 1952, "reads like a page from the Social Register.[36] In the 1970s, Norman Podhoretz, who turned *Commentary* magazine into a major neoconservative outlet, accentuated this class feeling. He described two groups: "a new and rapidly growing group of prosperous and well-educated people calling them-selves liberals [and] a less-prosperous and well-educated combination of groups, mostly in the working and lower middle classes."[37] Podhoretz whole-heartedly sided with the latter against the trendy counterculture of the former. Kristol himself boasted that the people who had helped launch *The Public Interest* with him "had themselves risen from the ranks of the urban poor." On the other hand, he said, those who were authoring the Great Society programs were "upper-middle class graduates of elite univer-sities who had been dazzled by trendy sociological theories."[38]

The neoconservative presentation of a "New Class" liberal agenda for America was now gaining clarity. Neoconservatives would describe the New Class as widely as possible and pose its prejudices and political agenda squarely against the countervailing notions of the rest of society, the broad social base. Social and economic class lines loomed large in this dichotomy as many signs indicated a political shift. What some called the "new managerial class," emerging from the college boom of the post–World War II years, had a cultural and political agenda quite different from lower middle- or working-class whites. The higher social group more likely opposed the war in Vietnam, supported civil rights, and advocated women's equality more than did the other.[39]

There is no attempt here to describe the neoconservatives as populists themselves. They did, however, have a critical role in preparing for a populist prejudice that gained ground in the Republican party throughout the 1970s. That fact, in turn, had everything to do with changes in the Democratic party. Neoconservatives individually had long identified with the Democrats, but the party's posture toward the 1960s counterculture and radicalism brought vigorous dissent and in several cases defection from the party. A critical turn occurred after the 1968 elections, when the party imposed new rules on delegate selection for its presidential conventions— a quota system, in short, for the inclusion of women and minorities. The symbolic outcome of the new requirements showed dramatically in 1972 when Mayor Richard Daley's group from Chicago was barred from the convention for failure to adhere to the affirmative-action requirements. Another group, led by Jesse Jackson, took its place.

This issue signified the declining power of the Democratic party's white, working-class base, with its leadership location in the labor unions and the big city political machines. Nor was that fact lost among a group of Democrats who identified with that contingent and now saw their party in outright betrayal. From this source came the Coalition for a Democratic Majority. It included Senators Henry Jackson and Hubert Humphrey, as well as Daniel Patrick Moynihan, Ben Wattenberg, Jeane Kirkpatrick, Michael Novak, and Norman Podhoretz. This group likened itself to Democratic loyalists in 1948 who defended the true party against radical insurgents headed by Henry Wallace. Kirkpatrick, for her part, saw a party changing from a tribal group of grassroots workers who worked the city wards and rang doorbells to an indiscriminate group of factions and narrow interests. The new Democratic party, she wrote, now spoke for the adversarial interests of the New Class— sophisticated, educated professionals, products of business school methods of market research and communications technology, a postindustrial Democratic party.[40] In 1979, Kirkpatrick wrote an essay she called "Why I Am Not a Republican." She spoke for disaffected Democrats who nonetheless could not join a party that still smacked of a country club lifestyle and lacked a broad vision for the common good.[41] Soon she would take a prominent post in the Republican administration of Ronald Reagan.

The ideological trek made by neoconservative intellectual Michael Novak supplies another lesson in the opening to populist conservatism. Novak was just coming off a sojourn with the Catholic Left in the United States when he authored his remarkable book of 1972, *The Rise of the Unmeltable Ethnics*. Novak gave it the subtitle *Politics and Culture in the Seventies*. The book had a somewhat populist cast insofar as it identified a particular victim class and an exploiting elite. For all that, Novak offered a fresh and singular thesis about the American situation. He wanted to draw attention to an underprivileged white group, one he labeled the PIGS—Poles, Italians, Greeks, and Slavs. It shared a close identity with the ethnic whites to whom Kevin Phillips looked for the basis of a new Republican strategy. These people, said Novak, people of tribal ways, blood ties, earthiness, a naturalistic and religious ethic accepting of things as they are, had long confronted the moralistic culture of the Yankee Protestant, bent on his own salvation and that of the world at large, given to rationalist reconstruction of the world and to philosophies of progress and amelioration. As part of the southern and eastern European group of immigrants, Novak, from his early years in Pennsylvania, had recoiled from the oppressiveness of Yankee cleanliness and perfectionist efforts. People of his roots, he said, had to learn to control their emotions, wash up, dress up, and chin up. From the corporate headquarters to the universities, Novak located a controlling elite, more suffocating in its dominant manner and presentation of self than in its economic entrenchment. But it was an elitist domination—heartless and soulless—nonetheless.[42]

*Unmeltable Ethics* had the appearance of a liberal or leftist sympathy. It offered a novel assault against the capitalist elite and joined New Left assaults against institutions of higher learning. But Novak learned from his own thesis, and he moved to the right. His shift began as he experienced more of the New Left movement in the United States. In its obsession with national sins and its appeal to a collective guilt, but also in its strident moralism and its fervent righteousness, Novak now saw the recurrence of the familiar Yankee-Puritan strain in American culture. "Left politics," Novak wrote, "is the last refuge of those wonderful people who brought us Prohibition." Novak had quite enough of the "politics of conscience" in any form.[43]

Throughout the 1970s and into the next decade, Novak moved into neoconservative prominence. In the aggressive liberalism that this group contested, Novak saw "profound class interest." In the Democratic reform group he saw the rise to ascendancy of a new generation, born to affluent parents and products of elite universities, young professionals in law, education, and the media. Furthermore, Novak perceived a breach between this New Class, with its airy and self-serving moralism, and the commonfolk majority. Novak coupled this charge with his emerging severe criticism of liberal public policy—civil rights, poverty, busing, and the Vietnam War.[44] Novak had once contrasted the courage and spirit of the young radicals with the white working class—corpulent, complacent, chauvinist in its unthinking patriotism, and racist. Workers, he said, found no higher spiritual fulfillment than, beer in hand, to lie supine before the television set.[45] In 1978, however, Novak described his own political shift: "I found that there were sources of health in American political traditions, and in the democratic majority . . . I became more hopeful about the democratic majority—those millions with beer cans watching football on television."[46] Two years later Novak announced his support for Ronald Reagan.[47]

One must be impressed, or vexed, at the conservatives' ability, in the 1970s, to turn almost every public policy issue into the dichotomy of the privileged elite against the ordinary rest. Consider the women's rights movement and its great symbolic cause, the Equal Rights Amendment. Invariably it became associated in the public mind with the abortion issue and day-care policies. Major opposition came from Phyliss Schlafly, earlier associated with the Goldwater movement and the heady crusade against the Wall Street-dominated Eastern Establishment in the Republican party. Now she had the support of the evangelical Right in fighting to reverse the successes in state legislatures made by ERA. Schlafly and conservative opponents of ERA advertised that the amendment nicely suited the needs of well-educated, career-bound women. Ordinary housewives, however, could only lose by repeal of laws that favored them in divorce settlements, for example. These appeals, in fact, did respond to demographic realities. As E. J. Dionne observed: "Many of the most ardent anti-feminists were concentrated among lower income whites—a group that had traditionally voted for Democrats and liberals." He summarized: "The result was a class war among women."[48]

In creating a right-wing populism, conservative advocates were succeeding more at the cultural front than at the economic in the early 1970s. In fact, the Nixon administration only made clear to many conservatives that more work needed to be done and their resolve would influence the critical shift in the Republican party later in the decade. Nixon, of course, could effect a populist tone with some skill. He appealed to the "real America" or the "forgotten American" or "the great silent majority" against the antiwar factions or the proponents of busing. He portrayed a situation in which a vociferous minority, much of it exercising power from the unelected federal judges, had stolen the country from its honest, hardworking, patriotic majority. Nixon, as noted, also responded to the challenge of the emerging populist Right led by George Wallace.

In terms of public policy, however, Nixon took measures that alienated many conservatives. For example, Nixon supported the Equal Employment Opportunity Commission and its "preferential treatment for minorities" in hiring, which action also incurred the opposition of white labor groups. He enforced this program by authorizing the EEOC to advance a strong affirmative-action program through the courts. Also, Nixon seemed to be hospitable toward the new environmental lobby in Washington. This cause seemed to many on the populist right a prime example of the new power held by the elite academic, managerial, and professional classes, a group, they believed, that also stood behind Ralph Nader and the consumer movement. The early years of the Nixon administration saw passage of the Clean Air Act, the Occupational Safety and Health Act, and the National Environmental Policy Act.[49] Nixon also scored low among conservatives on economic policy. In December 1969 he signed into law "the most progressive tax bill ever presented to Congress by a Republican president."[50] Only two years later this Republican president instituted wage and price controls, designed for a ninety-day duration and to be enforced by a pay board, a price board, and a cost-of-living council. Nixon's "New Economic Policy," engineered with Texan John Connally, proved to be pretty heavy-handed stuff. Thus conservative Michael Barone wrote in his massive chronicle, *Our Country* : "Connally's program brought more state direction to economic policy and did more to undercut the operation of free markets than anything done, except in war, by the Roosevelt, Truman, Eisenhower, Kennedy, or Johnson administrations." As Nixon said, "We are all Keynesians now."[51]

Populist conservatism in its ultimate and successful form, then, had yet a missing ingredient—the commitment to market capitalism. That inclusion would denote a remarkable achievement, for populism almost invariably looks to statist solutions; it has recourse to positive and protective legislation to reclaim government for the underprivileged masses against the elites who have conspired to deprive them of their power. A populism that championed laissez-faire solutions to America's economic ills—a populism that said government is not the solution, it is the problem—is indeed an arresting intellectual proposition. It is instructive, therefore, to return to the neoconservatives.

Irving Kristol once remarked that the New Left had much in common with the Old Right—a contempt for liberal democracy and capitalist progress.[52] Kristol could appreciate in the Old Left, with its commitment to socialism, an ideology that endorsed Western values of economic progress and modernity. Kristol separated himself from the Old Left basically on his conviction that socialism just did not work. His opposition was thus not moral but economic, although by the mid-1970s Kristol had moved sufficiently from his earlier leftism as to insist that a free society cannot exist without a free market.[53]

Kristol and other neoconservatives now faced a critical juncture. They had to make the best case they could for market capitalism. Kristol did so in a way that reflected democratic and populist standards. Capitalism, Kristol now argued, spoke for the ordinary citizen exercising his democratic economic rights at the local store. It honors the principle "one dollar, one vote." Capitalist economies flourish as the collective expressions of a free people doing in the marketplace what they do in the political arena. Kristol then attacked anticapitalist ideologies as inherently elitist. They voice the sentiments of those who recoil from the free choices of free people. Intellectuals and aesthetes, said Kristol, pronounce the democratic marketplace "vulgar" and, thus alienated, they have recourse to systems that replace the choices of ordinary people with reform programs that restrict that expression.[54]

Nonetheless, Kristol held a deep ambivalence toward capitalism, especially in its cultural effects. Essentially, Kristol celebrated the bourgeois ethic, which he associated with virtues like hard work, thrift, frugality, self-discipline, moderation, and delayed gratification. These elements, he believed, gave capitalism its moral legitimacy. They approximately related affluence to character, and for a long time they made bourgeois society likeable. But the bourgeois ethic, Kristol believed, had succumbed to the libertarian ethic. In discussing a problem addressed by Joseph Schumpeter in the 1940s, and pondered by Daniel Bell in the 1970s, Kristol recognized the "cultural contradictions" of capitalism. Parents who have gained success through bourgeois values, he said, cannot pass them onto the children born into the affluence their parents have attained. Bourgeois society then no longer reflects a bourgeois ethic. It reflects a capitalist ethic that knows few restraints, that pursues immediate gratifications. A credit-card culture takes over and debt caries no dishonor. Republican values erode and the consumer replaces the citizen. Harsh judgments indeed. Kristol, though, in defending capitalism, did not intend to engage in democratic flattery. "Look," he said, "I do not think that the United States is an altogether admirable place. . . . I think its society is vulgar, debased, and crassly materialistic. I think the United States has lost its sense of moral purpose and is fastly losing its authentic religious values."[55]

Kristol and other neoconservatives thus saw a breach between American bourgeois life and American traditional bourgeois values. The new rightist populism, however, would require overcoming that breach and cementing a union of the two. Populist conservatism awaited the critical role played by Ronald Reagan.

Reagan and his team perceived early on just how to strike the right chords to fashion a popular, vote-getting form of populism. For Reagan succeeded more than any one before him in making populism a rhetorically mainstream ideology. He merged several strands of 1960s and 1970s political language and fused them with a powerful symbolic message. Reagan envisioned an America liberated from the shackles of government by the recovery of the free enterprise system and an America restored to the traditional virtues of its citizens. Reagan's speeches of the 1970s show how this synthesis produced a populist conservatism.

Populism traditionally points to a government controlled by an elite and privileged group. The problem, then, is the liberation of government from this group and its return to its proper owners, the people. In Reagan populism, the problem is government itself. Reagan did not hesitate to list policy issues for which government control, direction, or intervention had made the matters in question worse than they were at the beginning. "It is time for us to realize," Reagan said in 1974, "we have had too much government, too much red tape, too many taxes, and too many regulations." In early speeches he had identified policy issues such as health, housing, farming, commerce, and education as examples of excessive government control. Reagan went after major bureaucratic enterprises in the federal government. He said of the Interstate Commerce Commission, "I challenge anyone to prove there is a need to continue the ICC or that it serves any useful purpose."[56] On this matter Reagan appealed to the basic materialistic interests of his audience. Government, he urged, constituted not so much a threat to liberty as to economic progress. It took its toll on Americans' pocketbooks. "Unnecessary restrictions, red tape, and regulations," said Reagan, "are robbing our people of the prosperity that is rightfully theirs." The unraveling of government and the liberation of business enterprise, Reagan urged repeatedly, assured a future of economic boom. "Private enterprise, not government, is the great provider." "There is only a very little time," said Reagan in apocalyptic warning, "to make the right decisions, to free the productive capacity of America, to loosen government's stranglehold on our economy and on our pocketbooks." "A conservative," Reagan specified, "states that the free market is the best mechanism ever devised by the mind of man to meet material needs."[57]

When Reagan labeled government the great problem, he drew on much of the anti-elitist rhetoric that had been building among the Right since the 1960s. He listed among the offenders "powerful academics," "fashionable left revolutionaries," "social engineers," "an arrogant officialdom," and assorted "experts" at all levels of government.[58] No wonder, said Reagan, that government pursued abstract or utopian ideals that simply defied common sense. Busing and affirmative action, among the critical policy issues, most dangerously reflected these habits. Reagan could thus employ another populist device by positing an unbridgeable gap between the good sense of ordinary people and the unreal notions of policy elites. Thus he could say: "The Americans who keep this country going—the ones who fight the wars; drive the trucks and raise the kids; the farmer and the fireman, craftsman, and cop, they are wondering . . . if the governmental institutions they have upheld and defended really care about them or their values."[59]

With considerable skill, Reagan related these matters to the changing political party system of the 1970s. As candidate for the Republican presidential nomination in 1976, Reagan reminded his audience that he had once been a Democrat. "But," he said, "the intellectual and political leadership of the Democratic party changed. The party was taken over by elitists who believed only they could plan properly the lives of the people."[60] Then in an address the next year, Reagan outlined a conservative strategy for a "New Republicanism." Here he precisely combined his two major themes—free enterprise (or economic conservatism) and social (and cultural) conservatism. To social conservatism, which embraced such policy issues as abortion, busing, and affirmative action, Reagan believed the Republican party could attract blue-collar, religious, and ethnic groups, ones traditionally associated with the Democratic party. For economic conservatism, which embraced issues such as inflation, deficit spending, and big government, Reagan looked to traditional Republican constituencies and independents. In a key rhetorical question, Reagan asked, "Isn't it possible to combine the two major segments of contemporary American conservatism into one politically effective whole?" Here, in fact, Reagan precisely summarized the major cultural and social shifts that had occurred in American politics over the previous decade. This "New Republican Party," as Reagan "envisioned" it, would no longer reflect a "country club big business image."[61]

Reagan's populism invoked a particular, traditional America. He would end forced busing and restore neighborhood and the local school. He would remove government intrusion that hindered the small, local businessman. But along with this trek back to an older America, Reagan also envisioned a bold breakthrough into the economic future. The liberation of business from government control meant a material cornucopia near at hand. Many elements of the Reagan career came together in this fusion— the world of Hollywood and its ethos of perpetual hope and promise, the modern technology of radio and television, and the material progressivism of General Electric media commercials ("living better electrically"). With

Reagan, instead of going back to the future, we go forward to the past. Thus political scientist Hugh Heclo, in summarizing the basic Reagan message, called it "a kind of space age, high technology version of Norman Rockwell's America."[62] Reagan biographer Garry Wills said that the Reagan message "works at sustaining the illusion that a world totally altered in its technology need not touch or challenge basic beliefs. . . . We are whisked off by Technicolor to Oz, only to make us end up claiming there is no place like the black-and-white farm in Kansas."[63]

One might well be in awe of Reagan's achievement here without at all affirming its ideological content or its political consequences in the 1980s. Reagan had borrowed from all the conservative strands that emerged in the 1960s and 1970s and he combined what he needed for his singular brand of conservatism. From the neoconservatives, for example, Reagan could fortify his critique of government and his skepticism of the liberal agenda in policy issues. Indeed, neoconservatives flocked to positions in the Reagan administrations.[64] Reagan, on the other hand, conveyed none of the neoconservatives' ambivalence toward unfettered market capitalism and the cultural contradictions of American capitalism. A conservatism that was both populist and pro-business constitutes the political legacy of the conservative movement that Reagan had pushed to ascendancy by the end of the 1970s. It should impress us for the significant historical shift it represents. What should one think of this unusual amalgamation? Does it signify an authentic conservatism?[65]

Some conservatives mistrusted the populist turn from the beginning. William F. Buckley, for one, though he could employ the populist rhetoric when so moved,[66] had resisted radical insurgency movements in the Republican party. He defended Rockefeller, denounced Wallace, and engaged in personal combat with Kevin Phillips. After writing *The Emerging Republican Majority*, Phillips became the intellectual champion of a "New Right," one that he called "populist," against an Old Right, one that he labeled "elitist." He had Buckley in mind. Phillips called for a Reagan-Wallace ticket in 1976.

Buckley resisted Wallace. Neither politically or intellectually, he said, would the conservative movement gain by an opening to "Wallace populism." He seemed almost embarrassed to have Phillips in the conservative ranks. He and his *National Review* co-defendants wanted a conservatism informed by scholarship and theory and refused to dichotomize the conservative rank-and-file by a division of the folk on the one hand and the learned ranks on the other. Buckley recoiled from Phillips's robust egalitarianism and anti-intellectualism. The *National Review* accused Phillips of "country and Western Marxism."[67]

Meanwhile, in the 1970s, columnist George Will endeavored hard to advance a distinctly nonpopulist kind of conservatism. Will wanted to link the American movement to its older roots in Europe. He appealed to Edmund Burke, Benjamin Disraeli, John Henry Newman, Otto von Bismarck, and Winston Churchill. He wrote in the American tradition of conservatives cited earlier—Babbitt, Kirk, Viereck. Will's conservatism celebrated the organic connections by which different peoples, of different classes and nationalities, found a preserving commonality. It honored ordinary people and local ways. But it trusted to a leadership class that must set high standards for emulation by all. Will called himself a "Tory" conservative. He saw in populism's inimical divisiveness and festering discontent a dangerously destabilizing presence. Furthermore, Will stood apart from conservatives who decried the welfare state and would submit the social classes to a brutal competitive economic order. Government, he insisted, had a proper role to play in saving society's weakest people from the ravages of modern industrial society. And he reminded readers that capitalism constituted the most revolutionary force of the twentieth century and had wreaked havoc on things true conservatives should hold dear—family farms, local governments, traditional craftsmanship, historic homes and buildings.[68]

The hybrid conservatism that Reagan had effected—populist and capitalist—Will considered suspect. He found it fitting that Reagan liked to quote the revolutionary Tom Paine: "We have it in our power to begin the world over again." No true conservative, said Will, holds so naive or so dangerous a faith.[69] Will found Reagan conservatism too cheery, devoid of any tragic sense, wholly negative about government,. and seeing only a realm of harmony and limitless material good in the private sector.[70]

Ironically, the most angry dissent from Reaganism came from Kevin Phillips. He concluded that the Reagan amalgam failed terribly. Surveying the scene in the middle of the Bush administration, Phillips described an outlandish situation, one in which Republican party politics, with Democratic acquiescence, had created new and dangerous disparities of wealth. Phillips's book of 1990, *The Politics of Rich and Poor*, expressed populist indignation, not at leftist intellectual elites this time, but at ostentatious wealth and a new political ethic that fostered it. He called the 1980s a "second Gilded Age." Furthermore, Phillips decried the economic gains made by the "money class" in the 1980s. His populism showed in his reference to recipients of "unearned income"—sources such as rents, dividends, capital gains, and interest. Phillips saw a specific design at work, for the growing gaps in wealth derived from the public policy of the 1980s. Lower corporate taxes, lower personal income taxes, especially for the rich, deregulation, easier rules for business mergers, liberalized depreciation benefits—these policies helped to create an economic free-for-all that gave advantages to the powerful. Phillips saw a profound change as aftermath of the Reagan revolution: "Establishment liberalism wasn't really the Establishment anymore. Values had changed. Social causes had faded. The dominant national elite had once again become *economic*—businessmen, investment bankers, entrepreneurs, people of high incomes of almost any origin."[71] Phillips could only gaze with angry disbelief that conservative populism had produced so unhappy an outcome.

If Phillips's views represented the judgments of populist conservatism from a populist view, those of Michael Lind represented the judgments of populist conservatism from a conservative view. Lind made his case with his 1996 book *Up from Conservatism*. Significantly, he dedicated it to Peter Viereck. Lind considered populist conservatism an impossible hybrid, an oxymoron. All that had transpired through 1996 to produce the so-called populist conservatism, he said, stood exposed by Pat Buchanan. Making his second run at the Republican presidential nomination, Buchanan decided to be a consistent populist. He showed establishment Republicanism to be only a bogus populism that had persuaded working-class voters to forget their economic interests and buy into a cultural crusade. Buchanan went after big corporations and their "down-sizing" programs, attacked NAFTA as a sell-out of American workers,[72] and he denounced immigration as well. But Buchanan, said Lind, had merely inherited a strident antigovernment and anti-elitist rhetoric that had inspired the insurgency since the 1960s. In its wake stood militia movements, burnings of abortion clinics, the Christian Coalition, and the National Rifle Association.[73] Lind wished above all to show, however, that the populist conservatism of the last three decades represented not true conservatism but fanatical and intemperate reactionism. Here Lind saw the upshot of the populist entry into conservatism. The whole thing was a mistake from the beginning[74]

When William F. Buckley Jr. introduced *The National Review* in 1955, he brought disparate segments of the conservative intellectual movement under one roof. Buckley made a successful effort at consolidation, but often proximity bred disaffection. At various points since that time, conservative factions have warred against each other—religious and metaphysical conservatives against agnostic, traditionalists against libertarians, "paleoconservatives" against neoconservatives. Along the way, too, such "fusionist efforts" as those led by Frank Meyer have sought to heal divisions or secure accommodations. The new populist conservatism effected by Ronald Reagan achieved its ultimate formulation in the 1970s and won significant political victories thereafter. As just noted, however, the compound had its own internal tensions; some said it did not even constitute a genuine conservative species at all. History may conclude that conservative population remained a rhetorical turn only, and that Reagan politics betrayed its own ideology. In late 1996, the "Gingrich revolution," perhaps conservative populism's best hope, seemed in jeopardy. Conservative populism, it would appear, can only go so far by proclaiming loss of faith in government and yielding completely to faith in "the people." Ultimately, it may be that conservative populism will need a more precise theoretical enhancement before its translation into politics can circumvent the political contradictions of the 1980s.

*University of Wisconsin–Milwaukee*

## Notes

1. I do not attempt in this article to offer a comprehensive overview of the conservative movement in the 1970s, but have taken a more precisely thematic focus. Thus I do not consider foreign policy issues or the place of the religious Right. For these subjects, see John Ehrman, *The Rise of the Neoconservatives: Intellectuals and Foreign Affairs, 1945–1994* (New Haven, 1995), and Jerome Himmelstein, *To the Right: The Transformation of American Conservatism* (Berkeley and Los Angeles, 1990), 97–128. For a review of scholarly literature on American conservatism since the mid-twentieth century, see William B. Hixson Jr., *Search for the American Right Wing: An Analysis of the Social Science Record, 1955–1987* (Princeton, 1992).

2. Irving Babbitt, *Democracy and Leadership* (Boston, 1924), 61.

3. Peter Viereck, *Conservatism Revisited* (1949; New York, 1962), 34–35.

4. Additional items in this literature would include Richard M. Weaver, *Ideas Have Consequences* (Chicago, 1949); Russell Kirk, *The Conservative Mind: From Burke to Eliot* (Chicago, 1950) and *A Program for Conservatives* (Chicago, 1954); Walter Lippmann, *The Public Philosophy* (London, 1955); and Allan Bloom, *The Closing of the American Mind* (New York, 1987). Among conservatives with a more expressed contempt for democracy and mass society, one would include H. L. Mencken and Albert J. Nock.

5. Michael Kazin, *The Populist Persuasion: An American History* (New York, 1995), 185–88.

6. William F. Buckley Jr., *God and Man at Yale: The Superstitions of Academic Freedom* (Chicago, 1951), 46–55, 22–23.

7. William F. Buckley Jr. and R. Brent Bozell, *McCarthy and His Enemies: The Record and Its Meaning* (Chicago, 1954), 317, 323, 330. Willmoore Kendall, a professor at Yale when Buckley arrived, also influenced the majoritarian ideology among conservatives, particularly in making the case against the open society, which Kendall associated with the liberal tradition of John Stuart Mill.

8. Arthur Schlesinger Jr., *The Vital Center: The Politics of Freedom* (Boston, 1949), 51–67.

9. Richard Hofstadter, *The Age of Reform: From Bryan to F.D.R* (New York, 1955), chaps. 1 and 2.

10. David Riesman and Nathan Glazer, "The Intellectuals and the Discontented Classes," in *The New American Right*, ed. Daniel Bell (New York, 1955), 73; Kazin, *Populist Persuasion*, 190–91.

11. C. Wright Mills, *The Power Elite* (New York, 1957), 262–68; John Patrick Diggins, *The Rise and Fall of the American Left* (New York, 1992), 224–26.

12. James Miller, *Democracy Is in the Streets: From Port Huron to the Siege of Chicago* (New York, 1987), 343–45.

13. Herbert Marcuse, *One-Dimensional Man: Studies in the Ideology of Advanced Industrial Society* (Boston, 1964), 20.

14. Mary C. Brennan, *Turning Right in the Sixties: The Conservative Capture of the GOP* (Chapel Hill, 1995), 7-8.

15. William F. Buckley Jr., *Up From Liberalism* (1959; New York, 1984), 125, 155-67.

16. Brennan, *Turning Right*, 8, 24-25, 35-36.

17. Ibid., 46, 71.

18. Dan T. Carter, *The Politics of Rage: George Wallace, the Origins of the New Conservatism, and the Transformation of American Politics* (New York, 1995), 23-24, 48-49, 52, 69, 76-77.

19. Ibid., 84, 206, 316, 344, 351-52, 368-69.

20. Ibid., 391, 394, 425, 432. E. J. Dionne states that in the Indiana primary contests of 1968 Wallace supporters tended to identify themselves as working class more than those supporting Hubert Humphrey or Richard Nixon. *Why Americans Hate Politics* (New York, 1991), 91; see also Thomas F. Pettigew, *Racially Separate or Together* (New York, 1971), 236-56.

21. Kevin P. Phillips, *The Emerging Republican Majority* (New Rochelle, N.Y.), 40, 44, 88.

22. Ibid., 167, 172, 179-82. Phillips identified early patterns of this trend in liberal urban-reform movements in the 1950s. Led by middle-class professionals (and often acting as reform "clubs" within the Democratic party), they were concentrated in the more affluent locations of the cities. As reform efforts, they worked against city machines with their working-class and ethnic connections. Kevin Phillips, *Mediacracy: American Parties and Politics in the Communications Age* (Garden City, N.Y., 1975), 21. Dionne writes of the reform movement: "Thus, the class war inside the Democratic party began not, as is often thought, in the struggles of the 1960s, but in the skirmishes of the 1950s." The reform group, Dionne adds, also became the dissenter Democrats who broke from Lyndon Johnson for Eugene McCarthy in 1968. Dionne, *Why Americans Hate Politics*, 45-46.

23. Phillips, *Mediacracy*, 17, 21, 26-27, 33. William Berman writes: "How ironic it was, then, that the major force for cultural change issued from a growing, relatively secure, postindustrial new class, while the main line of opposition to its program and values came from below." *America's Right Turn* (Baltimore, 1994), 15.

24. On the leftist background of the neoconservatives, see Gary Dorrien, *The Neoconservative Mind: Politics, Culture, and the War of Ideology* (Philadelphia, 1993), 19-67.

25. See Irving H. Welfeld, "Toward a New Federal Housing Policy," *The Public Interest* 19 (Spring 1970): 31-43.

26. See Larry E. Ruff, "The Economic Sense of Pollution," *The Public Interest* 19 (Spring 1970): 69-97.

27. See Martin S. Feldstein, "A New Approach to National Health Insurance," *The Public Interest* 23 (Spring 1971): 93-105.

28. See Marc J. Roberts, "Is There an Energy Crisis?" *The Public Interest* 31 (Spring 1973): 17-38.

29. See Martin Feldstein, "The Economics of the New Unemployment," *The Public Interest* 33 (Fall 1973): 3-42.

30. See Ralph W. Tyler, "The Federal Role in Education," *The Public Interest* 34 (Winter 1974): 164-87.

31. See Elliott Abrams and Franklin S. Abrams, "Immigration Policy—Who Gets in and Why?" *The Public Interest* 38 (Winter 1975): 3-39.

32. See Thomas Sowell, "Affirmative Action Reconsidered," *The Public Interest* 42 (Winter 1976): 47-65.

33. See Norton E. Long, "A Marshall Plan for the Cities?" *The Public Interest* 46 (Winter 1977): 48-58.

34. See Jude Wanniski, "Taxes, Revenues, and the 'Laffer Curve,'" *The Public Interest* 50 (Winter 1978): 3-16.

35. Mark Gerson, *The Neoconservative Vision: From the Cold War to the Culture Wars* (Lanham, Md., 1996), 95-96.

36. Quoted by Alexander Bloom, in *Prodigal Sons: The New York Intellectuals and Their World* (New York, 1986), 254–55.

37. Norman Podhoretz, *Breaking Ranks: A Political Memoir* (New York, 1979), 165–66.

38. Irving Kristol, "Skepticism, Moralism, and *The Public Interest*," *The Public Interest* 81 (Fall 1985): 33.

39. Berman, *America's Right Turn*, 9–10. The description of the New Class owed much to David Bazelon, a New York intellectual and affiliate of the radical Institute for Policy Studies. In 1966 he described a group of bureaucrats and intellectuals—managers, lawyers, social workers, consultants—who effectively determined liberalism's political agenda, from the expanding welfare state to massive investments in higher education. See Dorrien, *Neoconservative Mind*, 14.

40. Jeane J. Kirkpatrick, *Dictatorships and Double Standards: Rationalism and Reason in Politics* (New York, 1982), 53–54; idem, "America's Political System: The Rules of the Game Are Changing," *U. S. News and World Report*, 18 September 1987, 55–56 (an interview).

41. See Jeane Kirkpatrick, "Why I Am Not a Republican," *Common Sense* (Fall 1979): 34. E. J. Dionne Jr. has written: "Over the long run, the new party rules that emphasized participation led to an increasing role for the well-to-do and a declining role for the working and lower-middle classes." *Why Americans Hate Politics*, 49. He also confirms the neoconservative charge of a New Class takeover of the party and adds that "the 1972 results reversed decades of voting history." Ibid., 122.

42. Michael Novak, *The Rise of the Unmeltable Ethnics: Politics and Culture in the Seventies* (New York, 1972), 47, 86, 123, 126, 203, 245–46.

43. Quoted in J. David Hoeveler Jr., *Watch on the Right: Conservative Intellectuals in the Reagan Era* (Madison, Wis., 1991), 246.

44. Dorrien, *Neoconservative Mind*, 221.

45. Michael Novak, *A Theology for Radical Politics* (New York, 1969), 13, 17, 74, 21, 23, 29, 74, 60.

46. Michael Novak, "A Changed View of the Movement," *Christian Century*, 13 September 1978, 830.

47. Michael Novak, "Switch to Reagan for a Strong America," *Commonweal*, 24 October 1980, 102. And two years after this essay, in a book that showed Novak's full switch to market conservatism, he published *The Spirit of Democratic Capitalism* (New York, 1982).

48. Berman, *America's Right Turn*, 79–80; Dionne, *Why Americans Hate Politics*, 151, 107, 109 (the quotation).

49. Berman, *America's Right Turn*, 11–12.

50. Ibid., 12.

51. Michael Barone, *Our Country* (New York, 1990), 487–89, 492–93.

52. Gerson, *Neoconservative Vision*, 110.

53. Hoeveler, *Watch on the Right*, 99–100.

54. Ibid., 96–97; see also Irving Kristol, "When Virtue Loses All Her Loveliness—Some Reflections of Capitalism and the Free Society," *The Public Interest* 21 (Fall 1970): 3–15.

55. Irving Kristol, interview with Robert Glasgow, *Psychology Today*, 7 February 1974, 80; idem, "Capitalism, Socialism, and Nihilism," *The Public Interest* 31 (Spring 1973): 3–16.

56. [Ronald Reagan], *A Time for Choosing: The Speeches of Ronald Reagan, 1961–1982* (Chicago, 1983), 156–57.

57. Ibid., 147, 156, 160, 186. In the late 1970s corporate America made itself a major lobbying group in Washington with a very political agenda to fight the recent regulatory legislation: "Literally thousands of lobbyists came to town to work on behalf of [the] agenda for Fortune 500 companies, the Chamber of Commerce, and the National Federation of Independent Business." Berman, *America's Right Turn*, 70.

58. [Reagan], *A Time for Choosing*, 154, 177, 187.

59. Ibid., 169, 171, 188, 167 (the quotation).

60. Ibid., 176.

61. Ibid., 184, 189.

62. Hugh Heclo, "Reaganism and the Search for a Public Philosophy," in *Perspectives on the Reagan Years*, ed. John L. Palmer (Washington, D.C., 1987), 46.

63. Garry Wills, *Reagan's America: Innocents at Home* (New York, 1987), 148.

64. See the list compiled by Gary Dorrien, *Neoconservative Mind*, 10–11.

65. As possible predecessors for the kind of populist and laissez-faire conservatism I am describing here, it might seem that southern politics supplies a source. Powerful demagogues, especially those that appeal to a white, racist populace, do represent a significant strand in the American right-wing tradition. But this type invariably wanted at the very least to control business or did in fact attack big business as a populist device that inaugurated a political career. We have seen the case of Wallace in Alabama here. Huey Long in Louisiana attempted a grassroots effort against Standard Oil and learned from Theodore Bilbo of Mississippi the political advantages of denouncing the wealthy. See T. Harry Williams, *Huey Long* (New York, 1969), 71, 104–5, 152, 214–15. Leander Perez of Louisiana criticized federal control of business only that he might have more of the same in his own parish. See Glen Jeansonne, *Leander Perez: Boss of the Delta* (Baton Rouge, 1977), 101–20.

66. Buckley's most often-quoted lines to this effect spoke to Harvard liberal intellectuals: "I am obliged to confess," he said, "that I should sooner live in a society governed by the first two thousand names in the Boston telephone directory than in a society governed by the two thousand faculty members of Harvard University." Quoted in Hoeveler, *Watch on the Right*, 43.

67. See John B. Judis, *William F. Buckley, Jr.: Patron Saint of the Conservatives* (New York, 1988), 377–79. Phillips had written: we cannot "expect Alabama truck drivers or Ohio steelworkers to sign on with a politics captivated by Ivy League five-syllable word polishers." Quoted in ibid., 379.

68. See Hoeveler, *Watch on the Right*, 53–80.

69. George Will, *The New Season: A Spectator's Guide to the 1988 Election* (New York, 1987), 80–81.

70. George F. Will, *The Morning After: American Successes and Excesses, 1981–1986* (New York, 1986), 6.

71. Kevin Phillips, *The Politics of Rich and Poor: Wealth and the American Electorate in the Reagan Aftermath* (New York, 1990), 8–11, 75, 78, 80, 44–45 (the quotation).

72. Michael Lind, *Up from Conservatism: Why the Right Is Wrong for America* (New York, 1996), 5.

73. Ibid., 7–8.

74. For Lind's outline of a "true" conservatism, i.e., a "creative traditionalism" as presented by Peter Viereck, see ibid., 49–54.

## ALICE O'CONNOR

# The False Dawn of Poor-Law Reform: Nixon, Carter, and the Quest for a Guaranteed Income

In August 1969, President Richard M. Nixon approached the American people with a radical proposal to do what the federal government had never done before: guarantee a minimum level of income for every American family unable to provide one for itself. Eight years later, in August 1977, President Jimmy Carter announced a similar proposal for a federal guarantee of income, this time along with an expansion of public works jobs. Like Nixon before him, Carter soon abandoned his bill, and with it the quest for a federal income guarantee. Thus, inconclusively, ended a decade-long struggle to replace the nation's uncoordinated, incomplete collection of welfare programs with a single, comprehensive system of federal relief. This struggle took place against a backdrop of economic stagnation and demographic change that sent social spending soaring and made existing poor-relief arrangements seem increasingly obsolete. It also tapped into growing taxpayer resentment and a rising tide of popular animosity toward welfare. In part for these reasons, the quest for a guaranteed income marked the end of an era of liberal government activism against poverty, and ushered in a new era of poor-law reform. Welfare, not poverty, was the social problem of the 1970s. And the idea of a guaranteed income was the solution embraced by a new, more chastened and conservative, ideological center.

Of course, the obsession with fixing welfare was not new or peculiar to the 1970s. The 1960s, after all, had opened with a draconian welfare crackdown that put the town of Newburgh, New York, in the national headlines. And Congress, in 1962 and 1967, had made two attempts at welfare reform. The first of these, the Public Welfare Amendments, offered social work and rehabilitation as alternatives to relief. The second, known as the work incentive or WIN amendments, combined work requirements with incentives in the hope of moving more people off the rolls. Even the War on Poverty offered a kind of welfare reform, promising that the combination of opportunity and empowerment would greatly diminish the need for relief.[1] In proposing a guaranteed income, the Nixon and Carter administrations departed from this basic approach—extending, rather than restricting, eligibility for relief to more of the poor. At the same time, both Nixon and Carter used the welfare issue in their broader efforts to consolidate an electoral base among white, working-class, and suburban voters and to distance themselves from the "excesses" of big government liberalism—symbolized most powerfully in the "explosion" of the black, urban welfare rolls. Their criticisms of welfare thus heightened the distinction between the "dependent" and the "working" poor. Moreover, as working-class wages and employment prospects deteriorated, officials in both administrations looked to expanded government subsidies as alternatives to strategies emphasizing full employment or labor market reform. In this sense, the quest for a guaranteed income constricted the boundaries of antipoverty intervention, from employment and opportunity to welfare and welfare reform. In the process, the reformers of the 1970s built up a powerful case against the existing welfare system, and helped pave the way for the eventual triumph of a more restrictive and punitive version of poor law reform.

## The Case Against Welfare

On one level the story of the guaranteed income comes to us as an object lesson in the futility of planned social reform.[2] The story is neatly bracketed by two comprehensive proposals—Nixon's, called the Family Assistance Plan, and Carter's, called the Program for Better Jobs and Income—each with the weight of research and expertise behind it, and each a failure in political terms. In between these two episodes come several lesser-known proposals for welfare replacement, again with the imprimatur of Washington's analytic community and again unable to generate key political support. Nevertheless, the pursuit of "comprehensive" reform continued, as did the core of principles—equity, adequacy, administrative simplicity, dignity for the recipients of aid—upon which it was based. And political realities just as consistently defeated it, defying the logic of both comprehensiveness and reform. Indeed, legislation did bring about change in the 1970s, but it was incremental and unsystematic, and it left the existing system more complicated than ever. By the end of the decade, America's poor law, Aid to Families with Dependent Children, was still largely intact.

But just as important as this story of defeat and frustration is that of how and why welfare became such an object of scrutiny and animosity in the first place. Important to this story are the deeper social, economic, and demographic transformations that were operating to change both the "face" and the political meaning of welfare in the 1970s. The economy slowed down, inflation and unemployment went up, and wages for lower- and middle-class workers started their long-term decline. Divorce rates increased, out-of-wedlock births continued to rise, and the growing number of married women in the paid labor force made the American family look less like its 1950s ideal. Cities, already beset by postwar deindustrialization and suburban development, confronted the possibility of serious fiscal collapse. And the race question, following decades of black migration, was increasingly concentrated in depressed urban ghettoes. These structural shifts were reflected in the growing reliance on federal income maintenance programs to stave off increases in poverty. They also drew attention to the demographic "transformation" of AFDC, from a white widows' pension to a "subsidy," as some would have it, for never-married black urban "welfare mothers." Most of all, the economic and social dislocations of the 1970s drew attention to the Great Society's failure to deliver on its promises: of eternal economic growth, of universal prosperity without redistribution, of equal opportunity for all, and, especially, of an end to poverty in the affluent society. As newly resurgent conservatives in both parties sought to fill the political and ideological vacuum, mounting a case against welfare became a powerful political tool.

## The Case Against Welfare, Part One: The "Welfare Crisis"

"We face an urban crisis, a social crisis—and at the same time, a crisis of confidence in the capacity of government to do its job," said President Nixon when he first announced his program for welfare reform in August 1969. "Our states and cities find themselves sinking in Federal quagmire, as case loads increase, as costs escalate, and as the welfare system stagnates enterprise and perpetuates dependency."[3] As Nixon's words suggest, the crisis mentality around welfare played on themes—rising costs, taxpayer resentment, the prospect of a "dependent class," and even, to some degree, a fear of the "wandering poor"—that have accompanied poor-law reform throughout the ages. But the "welfare crisis" also reverberated with anxieties about the economy, race, family structure, and about whether and how government should respond that were particular to the post–Great Society era.

At first glance, the facts behind the "welfare crisis" were straightforward: growing enrollments and rising costs. Having expanded fairly steadily since the mid-1950s, welfare receipt rates took off in the 1960s, boosting relief rolls from approximately 7 million in 1960 to more than 14 million in 1975—and that was counting cash relief alone. Folding in recipients of in-kind benefits such as Food Stamps, Medicaid, and housing assistance, as many as 24 million people were receiving some form of means-tested benefits by the mid-1970s.[4] But it was not the in-kind programs that fueled concern about a welfare crisis. Nor was it aid to the elderly, blind, and disabled. Especially since Social Security benefits began to reach more of the elderly poor, those programs had been holding steady, or slightly declining over the decades. Even less was the simple persistence of poverty the motivating concern.[5] Instead, the "welfare crisis" was about the rise in "dependency" on one program in particular: the once-obscure Aid to Families with Dependent Children program. In 1970 AFDC accounted for 9 million cash relief recipients, triple what it had been a decade earlier and well on the way to its 1975 peak of 11 million. Total federal, state, and local spending on the program rose even faster, "quintupling" as a later analyst put it, to bring federal costs to more than $4 billion over the same period.[6]

"The issue of welfare," Daniel Patrick Moynihan wrote in 1973, "is the issue of dependency. It is different from poverty. To be poor is an objective condition; to be dependent, a subjective one as well." Dependency was "an incomplete state in life," he went on, "normal in the child, abnormal in the adult. In a world where completed men and women stand on their own two feet, persons who are dependent—as the buried imagery of the word denotes—hang."[7] For Moynihan, the "issue" of dependency was nowhere better captured than in the "silent transformation" of AFDC, from a relief program for white widows and children to "a subsistence program" for families of the unmarried, abandoned—and black. Only 6 percent of the 1963 caseload could be attributed to a father's death, Moynihan reported, down from 43 percent two decades earlier.[8] A higher proportion of these families were black—44 percent as opposed to 29 percent in 1948— and living in central cities.[9] "In short: from being a program designed to aid unfortunate *individuals*, AFDC gradually turned into a subsistence program for both individuals and for a *class*"—a black, urban, possibly "permanently dependent" lower class that was being propagated and raised by women. Fifty-six percent of welfare households had no "father figure" in sight, one study showed, and the consequences were borne out in a greater degree of psychological "impairment" in the children.[10] The development, in Moynihan's eyes, had all the ingredients of a demographic time bomb. Once the dirty little secret of the social work profession, the truth about welfare was out. AFDC had "mushroomed," according to *U.S. News and World Report*, into a "monster program" that surpassed all other cash poor-relief programs in enrollments.[11] "Dependency," reported *Newsweek* in a chart illustrating the proportion of welfare recipients to the population in several large American cities, was becoming "the cities' new math."[12]

Not surprisingly, the most populated states were hardest hit by what was now commonly referred to, in keeping with the atomic metaphors, as the welfare "explosion": almost half of all recipients lived in one of five industrialized states by the late 1960s, and New York and California alone accounted for more than 40 percent of caseload increases.[13] But, as *Newsweek's* chart suggested, the welfare crisis was virtually synonymous with another crisis—the "urban crisis"—that just a few years earlier had itself "exploded" on the streets of several major cities. Over the previous three decades, these cities had been fighting against the impact of deindustrialization, job and revenue loss, and white middle-class "flight" to the suburbs while at the same time becoming home to a vast wave of southern black, Appalachian white, and Puerto Rican migrants, who were themselves leaving depressed economic circumstances in search of jobs and opportunity.[14] While numerous studies have disproved the view that the newcomers were swelling the relief rolls, the demographic change brought about by postwar migration and suburbanization was inevitably reflected in urban welfare caseloads. It also fed into the widely shared fear, again challenged by studies at the time, that the more generous cities were serving as welfare "magnets" for the poor.[15] The nationwide AFDC population was more than 50 percent white, *Newsweek* reported in its 1971 cover story on welfare, but 90 percent of New York City's welfare recipients were either black or Puerto Rican. The comparable figures reported for nonwhite recipients were 80 percent in Detroit and 96 percent in Washington, D.C.[16] When combined with calculations that showed widening "dependency ratios" in cities, reports of the racial concentration of urban welfare rolls left an indelible impression: black newcomers were threatening municipal budgets with collapse. In 1970, New York Mayor John V. Lindsay refused to approve the city's $2.1 billion allocation for AFDC and Medicaid and threatened a lawsuit demanding full state and federal funding for the costs.[17] The suit followed closely on widely publicized reports that, in New York, as in hard-pressed states like Vermont, the welfare budget had surpassed the budget for education.[18] More than just a burden to the taxpayers, the reports implied, black welfare recipients were robbing the nation of its very future.

News of the welfare crisis had hit Washington in fits and starts since the early 1960s, creating the impetus for legislative amendments first in 1962 to enhance the "rehabilitative" aspects of the AFDC program and then in 1967 to institute work requirements and enrollment ceilings (unenforced, then repealed) among other reforms. [19] By early 1969, with AFDC growing faster than ever, welfare reform was getting top priority in the White House, as the new Nixon administration prepared to make it a centerpiece of the domestic policy agenda. "The sharply increasing costs of welfare and the growing number of people on the welfare rolls pose a threat to your Administration," top adviser Arthur F. Burns wrote the president portentously just weeks after the Inauguration. [20] Two years later, after Nixon's first reform attempt had failed, welfare was making national headlines. "Welfare Out of Control," "Welfare—The Shame of a Nation," "Welfare: Trying to End the Nightmare" warned *U.S. News and World Report*, *Newsweek*, and *Time* in simultaneous cover stories on February 8, 1971. The coincidence later confirmed the "state of alarm and perceived crisis" for Moynihan, who duly took note in his 1973 account of Nixon's Family Assistance Plan. "If it had happened before that all three national news magazines featured the same cover story, it surely was not on the subject of welfare." [21] What Moynihan failed to mention, however, was that the coincidence was considerably one of the administration's own making. Two weeks earlier, in his State of the Union Address, Nixon had stepped up the already overheated rhetoric against the welfare system, calling it, in words echoed in all three news stories, a "monstrous, consuming outrage—an outrage against the community, against the taxpayer, and particularly against the children it is supposed to help." [22] Having failed once with his proposal to replace welfare, Nixon seemed determined not to let it happen again.

As Nixon's urban affairs adviser, Moynihan himself had played a key role in making welfare one of the president's chief domestic policy initiatives. "I was in a position to encourage [the president's] interest, and did so," Moynihan recalled, referring to Nixon's request that his new urban affairs adviser prepare a report on the "New York welfare mess" in January 1969. Back in Washington after a brief academic hiatus in Cambridge, Moynihan used the occasion as an opportunity to recharge an argument—about the deterioration of the lower-class family structure and the perils of failing to address it—he had made four years earlier as a Labor Department official in the Johnson administration. [23] "From the wild Irish slums of the 19$^{th}$-century Eastern seaboard to the riot-torn suburbs of Los Angeles, there is one unmistakable lesson in American history," Moynihan wrote just after the outbreak of violence in Watts in 1965, "a community that allows a large number of young men to grow up in broken families, dominated by women, never acquiring any stable relationship to male authority, never acquiring any set of rational expectations about the future—that community asks for and gets chaos." [24] Insist as he might that he saw this as a problem faced by all urban lower-class populations, Moynihan had already done more than anyone to racialize the issue of changing family structure in his infamous report, on *The Negro Family*, written just before Watts in 1965. And it was in this report that Moynihan had drawn attention to a key indicator—a "measure of disintegration" within the Negro family—that would later figure prominently in his welfare report to Nixon. AFDC rolls were growing, he showed in a particularly dramatic graph, *despite* falling unemployment among nonwhite men. This development, Moynihan claimed, severed a once solid correlation between unemployment and welfare dependency—"among the strongest known to social science"—that had been in existence since the 1930s. Never mind that the correlation social scientists had been talking about was not between welfare and unemployment but between poverty and unemployment rates. Or that the AFDC program had never, from its inception, been considered to be a response to male unemployment. The trends showed, Moynihan claimed when he resurrected and updated the numbers for President Nixon in 1969, that "in the course of the 1960s the power of unemployment to account for dependency weakened and then vanished altogether."[25] And in case there was any doubt left about it, the graphs told another tale as well: welfare "dependency" was the problem of the Negro family.

"No one really understands why and how this has happened," Moynihan's report to Nixon finally concluded.[26] Others were not so hesitant to provide explanations. Higher welfare payments, migration for better benefits, and the "civil rights and War on Poverty atmosphere" of the 1960s were to blame, wrote political scientist Edward Banfield in a memorandum prepared for presidential adviser Arthur Burns. "I conjecture that some Negroes take a certain satisfaction in getting back at 'Whitey' via welfare," he added parenthetically. Moreover, higher benefits were creating disincentives to work and leading to family breakups, "especially among Negroes." The answer? Set benefit levels high enough to provide well for "the truly poor," Banfield recommended, but keep the appropriations low so that benefits would of necessity be strictly rationed. Ultimately, Banfield later confided in *Time* magazine, he would prefer to take steps "available only to an American dictator," such as those he had advocated in his book *The Unheavenly City*: repeal the minimum wage, enlist out-of-school youth in low-paying jobs or military service, institutionalize the "highly incompetent" poor, and put "problem families" in supervised housing.[27]

Although widely accepted within the administration and in the media, the idea of the "welfare crisis" was not without its detractors. Deftly subverting the usual hand-wringing over swelling rolls, sociologist and political activist Richard Cloward instead declared victory for the National Welfare Rights Organization (NWRO) and for the newly mobilized poor. Indeed, for this "NWRO militant," overloading the rolls was a conscious political strategy that would help bring the much-hated system to collapse. "All this talk about welfare crisis means is that poor people are finally getting something," he told *Newsweek*. "The rise in the welfare rolls is really a kind of reform itself."[28] Brookings Institution analyst Gilbert Steiner, hardly one to curry favor with militants, agreed. "The welfare poor became a major beneficiary of the militancy of the 1960's," he concluded, albeit "without contributing appreciably to the militancy," he wrote.[29] Other liberal analysts also depicted expanding rolls as something of an achievement: thanks to legal services, community action, and other programs initiated during the War on Poverty, local eligibility rules were less arbitrary, administration was more professionalized, and egregious local practices like midnight raids, sudden benefit cutoffs, and residency requirements had been found to be violations of recipients' constitutional rights.[30] When combined with more enlightened attitudes among caseworkers, these changes meant that a far higher percentage of those who were eligible—90 percent in the early 1970s as opposed to a mere 33 percent in 1960—were in fact receiving benefits in 1970.[31] One result, as Steiner pointed out, was that "the welfare poor are better off."[32] Thus, the idea that rising welfare rolls was on its face a bad thing, or that it signaled an *increase* in the number of families unable to provide adequately for their own needs, ignored the fact that more of the *already* eligible were now getting some help, and that it was actually helping.

Contemporary analyses also showed other aspects of the "welfare crisis" to be misleading at best. Writing in the *Public Interest*, Martin Rein and Hugh Heclo showed reports of the welfare tax burden to be greatly exaggerated: even in New York City, ground zero of the welfare "explosion," welfare spending had peaked at only 7.4 percent of the total budget and had *never*, in fact, exceeded spending for education. Nor were states paying significantly larger proportions of their budgets in welfare costs.[33] While considerable, the AFDC surge was but a small part of a much larger expansion of overall social welfare spending, with Social Security and "in-kind" programs such as Medicaid and Food Stamps leading the way. Together, these expenditures were responsible for holding the line against poverty as the economy went into recession in the early 1970s.[34] And while AFDC now included a much higher proportion of blacks than ever before, those proportions had leveled off since the early 1960s, challenging the idea that a growing class of permanently dependent blacks was causing the rolls to expand. Indeed, Rein and Heclo wrote, during the period of fastest growth, "*black as a proportion of all AFDC families changed very little, rising from 40 per cent to 43 per cent*" (emphasis in original).[35] Research could also show that the growth in single-parent families had been occurring since the 1950s and was spread throughout the population.[36] Overall, according to studies that were coming out at the time, the population counted as poor by official standards was much more diverse, and certainly more "temporary," than the "welfare crisis" imagery would suggest.[37]

And yet such critiques missed a fundamental point: the "welfare crisis" was never simply about numbers or proportions or even the expansion of the rolls. It was, to invoke Moynihan's distinction, more "subjective" than that: a qualitative change in the composition of the rolls, a black welfare matriarchy that was rapidly proliferating, a conspiracy of silence among liberal social workers "who decided, in effect, to say nothing ... in effect, to cover up."[38] Together, Moynihan concluded, using the tautological logic of his Negro family report, these behaviors formed a tangle of pathology that was taking on a self-perpetuating dynamic all its own. "The one inescapable fact was that welfare was a problem that had created itself," he wrote. "The rolls rise because they are there." And, thanks to the "vast bureaucratic machinery that depends on (the dependent poor) for its existence," there was no end in sight.[39] For a newly elected Republican president, eager to distance himself from the failures of the liberal regime, constructing a "welfare crisis" was a proposition with enormous political appeal.

### The Case Against Welfare, Part Two: The Welfare "Mess"

Like most manufactured crises, the one around welfare proved hard to sustain. Nevertheless, it tapped into a deeper reservoir of opposition and criticism that lingered long after the "explosion" in the rolls had subsided and the immediate sense of alarm had died down. Everyone, from the welfare rights movement to chambers of commerce, thought the system needed to be changed. No one, least of all the recipients, liked welfare the way it was. But by far the most vigorous critique came from economists, many of them associated with government research offices created during the Great Society era, who came to view welfare as a hopeless, complicated "mess." As the analytic vanguard of the War on Poverty, these economists had already created a base of knowledge and research technology to identify the causes and "cures" for poverty. When political priorities shifted from poverty-fighting to welfare reform, they used that knowledge to shift the focus of debate from "dependency" to the "working poor," and to advocate for a complete systemic replacement plan, featuring an expanded and rationalized federal income guarantee.

Analytic opposition to welfare can be traced to intellectual and political tensions dating back to the 1930s, when the Aid to Dependent Children program was originally relegated to residual status—the "widows and orphans" of the Social Security Act—within the broader structure of the emerging social insurance/welfare state. Having ceded much of the program's conceptualization to a "maternalist" network of social work professionals associated with the Children's Bureau, economists and other advocates of an insurance-based welfare state had little political or intellectual stake in paying attention as the program developed.[40] Besides, the thinking went, ADC would eventually "wither away" as more people came under the far preferable protective umbrella of social insurance, and the ever-capacious benefits of economic growth.[41] This attitude of "benign neglect" continued into the early days of the War on Poverty, when economists in Kennedy's Council of Economic Advisers devised a plan for bringing an end to poverty that reflected their basic faith in economic growth, high employment, and human capital investment. The plan also avoided, for reasons having to do with politics as much as principle, much mention of welfare or relief.[42] Things were beginning to change, however, as it became clear that, particularly in light of the demographic changes reflected in the rolls, AFDC would not simply "wither away" of its own accord. Nor were economists prepared to leave welfare in the hands of the social work profession, which had lobbied, as one analyst put it, for the "underresearched and oversold" 1962 amendments that "put more social work into public assistance."[43] Shortly thereafter, a much different orthodoxy, expressed primarily in the interagency commissions, staff background reports, and internal memos that were the stock in trade of the analytic subgovernment, was beginning to crystallize in policy-making circles: welfare was part of the problem, not the cure.

In contrast to Moynihan and others, the analysts tended to downplay the rise in dependency as the source of the welfare "mess." They also avoided much mention of race or immoral behavior, preferring to base their case on a more systemic, value-"neutral" view. Welfare, in this view, should be judged against the measurable standards of effectiveness, fairness, administrative simplicity, cost-benefit outcomes, and compatibility with the overall efficiency of the market economy. Welfare, it turns out, was a failure on all counts.

The list of indictments was impressive. The system was a "patchwork," to use the well-worn terminology, of categorically targeted cash and in-kind programs. Administered by overlapping federal, state, and local bureaucracies, it made for a "nightmare" of confusing regulations and wasteful paperwork. Despite all the effort and expense, welfare was woefully inadequate as a system of support, analytic critics noted, leaving out millions of poor people altogether and failing to bring those it did serve up to poverty levels. In sharp contrast to universal entitlements such as Social Security, welfare programs were demeaning to recipients, calling for continual proof of eligibility and offering inefficient "in-kind" benefits such as food stamps when straight-out cash would do. Even more glaring were the inequities in benefit levels that stemmed from welfare's federal/state structure, well documented in reports of huge disparities across the fifty states. In 1975, for example, when overall welfare spending was at its height for the decade, average monthly payments for a four-person family ranged from $60 in Mississippi to $497 in Hawaii. Although research remained inconclusive on the question, analysts suspected that the poor were being drawn to higher benefit states.[44] Local discretion had also resulted in a kind of matrimonial inequity across states, since the congressionally-approved AFDC-Unemployed Parent program, which authorized states to extend benefits to two-parent families, had been adopted in only half the states. Perhaps most galling to economists' sensibilities were the numerous "adverse incentives" created by these programmatic features. Welfare discouraged work, reports showed, by imposing a "marginal tax rate"—in the form of benefit reductions—of 66 percent for each dollar earned by recipients, even with the 1967 amendments allowing welfare recipients to keep more of their earnings. Unavailable to two-parent families in most states, welfare also created "a situation," as economist Harold Watts put it, "in which a father can best serve his family by deserting it."[45]

Of all the flaws in the welfare system, perhaps none was as egregious as its neglect of a group known to analysts as the "working poor": families making below-poverty wages and categorically ineligible for aid. The distinction contained in this formulation was important, drawing a line between "dependent" welfare recipients and the wage-earning poor that was loaded with unspoken reference to race and gender: the typical "working poor" family was two-parent, male-headed, and white. It also indicated the extent to which poverty had come to dominate the language of social policy—focusing narrowly on lack of income rather than labor markets, un- or "under" employment as a category of concern. Most significantly, the distinction recognized the right of a new class of claimants—the low-wage working class—to the benefits of public relief. Such an extension of relief could be seen as a revolution in welfare, violating, as it did, a prohibition against aid to the "labouring poor" that was as old as the poor laws themselves.[46] Of more immediate significance were its implications for the assumption, embedded in liberal social policy since the New Deal, that economic growth and modestly regulated labor markets were the most effective ways of providing for able-bodied, employable Americans. Extending relief to the "working poor" effectively acknowledged the inadequacies of this assumption and provided, as economist Robert Haveman noted, an occasion for making "the labor market itself ... a focus of policy debate."[47] But in the narrower confines of the case against welfare, the issue was fairness, not labor-market deficiencies, and almost inevitably it pitted the "deserving" against the "undeserving" poor.

In 1966, Watts testified, more than 90 percent of the "working poor" received no benefits at all.[48] While food stamps were covering substantial numbers by the early 1970s, working families in some states still stood to make less from employment than AFDC families "made" from being on welfare. "[T]here are literally millions of working men and working women whose after-tax income is less than the value of the cash, food and health benefits provided to AFDC families," announced Michigan Representative Martha W. Griffiths in summarizing the results of a three-year congressional study of the welfare system.[49] It was above all in the name of these families—unarguably the "deserving poor"—that analytic critics called for the radical overhaul of the outdated welfare system. And it was very much with them in mind that the economists advocated a particular solution to the welfare "mess": a guaranteed income, delivered in the form of a negative income tax.

Initially proposed by conservative economist Milton Friedman in the early 1960s, the negative income tax proposed to give people what they needed—cash—and to do it with as little government interference as possible.[50] Under such a plan, government transfer payments would be handled through the federal income tax system, and people with taxable income under some basic minimum would receive what amounted to refunds, or "negative taxes," that could be adjusted according to family size. Payment amounts would begin from a minimal standard for those with no other income at all, and diminish as income from earnings got higher, eventually phasing out altogether once a family reached some "breakeven" point. Thus, while free of existing "categorical" restrictions on eligibility for aid, the negative income tax could be targeted to the poor and fine-tuned to supplement rather than replace earnings from employment—preserving, in contrast to AFDC, an essential work incentive. "The advantages of this arrangement are clear!" Friedman wrote enthusiastically when he first laid out the idea. His reasoning underscored its appeal to economic values. "It is directed specifically at the problem of poverty. It gives help in the form most useful to the individual, namely, cash. It is general and could be substituted for the host of special measures now in effect." Perhaps most attractive from the economist's point of view, the negative tax "operates outside the market." And for Friedman, if not for other economists, it was a way to replace the welfare state altogether.[51]

Despite its conservative pedigree, it was liberal economists, convinced they had found an efficient way to "end poverty in the United States as we define it today," who took up the cause of the negative income tax in the mid-1960s. In a series of "five-year plans" projected to bring all Americans above the poverty line by the nation's bicentennial, economists and budget planners in the federal Office of Economic Opportunity proposed a gradual phase-in of a universal negative tax that would "substitute for the demeaning programs now lumped together under the head of Public Assistance." Envisioned as a supplement to existing employment, training, and community action programs in the War on Poverty, the negative tax would "not substitute for opportunity programs," the plan went on to say. "[B]y 1976, opportunity programs should be successful enough that they will establish those who can provide for themselves above the poverty level—well above this level."[52] Besides, the OEO planners were prepared to argue, in the affluent society the United States had become, the time had arrived to do what other Western societies had already done: recognize "a guaranteed income at the poverty level as a right in a wealthy country."[53]

Despite efforts to fit the idea within the framework of growth and opportunity, the chances of White House support for the negative tax were slim: it was too much like "the dole" for Lyndon Johnson's taste and, at $30 billion over five years, too costly for the Vietnam-drained federal coffers. Recognizing the politics of the situation, OEO economists were nonetheless persistent in their support. In 1967, they launched the first in a multi-million-dollar series of large-scale controlled social experiments that would, as one staff member put it, "determine the facts in this important innovation in social policy."[54] Started in urban New Jersey and eventually replicated in rural Iowa, North Carolina, Gary, Indiana, Seattle, and Denver, the experimental intervention was very much designed with the working poor in mind, and provided three years and more of income guarantees to selected (in New Jersey, exclusively two-parent) families. In addition to trying out this "revolutionary" approach, the experiments marked "a landmark in increasing the sophistication of Federal policymaking in general," one OEO staffer remarked, confirming the prominence of poverty research on the cutting edge of domestic policy.[55] Most important, they hoped, the income experiments would provide definitive scientific evidence for what the economists had long been trying to predict: how much, or how little, the guarantee of income would prevent the "deserving poor" from working at all.[56]

Bolstered by the high-visibility attention it was getting in analytic circles, by the late 1960s the negative income tax was gaining a broader base of support from congressmen and leading business figures as well as economists. It was also emerging as the lead proposal within the more wide-ranging movement for a guaranteed income, which spanned the political spectrum from Friedmanite conservatives to civil rights advocates on the left. Nevertheless, and despite strong support among his own advisers, Johnson would agree only to appoint a commission, led by business executive Ben Heineman, to study it in 1967.[57] By the time the Heineman Commission actually got under way in 1968, LBJ's intention to step down was public, and the future of existing antipoverty programs, let alone a proposal as dramatic as the negative income tax, was uncertain at best. And then, several months into the new Republican administration, the idea got a wholly unexpected boost: trumping an anticipated endorsement from the Heineman Commission, Nixon announced a more targeted, less generous, and, as OEO staffers liked to call it, more "workhouse"-like version of the scheme they had been promoting all along.

## The Futility of Reform

### Comprehensive Reform, Round One: The Family Assistance Plan

For all the behavioral issues buried in his talk of a "welfare crisis," Nixon came up with a plan—the Family Assistance Plan—that seemed much more attuned to the values of the analytic community. Assembled with the help of several "holdovers" from the Johnson administration, FAP was a proposal to extend basic cash benefits to a much larger pool of recipients than ever before. The key to the proposal was a version of the negative income tax that would work as both a basic income guarantee (or "floor," as those wary of guarantees preferred to call it) for the legitimately dependent poor and as an income supplement for low- wage working families. Accepting the analysts' logic, FAP was also pitched as a stabilizing factor that would keep two-parent families together and as a work incentive program to keep them in the labor force. Adding to the work-incentive idea, the plan included expanded day care and transportation, noting that these benefits would help welfare mothers get to work. FAP also promised equity across state boundaries, administering income maintenance as a federal program with a uniform benefit structure. But in key ways FAP was not to be confused with liberal guaranteed income schemes. ("This national floor under incomes for working or dependent families is not a 'guaranteed income,'" Nixon insisted in his announcement. Moynihan insisted that it was.)[58] The most obvious, and least convincing, was the requirement that able-bodied recipients, including mothers with children over six, register for work or training and face the threat of benefit reductions if they did not comply.[59] More important was the fact that FAP did not aim to eliminate poverty, nor even, in the Great Society sense, to attack "dependency" at its roots. It was, instead, a plan to rechannel dependency in a new, more Republican direction.

To many of its supporters, FAP was not to be judged as a political move but as a sensible, efficient way of providing the poor with the cash they needed without the stigma of interfering social workers; it was, in the title of one journalistic rendition, "Nixon's good deed."[60] There was also a certain appeal, as Moynihan was often to point out in promoting the idea inside the White House, to the prospect of stealing the liberals' thunder with a proposal that appeared even more radical than anything they had proposed in the past. "That only a Nixon could have done it—and not a Kennedy or Johnson—is one of history's ironies," Moynihan told *Newsweek* in a discussion about FAP. Echoing the theme, Nixon is reported to have aligned himself with "Tory men with liberal principles" when he put the new welfare plan forward in 1969.[61] But it was primarily as part of an evolving political strategy that welfare reform took on its greatest significance for the Nixon administration. The strategy was both symbolic and electoral: "welfarism"—constructed as big government, as black, and as urban—got to the heart of a much-weakened New Deal electoral coalition, and FAP was just the kind of proposal to drive the wedge in further. "Nowhere is the failure of government more tragically apparent than in its efforts to help the poor and especially in its system of public welfare," the president said in his August 1969 speech announcing FAP. Welfare, the product of "a third of a century" of centralization and "social experiment," was "a bureaucratic monstrosity" that imposed a "drastically mounting burden on the taxpayer." Welfare, by promoting "desertion" and nonwork, was antifamily and morally wrong. Welfare fostered dependency among the black urban poor. Worst of all, welfare was "unfair to the working poor," precisely those people, "forgotten" in liberal programs, whose votes Nixon had courted in the recent election. FAP would help to solidify the position of disaffected white working-class voters within the "emerging Republican Majority."[62] And it would "get rid of the costly failures of the Great Society," of which Nixon considered welfare (a New Deal program) "the worst offender."[63]

FAP was also significant as the centerpiece of a distinctively Republican, "unmistakably Nixon," alternative to Great Society "welfarism," known as the "New Federalism" and announced in the same speech that initially unveiled the new welfare plan in August 1969. Presented as a bid to "start power and resources flowing back from Washington to the states and communities," Nixon's reform package envisioned a reconfigured welfare state, in which the federal government held the purse strings but left it to states and localities to administer the wide range of services, housing, transportation, and community development programs the "Washington bureaucracy" had been accumulating since the New Deal. Nixon's plan also tried to assert greater White House control over policy decisionmaking, by consolidating the functions of proliferating social welfare agencies into a few "superagencies" under stricter Executive supervision.[64] In their place would be a more slimmed-down, efficient, and presumably less patronage-driven policy-making machinery that would also be subject to the fiscal discipline of an increasingly powerful Office of Management and Budget.[65] Significantly, the reorganization also featured an expanded role for policy analysis and "experimentation" in the federal government beginning, as Nixon announced in his New Federalism speech, with a remake of the OEO. Stripped of its controversial community action functions, in Nixon's hands the poverty agency would become a laboratory for research and innovation—and for more efficient, less "activist" government.

From the start, Nixon presented FAP as key to the realization of this larger agenda, a first, symbolic blow against the unwieldy, dependency-producing Washington bureaucracy that would offer "independence" and dignity for American families in need. Having lost at the hands of the Senate Finance Committee in 1970, Nixon once again gave FAP top priority in the reform package he presented in the 1971 State of the Union address—a package, including revenue sharing, block grants for community development and social services, and a complete reconfiguration of cabinet departments, meant to strike a dramatic departure from the "centralizing" tendencies of the past.[66] And yet, Nixon's reform plan did not propose to abandon the liberal legacy altogether: the 1971 budget, released soon after the reorganization plan, embraced a Keynesian commitment to expansionary spending and asked the Congress to accept "the concept of the full employment budget."[67] Nor did Nixon's reforms represent a repudiation of the state. The New Federalism was as much a plan to "streamline" and enhance as it was to "devolve" the powers of federal government. And while ridding federal government of the services and patronage networks associated with New Deal liberalism, it also proposed to expand federal largess where it mattered most: in the pockets of key voting groups.

Finally, while diminishing the power of the "old line" agencies such as Labor and HEW, Nixon's "administrative state" did enhance the position of analysts within those agencies—and, consequently, in the welfare-reform debate. The domestic reform program, to which FAP was a key, was thus meant to remold and rein in, but not entirely to repudiate, the liberal welfare state.

Despite some progress in implementing the broader reform plan, FAP once again got stalled in the Senate, thanks in no small part to the administration's own announcement of the attention-absorbing New Economic Policy in late summer 1971.[68] But FAP's internal problems were more than enough to weigh it down. Although initially appealing to proponents of greater fiscal relief for the states, the plan ultimately appeared simply to redistribute benefits from the more generous North to the stingy South: its basic guarantee of $1,600 for a four-person family represented less than what was available in many northern states and well more than what was available in the South. FAP also earned the ire of NWRO activists and other left-leaning advocates of guaranteed incomes for threatening to lower benefits for a large proportion of single mothers who were already on the rolls. Proposed benefit levels were equally threatening to southern conservatives, who immediately saw that they would undermine the pitifully low wage structure in the South. ("Who am I going to get to iron my shirts?" one southern Democrat is said to have wondered aloud.)[69] Nor could any amount of tough rhetoric from Nixon hide the fact that FAP was not "workfare," as he claimed, but a vastly expanded basic income guarantee: sanctions were included for those who failed to register for work, but they were never strong enough to satisfy advocates of work over the handout. Besides, as the 1967 WIN (for work incentive) amendments indicated, there was already a strong congressional contingency in favor of a more work-oriented approach to welfare reform. With the lines of opposition to FAP hardening, Moynihan urged the administration to make use of the preliminary findings from the New Jersey experiment—at that point, preliminary at best—to back up their case.[70] The turn to expertise was ineffective, however, and may even have backfired. The preliminary results for New Jersey, reporting no work fall-off at all, led a suspicious Senator John Williams from Delaware to order an investigation of the experiment itself. And then Williams, relying on charts "reluctantly supplied" by HEW, proceeded to make a devastating critique of FAP, demonstrating that it would not eliminate the so-called "notch" within which the working poor would lose more income from working than they would from remaining solely dependent on the dole.[71] FAP, it appeared, could satisfy none of the major constituencies competing to dominate welfare reform.

Meanwhile, as the 1972 election campaign heated up, welfare reform proposals proliferated, ranging from Democratic candidate Senator George McGovern's promise of a universal demogrant to Senator Russell Long's "workfare" proposals to create federal jobs—at welfare wages—for AFDC recipients. In this increasingly polarized atmosphere, Nixon's continued, if lukewarm, commitment to FAP took on yet another strategic significance: as a way of establishing the president as a man of the center. Nixon's advisers, urging him to "reassert your leadership on the high domestic priority of welfare reform," encouraged him to compromise with a bipartisan group of Senate centrists led by moderate Republican Abraham Ribicoff of Connecticut for a somewhat more generous bill in June 1972. That way, they argued, "McGovern's well publicized radical welfare proposals will be cut off from the bipartisan center coalition" just in time for the Democratic Convention. "Even if we lose," they reasoned, "we will be in the strongest possible position to exploit the issue: we will have done all we could to fight for real reform and the Democratic Congress killed the bill."[72] Setting the advice aside, Nixon stuck with HR 1 as originally proposed, but by then it was clear he preferred to let welfare reform die as quietly as possible. That year's Republican party platform took a stand against the principle of income guarantees—even though Republican-backed changes in Old Age Assistance programs would soon establish just that for the elderly. By the fall, the first presidential effort to achieve comprehensive welfare reform had been defeated. Nevertheless, the seeds of Nixon's domestic policy "revolution" had been planted: by 1974, community development, social services, and housing had been cashed out or "block granted," the federal government was providing more direct cash aid to individuals than ever before, and the social welfare bureaucracy, while still alive and well, was increasingly subordinated to the White House and the OMB.[73]

## Gearing Up for Round Two: The Income Supplement Program

While the prolonged struggle over FAP may have eroded political support for the negative tax, if anything it left the analysts more convinced of its worth than ever, and helped to create the foundations of expertise and research evidence that would keep the idea alive in the years following FAP's defeat. Analysts continued to build on those foundations through the mid-1970s, providing the background for a series of comprehensive welfare-reform proposals—most of them variations on the negative income tax—that gained support across the political spectrum. Backed up by a three-year Joint Economic Committee–sponsored study, Democratic Congresswoman Martha Griffiths proposed the Tax Credit and Allowances Act in

1974. That same year, Secretary of HEW Casper Weinberger put forward the Income Supplement Program, an even more streamlined version of the negative income tax that would, as the staff report accompanying it indicated, restore Milton Friedman's original concept of total welfare replacement.[74] Both of these proposals, announced virtually simultaneously, drew on the expertise of former Heineman Commission staff members, who had developed innovative modeling techniques for simulating the impact of various reform proposals, and of economists at the University of Wisconsin's Institute for Research on Poverty, which had been designated by OEO to conduct the New Jersey experiment.[75] Meanwhile, expertise on income-maintenance reform was becoming rapidly institutionalized within analytic networks: the three leading model-builders from the Heineman Commission had since gone to the Urban Institute, a nonprofit research organization that relied heavily on federal government contracts, where they developed and, later, marketed a series of increasingly sophisticated models for estimating the impacts of changes in the income-maintenance system. Soon a new set of acronyms, RIM (Reform in Income Maintenance), TRIM (Transfer Income Model), and, later, DYNAMISM entered the language of policy analysis. Alert to the growing government market in microsimulation, Mathematica Policy Research, a for-profit research organization, followed suit with MATH (Microanalysis of Transfers to Households).[76] IRP researchers also moved easily within these institutional networks, valued for their training in basic poverty research and, particularly as efforts to replicate the New Jersey experiment got under way, their exposure to pioneering social experimentation techniques. Most important, advocates of the negative income tax had a firm institutional anchor within the federal bureaucracy. In the early 1970s, analysts in the office of HEW's Assistant Secretary for Planning and Evaluation (ASPE) established the Income Security Policy division, staffed by several economists from the "reorganized" OEO, which became the leading source of government funding for research on poverty and welfare reform. Michael Barth, director of the ISP staff, was himself a veteran of the internal planning behind FAP.

This research network, and the growing body of evidence it was accumulating, seemed to portend well for the prospects of a negative tax, for both confirmed what the economists had felt all along: it was possible to design a simpler, fairer, more cost-effective alternative to the current welfare "mess," and, or so the New Jersey experiment seemed to suggest, a guaranteed income would not cause massive reductions in work effort.[77] Also encouraging for advocates of the change were new research findings indicating that the vast majority of people in poverty were there only temporarily and were not likely to make "dependency" a "way of life."[78] More-over, the planners at ASPE felt they had learned some political lessons from FAP, which they planned to use, as HEW Secretary Weinberger noted, to shift the debate "away from 'welfare reform' as such and towards what has become, in fact, the dominant function of the federal government—providing for the income security needs of the nation."[79] Thus it was with some confidence that analyst Laurence Lynn, writing in 1975, could say that "the sum total of experience with the existing system and the results of research on poverty have irrevocably altered the content of the welfare-reform debate in a manner that should be favorable to welfare reform."[80]

Lynn's prediction was premature, at least in the most immediate sense. Resisting an impressive array of analytic findings and background reports, President Ford rejected Weinberger's Income Supplement Program in fa-vor of a series of cost-saving reforms. Ford wanted budget cuts, not new spending, in light of his pledge to "whip inflation now," and he instructed Weinberger to come up with measures that would save "over $1 billion annually." The result was a series of administrative measures, packaged as a cost-saving "crackdown" on bureaucratic waste, loose eligibility require-ments, and "runaway husbands." Unhappy with Ford's rejection of his plan, Weinberger persisted in his argument that anything less than com-plete overhaul was no reform at all.[81] Weinberger later got vindication, of sorts, from a bipartisan group of prominent economists who took their plea to the White House and the front page of the *Washington Post*. "Funda-mental reform" had become an "imperative," they insisted in a letter to Ford in 1976. Calling for "equity, efficiency and prudence," they recom-mended that any new plan include a consolidation of all cash programs into one, "a federally-established floor" under all incomes, "equal treat-ment of intact and divided families," assistance for the working poor, and, picking up on old animosities toward the social work bureaucracy, a shift of administrative responsibility for income maintenance from HEW to "an appropriate agency," such as the IRS.[82] But the president's earlier decision was final. Sensing—unlike proponents of the negative tax—that the welfare debate was shifting, his own efforts at reform would be belt-tightening and restrictive, calculated to ward off, according to media re-ports, the "conservative tide" then sweeping the country.[83]

Ford's bow to more conservative forces was not the only sign of a com-ing shift in welfare politics. In its own way so, too, was a more subtle shift in the analytic case for reform. Earlier attached to an ambitious agenda that promised to end poverty in America, in the post–Great Society era the idea of a guaranteed income was instead tied more narrowly to the objec-tive of welfare reform. While the focus on welfare was to some degree of

Republican doing, it also expressed the mood of skepticism and disillusionment that gripped many Great Society liberals, and led them to embrace a kind of "bottom-line" realism in setting and evaluating policy goals. It also marked an erosion of faith among liberal economists, not only in the possibility of ending poverty, but in economic growth and opportunity as the means for bringing it about. In the 1960s, that faith had been criticized by advocates of large-scale government job creation, who charged that the aggregate growth strategists were blind to structural problems in the economy. In the 1970s, it was put to the test by economic slowdowns, rising inflation, and stagnating wages, leading once again to endorsements for more interventionist labor market and employment policies in response.[84] And yet, as inflation fears took over and unemployment rates shot up, the analysts in poverty circles increasingly focused on an expansion of welfare as the more expedient and efficient solution. Indeed, the chief appeal of the negative income tax, as Milton Friedman had said, was that it worked "outside the market." A government wage subsidy would provide income for low-wage workers without "interfering" in the labor market itself. Thus, even as they pleaded the case of the "working poor," poverty analysts were in effect pre-empting the broader debate about employment and wages, confining it instead to one about welfare reform.

At the same time, the institutionalization of the highly technical, presumably neutral approach to welfare reform embraced by the analysts represented the triumph of a style of policy making that was inherently hostile to the kind of "interest-based" policies associated with New Deal liberalism. And it was this combination, of chastised liberalism and technocratic style, that produced what turned out to be the culminating moment for the analytic approach to welfare reform: Jimmy Carter's Program for Better Jobs and Income.

## Comprehensive Reform, Round Two: The Program for Better Jobs and Income

By the time Jimmy Carter's comprehensive reform plan made its debut in August 1977, the policy environment had grown infinitely more complicated than it had been when Nixon first announced FAP eight years, almost to the day, earlier. The first complicating factor was the slew of piecemeal initiatives that had been added to the system since the early 1970s, each in its own way an attempt to achieve some piece of the comprehensive reform agenda: Social Security benefits were indexed to inflation, greatly improving benefit levels and accelerating poverty reduction among the low-income elderly; the Supplemental Security Income program (SSI) federalized cash assistance for the aged, blind, and disabled, essentially providing a minimum income guarantee for one whole category of the "deserving" poor; the Earned Income Tax Credit (EITC) provided a graduated wage subsidy for low-income workers with children; the Food Stamp program was liberalized, with provisions that made it, as Brookings Institution analyst Richard Nathan noted, a "mini-negative income tax" for the poor.[85] Clearly the scope, as well as the costs, of federally funded income maintenance had expanded dramatically, making it the nation's principal weapon against poverty. Not all incremental welfare reforms moved in a liberalizing direction, however. Some hoped to tighten the rules: the 1971 Talmadge amendments required states to put more of their recipients into the already-existing work incentive or WIN program; and the Child Support Amendments, passed in 1975, significantly expanded the federal role in establishing paternity, locating fathers, and collecting support for AFDC children.[86] In 1973, Congress also added another new component to the system of social provision with the Comprehensive Employment and Training Act, the first direct federal job-creation program since the Great Depression, and a sign of mounting concern over rising unemployment.[87] When added together, these changes lent support to the conclusion that welfare, as well-informed observers noted, "is already more reformed than most people think."[88] It also cautioned against yet another effort at comprehensive reform. "[T]he beginning of welfare wisdom," cautioned advocates of a more "incrementalist" strategy, was that "idealized systems cannot be achieved, no matter how ambitious the legislation."[89]

Adding to the system's complexity as a caution against comprehensive reform was increasing evidence of rifts within the analytic community about what such a reform might look like. Reflecting long-standing intellectual and institutional differences between the two agencies, these rifts came to the surface in the struggle between HEW's ASPE and its more recently established analytic counterpart in the Department of Labor, ASPER, during the development of Carter's welfare-reform plan.

Throughout the 1970s, thanks in part to provisions for research in the CETA legislation, Labor's ASPER had been building up the research networks around issues of unemployment and labor market policy. These networks, along with the backing of the forceful and respected Labor Secretary Ray Marshall, strengthened the agency's hand in its long-standing advocacy of job creation as the best approach to welfare reform.[90] Having lost the battle for a job-creation strategy during the War on Poverty, labor analysts were determined not to cave in to the straight income approach favored by the analysts at HEW. In the first place, the labor analysts disliked the idea of lumping everyone together in a single undifferentiated cash supplement plan such as the negative income tax. Income from work was more desirable than income from the government, they reasoned, and should be recognized as such. Labor analysts were also fearful of the deadening effects such "dependency" would have on labor's political voice. Everything should be done to avoid simply putting the working poor on the dole. At the same time, the labor analysts had become increasingly concerned about the inequities and gaps in the welfare system, and were eager to ensure that reform was coordinated with a program to assist the working poor. Their answer was to introduce an entirely new, in some ways antithetical, "track" into the idea of welfare reform by guarantee: government jobs for those who could reasonably be expected to work; cash grants for those who could not.[91]

In a reprise of battles from the 1960s, the job-guarantee proposal was greeted with skepticism from negative-income-tax advocates at HEW and became a major point of contention with DOL. In the 1960s, the battle had been decided by LBJ's refusal to spend the kind of money required to create jobs for the poor. This time, it erupted into analytic warfare. Assigned to work together in planning for PBJI, Labor and HEW came up with rival microsimulation models and conflicting cost estimates to back up their opposing plans.[92] It was only after news of the infighting had become public knowledge that the planning group came to something of a détente, appropriately enough after both sides agreed to use the same model, known as the KGB (albeit without reference to the Soviet spy agency). Their efforts were reflected in a lengthy, detailed document known to White House officials as the "monster memo," laying out the components of what eventually became PBJI.[93]

The final complication, as ever, was the divergent array of constituent groups with a stake in any effort at reform. Conservative congressional leaders wanted tighter work requirements and had been advocating expanded "workfare" for years. Labor wanted jobs, as well as assurances of adequate wages and income guarantees. Representatives of state and local interests, who found a spokesman in New York Senator Daniel Patrick Moynihan, were chiefly interested in fiscal relief, administrative simplicity, and national minimum standards. And although not nearly so well organized as they had been a few years earlier, welfare rights advocates remained centrally concerned about benefit inadequacy and were wary of efforts to impose further work requirements.[94] Overriding all of these factors were two basic considerations: popular sentiment, of which the president was acutely aware, that welfare was too costly and that Washington "special interests" were at least partly

to blame; and economic uncertainty, amidst the twin threats of inflation and unemployment, that made Carter reluctant to endorse any
plan requiring significant new spending.[95]

In its own way the Carter plan sought to steer among—even capitalize on—the various factors complicating welfare reform. For one thing,
the themes of bureaucratic waste and Washington "interests" gave Carter
something to run on: welfare, as he emphasized in his election campaign, was a complicated, bureaucratic, special-interest-laden "mess"
that needed a complete "overhaul." At the same time, his reform plan
was nothing if not a reflection of Washington expertise—splitting the
difference, rather than choosing between the two major factions in his
Cabinet—and an effort to offer something for each of the major interest
groups involved. Finally, Carter insisted that the actual development of
the plan would be a model of efficiency (he insisted on a series of
nearly impossible deadlines), open to public view and input (planning
included an unprecedented public outreach effort), and would not result in more government spending. [96] All of this came together in an
enormously complex three-part proposal: a basic federal income guarantee that collapsed all existing cash programs into one; a new program of government-created jobs, offered as "last resort" employment
for able-bodied recipients; and a wage supplement, in the form of an
expanded EITC. Together, these components were meant to operate as
a three-tiered, or "triple track," system that differentiated among different groups of the poor: outright grants for those (including the aged,
disabled, and mothers with children under six) who were not expected
to work; work-conditioned grants for able-bodied dependents, with benefit reductions for those refusing to work; and an expanded EITC for
the low-wage "working poor," designed to make private-sector employment more attractive than "dependency" on the minimum-wage-scale
public service jobs.[97]

In the end it was precisely these complications that brought about
PBJI's quick demise on the Hill. Initially greeted with modest enthusiasm, the proposal began to fall apart in fairly predictable ways once the
major players read the fine print. The income provision, in a replay of
FAP, was too high for conservatives and too low for welfare rights advocates. The jobs proposal left many questions unanswered, beginning
with how they would be created, what they would look like, and where
the private-sector slots would come from. Meanwhile, the administration was backing away from its earlier commitment to public job creation as a means of economic stimulus, making it clear that the "jobs"

component of PBJI would remain a stigmatized "less desirable" alternative to low-wage private-sector employment.[98] Fiscal relief was uneven, once again leaving several northern states feeling dissatisfied.[99] And the internal administration sniping continued, complicated by the fact that no one, analysts included, could get the facts straight. Forced to back down on its original estimate of an additional $2.8 billion in costs, the administration was deeply embarrassed when the Congressional Budget Office—using the ubiquitous KGB model—came up with a figure of $17.4 billion a few months later.[100] HEW analysts were later taken by surprise when Moynihan, citing findings from their own income-maintenance experiments, withdrew his support for the negative income tax on the grounds that it caused marital instability.[101] Even Carter's efforts to tap into populist antiwelfare sentiment seemed to backfire, as "tax revolt" fever overwhelmed any notion of rational government reform.

But perhaps most telling in the fall of Carter's welfare reform was its fate at the hands of his own internally-conflicted domestic agenda, in which social policy goals—including such measures as national health insurance, job creation, and urban revitalization—were continually confounded by his insistence on a stance of fiscal conservatism and his desire to divest himself of associations with "big government" liberalism. By the end of 1978, PBJI was long gone, and with it the prospects for welfare reform analytic-style. After a decade of trying, the quest for comprehensive, systematic expansion of the nation's income-maintenance system had finally come to an end.

## A New Day Arrives

PBJI rang the death knell for a distinctive, and what in retrospect appears to be quixotic, vision of welfare reform. While it built in important ways on ideas and policy developments from the 1960s, this vision was very much a product of the 1970s, a time of heightened economic insecurity, growing popular resentment of the burdens imposed by big government, and, always just beneath the surface, backlash against the groups—blacks and welfare recipients among them—who were deemed to have benefited most from Great Society programs. Amidst such volatile forces, the idea of sweeping welfare reform seemed a grand one: a single, inclusive system for assuring all Americans, on an equal basis, at least a minimum level of protection from want. Indeed, for a brief period beginning in the late 1960s, the idea of replacing welfare with a minimum-income guarantee was very much about expanding the rights of all citizens to include the right to a decent income at or above the poverty level. But in its 1970s version, this vision of reform was attached to a much different agenda, of welfare state retrenchment and political realignment, that engaged both parties in a search for alternatives to New Deal liberalism and that shifted the political center significantly to the right. By the time his welfare-reform efforts were over, Jimmy Carter was repudiating Keynesian economic principles and cautioning Americans that they should not look to government to find them a way out of poverty.[102] Seen in this light, FAP and PBJI were more significant as efforts to streamline and diminish the political apparatus of the New Deal welfare state, and as electoral appeals to disaffected Democratic voters who were not getting their "fair share" of government largess. In turning to federal relief as a response to problems caused by wage deterioration, urban deindustrialization, labor market restructuring, and family instability, they also represented a retreat from the liberal commitment—however partial and problematic—to eliminating poverty through economic growth and opportunity.

The political failure of the guaranteed income did not spell the end of welfare reform. Indeed it opened the door to a dramatically different approach. Orchestrated by California Governor and presidential candidate Ronald Reagan, that approach started locally, was explicitly ideological rather than analytical, and had as its ultimate objective the complete dissolution of the liberal welfare state. It shunned the "philosophy" and principles of the income guarantee in favor of a system that was temporary, highly targeted, deliberately ungenerous to the able-bodied poor, and unafraid to weed out all "chisellers" (strikers, illegal aliens, and students) from the government rolls. As a "blueprint for national welfare reform," Reagan said in 1974, his California plan envisioned an end to overbearing federal regulation and a return to the principles of local autonomy in charitable provision.[103] California welfare reform also envisioned, as was increasingly evident on the campaign trail in 1976, a way to save taxpayers billions of dollars by eliminating federal support for the poor. And it promised to stop subsidizing the "welfare queen," who by then had become a featured player on the campaign trail.[104]

This, a decentralized privatized system to which only the "truly needy" need apply, was the welfare-reform vision that eventually emerged triumphant from the 1970s. And in making welfare the issue when more fundamental social and economic problems were at stake, the proponents of the guaranteed income had, however inadvertently, played a role in bringing it about.

*University of California, Santa Barbara*

## Notes

1. Alice O'Connor, "Neither Charity Nor Relief: The War on Poverty and the Effort to Redefine the Basis of Social Provision," in Donald T. Critchlow and charles H. Parker, eds., *Always With Us: A History of Private Charity and Public Welfare* (Rowman & Littlefield, forthcoming).

2. This theme has by now become a perennial in welfare reform, as Daniel P. Moynihan reminded economist David Ellwood, who was appointed Clinton's Assistant Secretary for Planning and Evaluation at HHS in 1993. "So, you've come to do welfare reform," Ellwood quotes Moynihan as saying at the time, "I'll look forward to reading your book about why it failed this time." Ellwood, "Welfare Reform As I Knew It," *American Prospect*, May–June 1996, 22.

3. Richard M. Nixon, Television Address, 8 August 1969.

4. For estimations of cash programs, see James T. Patterson, *America's Struggle Against Poverty, 1900–1994* (Cambridge, 1994), 171; Robert J. Lampman to Arthur F. Burns, "The Recent Increase in the Number of AFDC Recipients," Burns Papers, Box A32, Folder 10, Gerald R. Ford Presidential Library. On in-kind benefits, see Laurence E. Lynn Jr., "A Decade of Policy Developments in the Income Maintenance System," in Robert H. Haveman, *A Decade of Federal Antipoverty Programs: Achievements, Failures, and Lessons* (New York, 1977), 55–117, and Gary Burtless, "Public Spending for the Poor: Trends, Prospects, and Economic Limits," in Sheldon H. Danziger and Daniel H. Weinberg, *Fighting Poverty: What Works and What Doesn't* (Cambridge, 1986), 22–23.

5. Poverty rates had been declining—largely due to increased social welfare spending—since the early 1960s.

6. Lynn, "Income Maintenance," in Haveman, 85; Burtless, "Public Spending for the Poor," 21.

7. Daniel Patrick Moynihan, *The Politics of a Guaranteed Income* (New York, 1973), 17.

8. Daniel Patrick Moynihan, "The Crises in Welfare," *The Public Interest* (Winter 1968): 13.

9. Ibid., 13–14.

10. Moynihan, *The Politics of a Guaranteed Income*, 90.

11. "Welfare Out of Control," *U.S. News and World Report*, 8 February 1971, 32.

12. "Welfare—The Shame of a Nation," *Newsweek*, 8 February 1971, 23.

13. Lampman, "AFDC Recipients," 5; Patterson, *America's Struggle Against Poverty*, 178.

14. On the history of migration to the cities, see Nicholas Lemann, *The Promised Land: The Great Black Migration and How It Changed America* (New York, 1991); Jacqueline Jones, *The Dispossessed: America's Underclasses from the Civil War to the Present* (New York, 1992), 205–65; Joe W. Trotter Jr., "Blacks in the Urban North: The 'Underclass' Question in Historical Perspective," in Michael B. Katz, ed., *The "Underclass" Debate: Views from History* (Princeton, 1993), 55–84.

15. For a review of the sociological literature on migration, poverty, and welfare, see William Julius Wilson, *The Truly Disadvantaged* (Chicago, 1987), 177–80. See also Jacqueline Jones, "Southern Diaspora: Origins of the Northern 'Underclass,'" in Katz, ed., *Underclass Debate*, 44–45. The question of whether differential welfare benefits stimulate migration has also been a subject of continued debate and shifting views in the literature. While several more recent studies find support for the proposition, research in the early 1970s generally found no evidence that benefit levels were causing migration. Larry H. Long, "Poverty Status and Receipt of Welfare Among Migrants and Nonmigrants in Large Cities," *American Sociological Review* 39 (February 1974): 46–56. For a more recent view, see Paul Peterson and Mark C. Rom, *Welfare Magnets: A New Case for a National Standard* (Washington, D.C., 1990).

16. *Newsweek*, 8 February 1971, 23–24.

17. Ibid., 22.

18. Martin Rein and Hugh Heclo, "What Welfare Crisis?—A Comparison Among the United States, Britain, and Sweden," *Public Interest* (Fall 1973): 65-66.

19. Gilbert Steiner, "Reform Follows Reality: The Growth of Welfare," *The Public Interest* (Winter 1974): 47-65.

20. Arthur Burns to Nixon, 11 February 1969, Burns Papers, Box 32, Folder 10, Ford Library.

21. Moynihan, *The Politics of a Guaranteed Income*, 6.

22. Nixon, State of the Union Address, 22 January 1971.

23. Moynihan, *The Politics of a Guaranteed Income*, 80; Gareth Davies, *From Opportunity to Entitlement: The Transformation and Decline of Great Society Liberalism* (Lawrence, Kan., 1996), 215.

24. Moynihan, "The Case for a Family Policy," reprinted in *Coping: Essays in the Practice of Government* (New York, 1973), 76.

25. Moynihan, *The Politics of a Guaranteed Income*, 82-84.

26 Moynihan, quoted in Arthur Burns memorandum to President Nixon, February 11, 1969, Burns Papers, Box A32, Folder 10, Ford Library.

27. Edward C. Banfield, "A Memorandum on the Welfare Problem," Burns Papers, Box A32, Folder 11, Ford Library; *Time*, 8 February 1971, 22. For Banfield's proposals for dealing with the "underclass" problem more generally, see *The Unheavenly City* (Boston, 1970) and *The Unheavenly City Revisited* (Boston, 1974).

28. *Newsweek*, 8 February 1971, 26. For more on the welfare crisis as the result of a strategy employed by the NWRO, see Frances Fox Piven and Richard A. Cloward, *Regulating the Poor: the Functions of Public Welfare* (New York, 1993), 330-38.

29. Gilbert Steiner, "Reform Follows Reality," 64.

30. Lampman, "AFDC Recipients."

31. Patterson, *America's Struggle Against Poverty*, 179.

32. Steiner, "Reform Follows Reality," 65.

33. Rein and Heclo, "What Welfare Crisis?" 66. On welfare and the urban crisis, see also Michael B. Katz, *In the Shadow of the Poorhouse* (New York, 1986), 280-83.

34. Rein and Heclo, "What Welfare Crisis?" 63-64.

35. Ibid., 75.

36. For a review of trends in single parenthood, see Irwin Garfinkel and Sara S. McClanahan, *Single Mothers and Their Children: A New American Dilemma* (Washington, D.C., 1986), 45-85.

37. This new image of poverty, sharply different from the "other America" that informed the War on Poverty, was largely the result of the Panel Study of Income Dynamics, a longitudinal survey of households beginning in the late 1960s, that by the early 1970s was publishing the results of its first wave of surveys. See also Lynn, "Income Maintenance," in Haveman, 98-99.

38. Moynihan, "The Crises in Welfare," 15. On the significance of the imagery of the black welfare mother, see Jane Sherron De Hart, "The Welfare Mother as Racialized 'Other': Public Assistance, Citizenship, and National Identity," in *Defining the Nation: Personal Politics and the Politics of National Identity* (Chicago, forthcoming), chap. 6.

39. Moynihan, *The Politics of a Guaranteed Income*, 93.

40. On the ideological and gender dimensions of the contrast between social insurance and welfare, see Linda Gordon, *Pitied But Not Entitled, Single Mothers and the History of Welfare, 1890-1935* (New York, 1994), 145-207.

41. Gilbert Y. Steiner, *Social Insecurity: The Politics of Welfare* (Chicago, 1966), 18-47.

42. Carl Brauer, "Kennedy, Johnson, and the War on Poverty," *Journal of American History* 69 (June 1982): 95-119.

43. Steiner, "Reform Follows Reality," 55-56, and *Social Insecurity*, 141-75.

44. Joel Haveman and Linda E. Demkovich, "Making Some Sense of the Welfare Mess," *National Journal*, 8 January 1977, 44.

45. Harold Watts, Statement before the Fiscal Policy Subcommittee of the Joint Economic Committee of Congress, 13 June 1968, Institute for Research on Poverty Archives, Madison, Wis.

46. Of course, public assistance for the working poor was not without precedence, having been used in the past to maintain minimal living standards while keeping wages low. The most famous, if short-lived, example was a late eighteenth-century scheme of wage subsidies implemented at Speenhamland, England, which helped to maintain a low-wage structure while warding off food riots among the poor. As noted by Moynihan, Piven and Cloward, and others, Nixon's FAP would operate in much the same way. Piven and Cloward, *Regulating the Poor*, 29–32.

47. Robert Haveman, Introduction, in Haveman, ed., *A Decade of Anti-Poverty Programs*, 17.

48. Watts, JEC Statement.

49. *National Journal*, 19 October 1974, 1565.

50. Milton Friedman, *Capitalism and Freedom* (Chicago, 1962); Christopher Green, *Negative Taxes and the Poverty Problem* (Washington, D.C., 1967).

51. Friedman, quoted in Green, 58–59.

52. Office of Economic Opportunity, "National Anti-Poverty Plan, FY 1968–1972" (June 1966), vii. Shriver Papers, Lyndon Baines Johnson Presidential Library.

53. "National Anti-Poverty Plan," iv.

54. Robert Levine to Sargent Shriver, 6 May 1967, IRP Archives.

55. Levine to Theodore Berry, 7 June 1967, IRP Archives.

56. Alice O'Connor, "Social Research as Social Policy: The New Jersey Negative Income Tax Experiment," paper presented at the APPAM meetings, November 1995; Walter Williams, *The Struggle for a Negative Income Tax: A Case Study* (Washington, D.C., 1972). The results of the experiments are reported in Harold Watts and Albert Rees, eds., *The New Jersey Income Maintenance Experiment* (New York, 1977).

57. On Johnson's resistance to the idea, see Davies, *From Opportunity to Entitlement*, 161.

58. Moynihan, *The Politics of a Guaranteed Income*, 218–20.

59. Although Nixon promoted his plan as "workfare and not welfare," critics at the time noted that its proposed sanctions—benefit reductions for the adult nonworker, but not absolute cutoffs—were not as tough as they might be. Nor did the prospects for getting nonworking recipients into jobs look very promising. Evaluations of the HEW-Labor administered WIN program showed that, due to a combination of inadequate day-care and transportation facilities, interagency squabbling, and a high degree of disability among recipients, WIN was having trouble filling its existing training slots, let alone placing enrollees in jobs. "Administration Welfare Reform Woes Increased by Record of WIN Program," *National Journal*, 24 January 1970, 162–64.

60. Vincent J. Burke and Vee Burke, *Nixon's Good Deed: Welfare Reform* (New York, 1974).

61. Moynihan quoted in *Newsweek*, 8 February 1971, 26; Nixon quoted in Jill Quadango, *The Color of Welfare: How Racism Undermined the War on Poverty* (New York, 1994), 123.

62. Davies, *From Opportunity to Entitlement*, 216–18; Quadango, *The Color of Welfare*, 117–34; Nixon Televised Address, 8 August 1969; Kevin Phillips, *The Emerging Republican Majority* (New York, 1969).

63. Nixon quoted in Laurence Lynn and David Whitman, *The President as Policymaker: Jimmy Carter and Welfare Reform* (Philadelphia, 1981), 18.

64. For a discussion of Nixon's reorganization plans, see Richard Nathan, *The Plot That Failed: Nixon and the Administrative Presidency* (New York, 1975).

65. Hugh Heclo, "OMB and the Presidency: The Problem of 'Neutral Competence,'" *Public Interest* (Winter 1975): 80–98.

66. *Time*, 1 February 1971, on Nixon's speech.

67. On Nixon's pattern of selectively preserving certain liberal tenets, see Davies, *From Opportunity to Entitlement*, 218. Nixon referred to the "full employment" budget in his 1971 State of the Union address.

68. Lynn and Whitman, *The President as Policymaker*, 28–29.

69. On southern opposition to FAP, see Lynn and Whitman, *The President as Policymaker*, 26; and Quadango, *The Color of Welfare*, 129–31.

70. Williams, *The Struggle for a Negative Income Tax*, 20.

71. O'Connor, "Social Research as Social Policy." On Senator Williams and the "notch" effect, see Lynn and Whitman, *The President as Policymaker*, 26.

72. Elliot Richardson and James Hodgson to Nixon, 2 June 1972, Needham Papers, Box 6, Ford Library.

73. Nathan, *The Plot That Failed*, 70–76. By 1977, Nathan notes, the White House role in domestic policy was virtually "nonexistent" because of Watergate. Nevertheless, Nixon had succeeded in establishing the mechanisms of adminstrative control over the bureaucracy.

74. Department of Health, Education, and Welfare, "Income Supplement Program" (Washington, D.C., 1974); *National Journal*, 19 October 1974, 1559–66.

75. *National Journal*, 19 October 1974, 561.

76. The evolution of these models is discussed in detail in Kenneth L. Kraemer et al., *Datawars: The Politics of Modeling in Federal Policymaking* (New York, 1987), 38–62.

77. Watts and Rees, *The New Jersey Income Maintenance Experiments*, vol. 2.

78. Lynn, "Income Maintenance," in Haveman, 116.

79. Secretary Weinberger to President Gerald R. Ford, 20 December 1974, White House Operations Collection, Cheney Files, Box 13, Gerald R. Ford Presidential Library.

80. Lynn, "Income Maintenance," in Haveman, 117.

81. Weinberger to Ford, 7 January 1975, and Kenneth Cole to Ford, 15 January 1975, both in Needham Papers, Ford Library, Box 6.

82. The letter, which was sent to Ford by Princeton University economist Albert Rees, was also signed by Princeton's William J. Baumol, Wisconsin economist and pioneer poverty researcher Robert J. Lampman, Joseph Pechman of the Brookings Institution, Nixon CEA Chair Herbert Stein, James Tobin of Yale, and Harold Watts of Columbia University, who had been a principal investigator in the income-maintenance experiments. Rees to Ford, 8 April 1976, W. Allen Moore Papers, Box 4, Ford Library.

83. *U.S. News and World Report*, 22 December 1975, 17–19.

84. For a discussion of the movement in the 1970s for expanded labor market and employment policies, see Margaret Weir, *Politics and Jobs* (Princeton, 1992), chaps. 4–5.

85. Frederick Doolittle, Frank Levy, and Michael Wiseman, "The Mirage of Reform," *The Public Interest* (Spring 1977): 67. For a review of changes in income-maintenance programs up to the mid-1970s, see Lynn, "Income Maintenance," in Haveman.

86. Patterson, *America's Struggle Against Poverty*, 176; Garfinkel and McClanahan, *Single Mothers and Their Children*, 118–19.

87. Weir, *Politics and Jobs*, 117–19.

88. Doolittle et al., "Mirage," 63.

89. Ibid., 63. For an earlier case for the incrementalist approach, see Henry Aaron, *Why Is Welfare So Hard to Reform?* (Washington, D.C., 1973).

90. Weir, *Politics and Jobs*, 110; 123–25.

91. Lynn and Whitman, *The President as Policymaker*, 49–51.

92. Kraemer, *Datawars*, 126–43.

93. A description of the KGB model is in a paper by the model's creators (listed in reverse order here): David Betson, David Greenberg, and Richard Kasten, "A Simulation of the Program for Better Jobs and Income," Technical Analysis Paper #17, Office of Income Security Policy, HEW, January 1979. On the "monster memo," see James T. Patterson, "Jimmy

Carter and Welfare Reform," in Gary Fink and Hugh Graham, eds., *The Carter Presidency: Policy Choices in the Post–New Deal Era* (Lawrence, Kan., forthcoming).

94. Lynn and Whitman, *The President as Policymaker*, 36–40.

95. For an overview of Carter's economic policy, see Bruce Schulman, "Slouching Toward the Supply Side: Jimmy Carter and the New American Political Economy," in Fink and Graham, *Carter Presidency*.

96. HEW, *Report on the 1977 Welfare Reform Study*, May 1977.

97. HEW Press Release, "Welfare Reform," 6 August 1977, IRP Archives; James R. Sloney et al., "The Better Jobs and Income Plan: A Guide to President Carter's Welfare Reform Proposal and Major Issues" (Washington, D.C., 1978).

98. Weir, *Politics and Jobs*, 127–28.

99. Linda E. Demkovich, "Welfare Reform: Can Carter Succeed Where Nixon Failed?" *National Journal*, 27 August 1977, 1328; Sheldon Danziger, Robert Haveman, and Eugene Smolensky, "Welfare Reform Carter Style: A Guide and a Critique," report prepared for the Joint Economic Committee, 10 October 1977.

100. Demkovich, "The Numbers Are the Issue in the Debate over Welfare Reform," *National Journal*, 22 April 1978, 633.

101. *New York Times*, 16 November 1978, A23.

102. Schulman, "Slouching Toward the Supply Side," 28.

103. Ronald Reagan to Gerald Ford, 20 December 1974, with attached "California's Blueprint for National Welfare Reform," September 1974, Cheney Files, Box 13, Ford Library.

104. "Reagan Trips over Sally on Welfare Queen," *Washington Star*, 4 February 1976, photocopied in Needham Papers, Box 5, Ford Library.

JOHN T. WOOLLEY

# Exorcising Inflation-Mindedness: The Transformation of Economic Management in the 1970s

In late August 1994, Alan Blinder was concluding his second month of service as vice-chairman of the Federal Reserve Board. A former member of the CEA and a distinguished economist, Blinder had achieved a reputation as a "hard-headed liberal economist."[1]

Blinder spoke that August before an annual gathering, sponsored by the Federal Reserve Bank of Kansas City, in Jackson Hole, Wyoming. In attendance were the elite of the world's central-bankers. In his remarks, Blinder said something that was almost unthinkable to his central-banking colleagues. Blinder proposed that the Federal Reserve should have a short-term employment objective in addition to an inflation objective.[2] That is, Blinder proposed that the central bank should try to promote greater employment just up to the point at which inflation starts to accelerate.

The more orthodox position had been offered by Fed Chairman Alan Greenspan—that any short-term trade-off between inflation and unemployment was "ephemeral." Moreover, Greenspan had argued, "Monetary policy which fails to focus on the long-term requirement of achieving price stability is inevitably going to find itself in a position where inflation emerges."[3]

Had Blinder made his remark in the early 1970s, they would have hardly seemed noteworthy. By 1994, views and politics had changed so much that Blinder's remarks were taken as indicating that he was "soft on inflation."[4] An uproar ensued that was reported prominently in every major U.S. newspaper and even provoked an editorial in the *Wall Street Journal*.[5] *Newsweek* columnist Robert Samuelson proclaimed that Blinder's "biases" seemed to be "on the side of risking more inflation."[6] Expressing a widely held conclusion about the past, Samuelson added, "It is precisely this attitude that got us into trouble in the '60s and '70s."

Samuelson's views, though perhaps overstated, reflect much of the conventional wisdom about the origins of economic problems of the 1970s. The conventional wisdom is at best partial and at worst simply wrong about the importance of "biases." It is surely true that the events that shaped Samuelson's judgment—and our now-powerful conventional wisdom—are rooted in the late 1960s and early 1970s. In the 1970s, choices were made that have proven largely irreversible. In terms of economic management, the story of the 1970s is a story of repeated policy failure and of a search for effective policy strategies from a progressively more restricted menu of choice.

Today macroeconomic policy is dominated by assumptions and shaped by institutional relationships that are profoundly different from those of 1970. In management of the economy, the 1970s marked the undoing of a set of ideas and institutional relationships that had previously characterized postwar economic governance. By the close of the 1970s we had not fully defined an alternative mode of economic governance, but the main course of future developments could be discerned.

The biggest single change had to do with inflation. In the 1970s, economic policymakers lost faith in their ability to exploit the Phillips curve as a guide to economic policy making. The effect of this was to shift discussion and debate about inflation from concern with "trade-offs" and to frame the inflation issue as one that should be examined in isolation. Moreover, inflation came to be seen as the dominant policy problem.

Discretionary fiscal policy (especially deficit spending), once seen as an essential element of macroeconomic management, came to be seen as too unwieldy and clumsy to figure centrally in a stabilization program. The risks arising from politics and gridlock seemed to imply that discretionary fiscal policy was likely to be a source of economic instability, not the reverse.[7]

Policymakers lost faith in the efficacy of wage and price controls—including voluntary guidelines and "jawboning." Indeed, policymakers began to question the idea that there were any short-term government policies, other than monetary policy, that were effective in controlling inflation. Thus, the problem of inflation—the macroeconomic problem—came increasingly to be viewed as primarily a problem for long-term supply-oriented policy and for monetary policy and the Federal Reserve.

Economic policy and its evolution and development are by no means simple reflections of the consensus views of economists or of any distinctively coherent position in economic theory. Policymakers often have little patience for repeated testing of economic hypotheses when they appear to have been falsified. In the world of politics, rarely can economic policy experiments be put to clear and extreme tests. On the other hand, policymakers are almost always guided by some kinds of ideas, often ones that are regarded by experts as demonstrably inadequate. The story of economic management in the 1970s is the story of a struggle to adapt to policy failure.


## The Inflation Problem Circa 1970

At the start of the 1970s, inflation was not an issue that aroused great passions except among old-guard Republicans.[8] Their analysis, the traditional conservative view, was that the growing inflation of the late 1960s was due to profligate social spending and budget deficits.[9] Beginning in the 1970s, the conventional wisdom in the economics mainstream was that various benefits could be derived from moderate inflation. For example, inflation "greases the wheels of the labor market" if it allows adjustments in the relative real wage of different occupations without explicit pay cuts for particular workers. This general view was encapsulated in the Keynesian notion that there was a "Phillips-curve trade-off" between employment and inflation.[10] The Phillips curve embodied the optimistic notion that policymakers could choose combinations of inflation and unemployment that seemed most appropriate in light of the relative costs of inflation and unemployment. A choice for lower unemployment and higher inflation could be reversed after a few years and the economy could return to essentially the same combination of inflation and unemployment that would have prevailed earlier.

The logic of the Phillips curve did not hold that *any* combination of inflation and unemployment was attainable. The trade-off implied that below some level, perhaps "full employment" (a term used very rarely in official documents), inflation would increase rapidly. Similarly, the trade-off implied that reducing inflation below some basic level would require very high levels of unemployment.

This view was not, and never had been, embraced by traditional conservatives who viewed inflation as an unalloyed evil—a covert mechanism for redistributing income or taxing wealth. In this view, inflation was not merely costly but *wrong*.

The official embrace of the Phillips curve was documented in the final report of the Johnson Administration Council of Economic Advisors in 1969. That report included a Phillips-curve diagram based on annual data from 1954–68. Arthur Okun, then-chairman of the CEA, later observed that in early 1969 "there was absolutely nothing to suggest that there had been an upward shift of the Phillips curve, a structural deterioration in the labor market." He recalled thinking that "you can go down that curve just as you went up that curve." That is, the Phillips curve seemed a reliable guide to policy, and movement in both directions along the curve seemed possible.[11]

At the outset of the Nixon administration, policy thinking was still dominated by the concept of the Phillips curve. Nixon's first CEA Chair, Paul McCracken, observed that "our theory of inflation . . . would have been pretty much just the Phillips curve logic."[12] And, after all, it was Nixon himself who announced in January 1971, "I am now a Keynesian in economics."[13]

Versions of the Phillips curve for the 1960s and 1970s are shown in Figure 1, using monthly data. An obvious retrospective fact is that the 1960s were a period of astonishing economic orderliness by contrast to the 1970s. It is not surprising that the comparative unruliness of the 1970s would have tested the faith of policymakers in the empirical relationships they thought they could rely on, and would test the faith of citizens in their policymakers.

## Optimism About Capacity of Government

We commonly recall the early 1970s as a period of intense turmoil, domestic conflict, and failure in war. But it was, in some respects, a high watermark in confidence and optimism about the ability and responsibility of government to shape economic outcomes. That optimism would largely have dissipated by the end of the decade. It is important to be reminded of the ambition that was evident at the outset. The country had just completed a decade of considerable success in managing the economy by confident economists who did not shrink from using the phrase "fine tuning." The welfare state had been dramatically expanded.

President Nixon proposed in 1969 a government role in developing a "supersonic transport," and he supported this program enthusiastically. In 1970, the imminent collapse of the Penn Central Railroad provoked great concern in the White House and serious discussions about how to provide an emergency loan to the failing firm.[14] Eventually, the Federal Reserve, under Arthur Burns, intervened in extraordinary ways to stabilize financial markets after the bankruptcy of the Penn Central Railroad. Both Nixon and Burns, like many in government, supported a bailout for the Lockheed

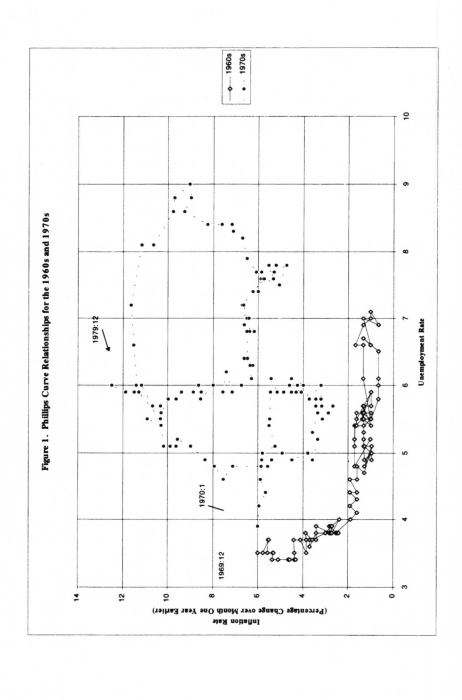

Figure 1. Phillips Curve Relationships for the 1960s and 1970s

Corporation in 1971, and Burns promoted the creation of a dedicated "bailout fund" that would have ongoing authority to issue loan guarantees to big companies in trouble.[15]

In the legislature, Senator William Proxmire proposed to authorize the Federal Reserve to formally allocate credit, and the Joint Economic Committee called for formalizing a long-term unemployment objective of 3.0 percent. The federal government adopted a large number of new regulatory statutes, principally with respect to worker health and safety, pollution control and environmental quality, and consumer protection and product safety.

## The President Decides to Control Wages and Prices

In the early 1970s, direct controls on wages and prices were in widespread use in the industrial world.[16] The Kennedy and Johnson administrations had used wage and price "guideposts," which many economists believed had been helpful in achieving the good inflation and unemployment record of the 1960s.[17] In late 1968, Johnson's Cabinet Committee on Price stability had recommended a return to official guideposts, and many observers argued that with proper leadership such programs could contribute significantly to price stabilization.[18]

The Nixon administration entered office proclaiming that inflation was a major policy concern, third only after the Vietnam War and reestablishing domestic law and order.[19] Moreover, the administration believed, inflation-fighting was a matter of getting fiscal policy and monetary policy right, not a matter of controls—which Nixon emphatically rejected.[20] William Safire, Nixon's speechwriter, characterized Nixon's position as one of

> fierce opposition to wage and price controls; in every economic speech I had ever worked on with him, there was a boilerplate paragraph on the horrors of wage and price controls, how they would lead to rationing and black markets and a stultifying government domination of the economy.[21]

In one of the more complex and troubling reversals by any postwar politician, Nixon retreated from his prior pledge and abruptly instituted wage and price controls in August 1971.

Why did the Nixon administration adopt controls? Clearly ideas were essential—controls seemed available, feasible, and plausible. They were in use elsewhere. Analysts perceived important rigidities in the institutions of wage bargaining and argued that it was difficult to reduce inflation substantially in that institutional context without incurring unacceptable costs. Controls could address behavior in those institutions in a relevant way. This belief combined decisively with the determination of President Nixon to be reelected and his view that U.S. electoral institutions punished incumbents for high rates of unemployment.

Still, from the perspective of the late 1990s, it seems astonishing that an inflation rate of 4.25 percent (and falling) and an unemployment rate of 6 percent (and roughly steady) should provoke a dramatic act of crisis proportions—invoking general wage and price controls. Mandatory controls had previously been a wartime expedient, rejected and avoided in peacetime.[22]

Viewed from 1971, things look somewhat different. Based on monthly data (as in Figure 1), in the 228 months from January 1950 until Nixon took office in January 1969, the unemployment rate had exceeded 6 percent only about 13 percent of the time (in 30 out of 228 months). In the same period, inflation for the prior year had exceeded 5 percent only about 6 percent of the time (13 out of 228 months). Based on the Phillips curve of the 1960s, with unemployment above 5 percent, inflation should have been well below 2 percent. Instead, it seemed to be stuck above 4 percent.

Nixon was basically constrained by Phillips-curve logic. He believed that inflation was an evil that should be opposed, but he knew, based on recent history, that such high levels of inflation should have been consistent with lower levels of unemployment. He believed that lower unemployment was essential for his reelection. His goal was to get a lower level of unemployment without higher inflation. He and his advisers were perplexed by the fact that the Phillips-curve relationships did not hold. The idea emerged that controls could be used on a short-run basis to shock people out of their inflationary ways of thinking and, presumably, back onto the old Phillips curve.

By mid-June 1971, the president's CEA chairman, Paul McCracken, was still publicly insisting that the administration would not adopt controls. But privately, McCracken had advised the president that "we must be prepared at a suitable time to use the ultimate weapons of wage and price controls." These controls would be temporary, and would provide an opportunity to "exorcise the inflation-mindedness that has given us a situation where the price-cost level is rising because the price-cost level is rising."[23]

In congressional testimony in late July 1971, Arthur Burns expressed views that many economists uneasily shared. He proclaimed that "the rules of economics are not working in quite the way they used to," meaning, basically, that the expected Phillips-curve relationships were not holding. "Despite extensive unemployment in our country," Burns observed, "wage rate increases have not moderated. Despite much idle industrial capacity, commodity prices continue to rise rapidly."[24]

As the summer of 1971 wore on, Nixon had more and more reason to fret about his electoral prospects. A Harris poll taken in early August reported that only 22 percent of the public approved of Nixon's handling of the economy and fully 62 percent believed the nation was still in a recession.[25] It appeared likely that he would end up in a race against a seasoned Democrat such as Edmund Muskie or Birch Bayh.

## Support for Controls

In early 1971, the notion of instituting a formal system of controls was very much in the air. For the past year, there had been vigorous and public advocacy of an "incomes policy" by Fed Chairman Arthur Burns. What exactly Burns had in mind was often obscure, but his public advocacy of this goal in the face of firm White House rejection of "controls" was a source of conflict and tension.[26] Others, including several former officials, began in 1970 to speak out in support of guidelines.[27] In early 1971, the White House experimented with partial and tentative bits of income policy—issuing "inflation alerts"; jawboning the steel industry about wages; and temporarily suspending the Davis-Bacon Act.[28]

Congressional Democrats pressed vigorously for controls and worked to extend the president's authority to impose wage and price controls. The proposal to extend the president's authority was eventually embraced by the administration, with a pledge by John Connally that the administration would not use controls "short of an all-out national emergency."[29] AFL-CIO President George Meany offered to cooperate in wage and price controls provided they were applied across the board. Representative Henry Reuss (D-Wis.) called for an "across the board freeze on wages prices and salaries until permanent voluntary price-wage incomes policy was agreed."[30]

In May 1971, Congress passed, and Nixon signed without hesitation, legislation extending the president's discretionary authority to establish wage and price controls.[31] Between April and the end of July 1971, the New York Times editorialized at least fifteen times in favor of stronger incomes policies or some form of formal controls. Even some business leaders had concluded that controls appeared to be the only recourse in the face of strong wage pressures.[32]

Well before the debate about controls intensified in 1971, polls had showed that there was significant public support for price controls. A University of Michigan poll of consumers showed 45 percent agreeing that the government should control prices to slow down inflation.[33] Gallup polls showed support steadily increasing in the 1970s, and it exceeded 50 percent in favor in July 1971.[34]

## Intellectual Ferment and the Rejection of Controls

Nixon imposed wage and price controls in August 1971 and simultaneously suspended convertibility of the dollar into gold. His "New Economic Program" involved a newly stimulative budgetary policy. The effect was electric in terms of public opinion and effective in terms of temporarily promoting further economic expansion at low inflation. It also involved falling into the trap of excessive expansionism.[35]

One thing was clear. Even before the end of wage and price controls, both politicians and economists agreed that the experience was ultimately a negative one—and overwhelmingly disagreed with the proposition that wage and price controls should be used again to control inflation.[36]

Some of the conclusions were "facts" that did not actually require the experience of controls—for example, that controls caused distortions. Some were reactions against the sheer difficulty of extracting the economy from controls.[37] Other analyses led to the conclusion that controls only suppressed inflation temporarily, and that immediately following the end of controls prices had rebounded to compensate for losses that had occurred during the controls period.[38]

Congress allowed the president's authority to impose wage and price controls to expire in April 1974, and efforts in the prior year to renew, extend, and strengthen price controls were handily defeated. This proved to be a fateful and important act. Without standby authority for controls in place, any future administration considering controls would have to request new statutory authority. The debate itself would signal to price-setters that they should urgently raise their prices as quickly as possible in order to position themselves favorably for potential controls—thereby worsening the very inflation problem controls would be designed to cure. This prospect discouraged incipient discussion of controls later in the Carter administration.[39]

Three years after imposing wage and price controls, Nixon himself "was vigorously denouncing his own 'discredited patent medicine of wage and price controls.'"[40] At a November 1974 conference attended by economists and price controllers, devoted to the topic of controls, "the virtually unanimous judgment of the conferees was that experience with wage-price policy over the thirty-year period had been unsatisfactory."[41]

The expense, trauma, and emotional energy that had been poured into wage and price controls proved, ultimately, to have gone almost for nothing—save the reelection of Richard Nixon. The legacy of this peacetime experiment with controls was in many ways historic: it involved a commitment on the part of virtually all relevant policymakers to forgo generalized wage and price controls in the future. By 1980, only a handful of conventional economists supported controls.

Keynesian economists were hardly passive in light of the inadequacy of their models in predicting the stubborn conditions that provoked Nixon into controls. There were ongoing efforts by Keynesians to come to grips descriptively with the economic changes and failures at the time. These efforts went in many directions. One involved identifying sources of price pressure in internationally traded goods, and emphasizing inflation dynamics other than excess-demand, wage-price spiral stories that had previously been so influential. Significant inflation arising from farm and food prices in 1971 was a "new phenomenon."[42] External shocks had contributed "an alarming number of upward jolts to prices."[43] Other efforts focused on trying to unravel the apparently unstable demand for money that had made it so difficult to anticipate the effects of monetary policy.[44]

## The Ford Failures

By the time Gerald Ford ascended to the presidency (August 1974), there was no new consensus to replace the old. Moreover, shocks were about to hit the economy that nobody anticipated and the effects of these shocks could not be well forecast.

When Ford took office, two important developments lay ahead in the political economy of macroeconomic management. Neither was a necessary consequence of the experience of the Nixon years. Rather, they required the experience of further failure. The first was a further weakening of faith in the concept of the Phillips curve and the ability of the government to use discretionary policy to balance inflation and unemployment at acceptable levels. The second, closely related to the first, was the de facto assignment of the inflation-management problem to the Federal Reserve. The first change was hastened in surprising ways by the Ford administration. Both were quite thoroughly accomplished by the end of the Carter administration.

The Ford administration began with an unambiguous internal consensus on the primacy of the inflation problem. This reflected Ford's traditionally conservative orientation and that of his top advisers, characterized by an emphasis on budget balancing and a determination to adhere to a goal of reducing inflation.[45] Ford began his term with a declaration that inflation was "domestic enemy number one" and he called an "Inflation Summit" to discuss ideas about how to deal with inflation.[46] Ford proposed a voluntary program to "Whip Inflation Now," and citizens were encouraged to show their support by wearing "WIN Buttons."

Even more memorable, however, was the spectacular failure of economic forecasts in the fall of 1974 to anticipate that a deep recession was just around the corner.[47] This was not a failure just of government forecasts. Former Nixon adviser George Shultz commented in September 1974 that all the available economic forecasts "could be covered by a hat."[48] None of those forecasts suggested that unemployment would be at 9 percent the following May. Herbert Stein advised in August 1974 that Ford should "try to be careful that the unemployment rate does not rise *much* above 6 percent."[49] Arthur Burns wrote from the Fed that "the nation is in the grip of a dangerous inflation" and urged the president to articulate a "firm anti-inflationary policy."[50] Stein reported to Ford forecasts of unemployment for mid-1975 ranging between 5.5 and 6.5 percent.

Ford committed himself in a congressional speech in early October to a quite traditional anti-inflation, budget-balancing program. He at first refused to budge from that program despite rapidly developing information of further deterioration in the economy. Only a month later, in early November 1974, the White House admitted that the economy probably was in a recession. Projections provided to President Ford in late November anticipated unemployment in the first half of 1975 in the 7 to 7.5 percent range.[51]

The administration realized, of course, that in only three months economic conditions had become far worse than it had thought remotely possible. Gloomy updates of forecasts gave way to even more gloomy economic outcomes. By the end of 1974, the president's advisers were recommending temporary stimulus.

Much of these economic woes could be traced to supply shocks in both food and energy prices.[52] The revealing graph in Figure 2 shows the course of energy prices and all consumer price inflation for the period 1960–89. The increases in energy costs were stunning. These shocks provoked, in worst form, the old problem that had driven Nixon to impose controls—stagflation. Within a few months of declaring that inflation was "the problem," Ford was forced to deal with a 50 percent increase in unemployment. His response, again, was largely traditional and focused on mild budgetary stimulus.

Ford left monetary policy and the Fed largely to its own devices. As it developed, that meant keeping policy quite restrictive—although policy was possibly more restrictive than the Fed initially realized or intended.[53] Both strategies produced conflict with Congress. Congress struggled with Ford for a larger economic stimulus and attacked the Fed for its restrictive policy.

The Ford administration's experience of failure, reversal, and retreat raised a number of issues that were not resolved prior to the transfer of power to the Carter administration. These involved the viability of any policy based on a sophisticated discretionary fiscal policy in conditions of divided government. Throughout 1975–76, Congress and the administration were substantially stalemated on the design of a fiscal policy that each side believed was essential to recovery. It was impossible to avoid the question of whether it was reasonable to expect that any timely adjustment of discretionary taxing and spending could be implemented consistent with Keynesian policy prescriptions.

Further, the de facto reliance on monetary policy for stabilization and the apparent insensitivity of Fed officials to unemployment provoked a huge controversy. The Fed was subjected to a wide range of attacks, which were unnerving to Fed officials even though only one relatively mild reform actually passed into law.[54] That reform was a resolution requiring the Fed to submit periodic reports to Congress and to announce publicly its target ranges for monetary aggregates. How the Fed would balance the inflation and unemployment objectives was, however, very much unresolved.

There was still a widespread belief that inflation had important psychological or institutional origins that could be appropriately addressed through techniques of persuasion. Thus, the administration proposed, and Congress adopted, legislation creating the Council on Wage and Price Stability. The council was intended to "monitor inflation," to propose voluntary guidelines for private-sector pricing behavior, and to conduct studies on inflation. Could persuasive techniques alone, without sanction or threat, be used to intervene to shape the formation of expectation of inflation in a favorable direction? Could the effects thus achieved be large? Clear answers were not possible within the tenure of the Ford administration.

The intellectual debates among economists raged on. The divisions between monetarists and Keynesians were further highlighted by the forecasting errors that flowed from external shocks. This ferment was of no direct consequence to the mass public, but it contributed to an elite anxiety that was inescapable.

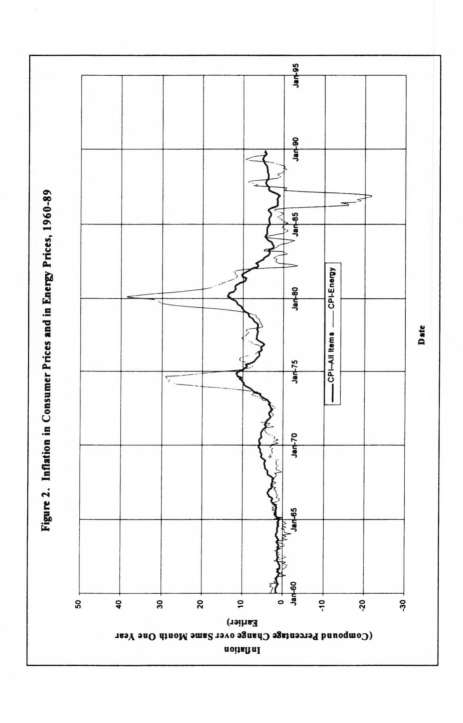

Figure 2. Inflation in Consumer Prices and in Energy Prices, 1960-89

## The Carter Failures

Carter-era policymakers had to try to resolve the dilemmas remaining from the Ford years. Virtually without exception, they met with failure. The focus of policy switched back to unemployment, which seemed to be declining too slowly, even though inflation remained stubbornly above the Nixon lows. Carter had committed himself in the presidential campaign to getting the economy moving again, so providing adequate economic stimulus was naturally a major concern. The Carter economic team forecast that very rapid rates of economic growth were possible without accelerating inflation, but they expected that further gains in reducing inflation were unlikely.

The Carter team had problems from the beginning in developing coherent Keynesian stabilization programs because Carter was basically a traditionalist—he opposed inflation. As a fiscal conservative, Carter was leery of enlarging the federal budget deficit; as a traditionalist, he embraced the belief that deficits were "one of the root causes of inflation and unemployment."[55]

The inflation problem was eventually assigned once again to the Council on Wage and Price Stability. The council, together with other Carter advisers, identified dozens of changes, in both the public and private sector, that could help reduce inflationary "biases" in the economy and "decelerate" inflation.[56]

Most of Carter's economic team regarded fiscal policy as an important component of economic stabilization, and they initially proposed a variety of "fine-tuning" fiscal adjustments. Carter's solution to the problem of monitoring the Federal Reserve was, eventually, to appoint a new Fed chair with whom he could work closely.

As events would have it, not a single element in the Carter economic program evolved smoothly. Very early in his term, Carter agreed to a fairly complicated economic stimulus package that included a jobs-creation program, investment tax credit, Social Security tax rebate, and an individual tax rebate of $50 per person.[57] The tax-rebate proposal enjoyed only lukewarm support among many Carter advisers, and it was received coolly at the Fed and in Congress, and with mild derision from others.[58]

In principle, these reactions were of little importance. However, economic circumstances changed very quickly—the mirror image of Ford's problem. Within three months of advancing his initial stimulus package, Carter decided that the additional stimulus that would flow from the $50 rebate would not be necessary, because inflation appeared to be higher than expected. Consequently, Carter withdrew the rebate proposal together with the investment tax credit proposal.[59]

In one quick and regrettably memorable act, Carter had recapitulated the problems of his predecessors. He switched his main priority from economic stimulus to controlling inflation. Carter later wrote that "after a few months, the threat of rising inflation and budget deficits preyed on my mind."[60] When the economy actually slowed substantially below expectations in the third quarter, Carter had no fallback position. His forecast had failed; his plan had proved to be neither durable nor reliable, and substantial political damage had been incurred because of the switch.[61]

The Carter administration's basic plan for coping with inflation was initially not entirely clear. CEA Chairman Charles Schultze later observed that "we were always, in terms of an anti-inflation program, six months to a year behind the game."[62] In the long run, Carter had committed himself to balance the budget, and he repeatedly emphasized that he thought this was an important signal of his commitment and determination to fight inflation.

To deal with the wage-price spiral, which Carter thought was a major cause of inflation, he relied on the old voluntary-guidelines approach. This project did not get under way until early 1978, when the administration unveiled a program emphasizing government efficiencies and a program to encourage private-sector cooperation in price "deceleration." As 1978 progressed, the inflation outlook rapidly deteriorated, forcing administration economists to scramble for more forceful ways to act.

The administration's next solution was to move to increasingly specific and focused guidelines and targets for price and wage increases. Failure to comply would result in "investigations" of firms and demands for information to justify price increases. Firms out of compliance would be excluded from government procurement. Huge amounts of energy went into planning and selling the program to business and the American public.

By early 1979, inflation was rapid and exceeded the wage and price guidelines in place. The guidelines were proving difficult to administer, and there seemed to be growing public skepticism about the willingness of the administration to confront violators. It was already clear to Carter economists in March that their current policy course was highly likely to be exposed in the near future to be "an obvious failure."[63] In June 1979 a federal court struck down the administration's use of eligibility for government procurement contracts as an enforcement mechanism for the guidelines. Overwhelmed by events, the guidelines program gradually faded into obscurity.[64] The initiative and responsibility for fighting inflation shifted decisively to the Federal Reserve.

Carter and his advisers had acted on the assumption that the inflation they confronted did not arise from demand pressures but from supply shocks and rigidities in the labor market. Thus, initially, the Fed's ability to restrain demand through monetary restraint seemed not to be a central element of the inflation solution.

Nonetheless, relations with the Federal Reserve began rocky and eventually foundered as well. Throughout 1977, Carter's economists tangled in public with Arthur Burns. Burns criticized fiscal policy and what he saw as Carter's inability to bolster business confidence. However, the record showed that monetary growth was quite rapid in 1977— in fact above the Fed's target ranges—while at the same time interest rates were rising.[65] The Fed's chief economist later observed that this rapid growth in money, and its continuation through 1978, eroded the credibility of monetary policy.[66]

When Burns's term expired in early 1978, Carter replaced him with businessman G. William Miller. Under Miller's leadership, monetary expansion continued to be rapid.[67] In late 1978, inflation markedly accelerated, and the dollar came under sharp pressure in foreign-exchange markets. A package of monetary tightening measures proved to be not enough to cope with inflationary expectations. Indeed, in early 1979, Washington witnessed one of the few unambiguous instances of the White House publicly pressing the Fed for tighter policy.[68]

By mid-1979, Carter faced a hopeless situation. His main anti-inflation strategy—wage and price guidelines—was an obvious failure. His chairman of the Federal Reserve had provided a monetary policy that Carter's own economists thought was inflationary. His budget-balancing objectives were receding from his grasp. The ability of his advisers to correctly foresee and identify a strategy for successful stabilization appeared to be most limited.

In this situation of crisis, the critical changes began that have endured to today. In order to try to reassure financial markets, Carter had to appoint someone with unquestioned central-banking ability and proven determination to fight inflation. That person was Paul Volcker.[69] In early October, Volcker announced a policy of monetary targeting that served many purposes. It temporarily silenced the monetarists, a vocal group of critics; it drew positive notice as an indication of the Fed's anti-inflation commitment; and it provided a rationale for the very high interest rates the Fed believed would be necessary to deal with inflation. This began the enduring practice of assigning the inflation problem primarily to the Federal Reserve and monetary policy.

Next, the administration ended any possible future consideration of price controls by exploiting the only remaining authority it had in that regard—an authority to recommend to the Federal Reserve that controls be put in place on consumer credit. "The program itself was mild, but the psychological impact on the public was strong—leading to a sharp run-down in debt, the money supply and interest rates after inception followed by a ballooning of all three after rescission."[70] The economy slumped into a brief, sharp recession. Charles Schultze later guessed that "we got the steepest decline in GNP in one quarter in our history. . . . It gave us a quicky recession, which didn't do much good."[71] What did happen, how-ever, was that Congress voted in June to remove the president's authority to recommend credit controls. Thus U.S. experimentation with general-ized formal economic controls came to an ignominious end at the same time that informal guidelines were "fizzling."[72]

Evidence is compelling that starting in this period the problem of inflation acquired an enduring negative prominence. On the one hand, we have the views of Reagan-era reformers who felt they were initially stymied by "inflation hysteria," which certainly had its roots in the 1970s.[73] Data from Gallup poll questions about the "most important problem" from 1971 to 1984 (see Fig. 3) show that inflation concern rose extremely rapidly relative to concern about unemployment con-cern as actual inflation increased relative to unemployment. This ap-pears to have been reinforced by the nature of communications in the elite media[74] and, perhaps surprisingly, systematically in the public analyses of the President's Council of Economic Advisors.[75] In short, national attention had been fixed on inflation in a way that would persist and condition the conduct of policy for the next generation.

One lasting positive legacy of the 1970s was an emphasis on long-term strategies to improve productivity and efficiency. It was, in many ways, the only way out for policymakers, who could not forecast the economy because of shocks. In the Carter years, this took several forms, including ongoing efforts to fight inflation by deregulating industries such as the airline and trucking industries. In the longer haul this evolved into a generally positive—if also largely ambiguous—search for so-called "supply-side" strategies. This development was clearly evident in Carter administration policy discussions, and it was echoed in posi-tive tones on Capitol Hill in Joint Economic Committee reports start-ing in 1979.[76]

In economic management, the 1970s were years of lost faith and dashed hopes. The transformation in thinking and practice was quite remark-

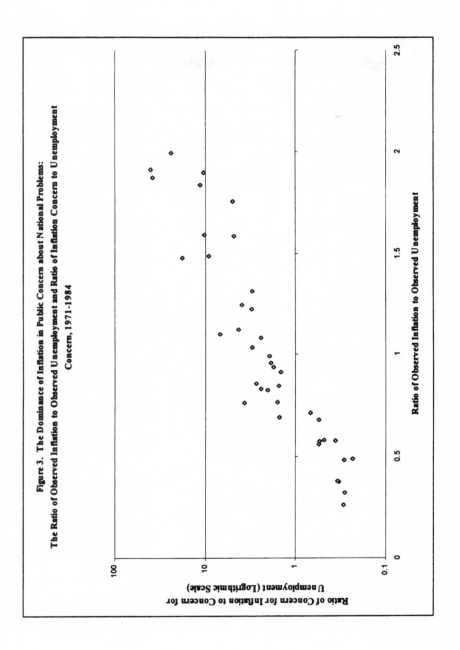

Figure 3. The Dominance of Inflation in Public Concern about National Problems:
The Ratio of Observed Inflation to Observed Unemployment and Ratio of Inflation Concern to Unemployment Concern, 1971-1984

able. Policy options were permanently transformed. No longer would those wishing to be taken seriously in policy debates suggest any kind of formal controls on prices, wages, or credit. Even guidelines seemed a fruitless gesture. Markets and market efficiency were the default option.

Inflation had secured a prime place as the most evil of macroeconomic evils. To be sure, the notion persisted that budget deficits were a leading cause of inflation. However, the job of fighting inflation had been, in fact, assigned to monetary policy and the Federal Reserve—probably never to be retrieved by fiscal managers. The dilemmas of having such important matters handled in a largely undemocratic institution remained to be addressed.

Economic theory still had a place for a "short run" Phillips-curve trade-off, but it was the strong consensus that this trade-off could not be used for any good purpose. In part, this consensus arose from the preoccupation with inflation, which was held to be inexorably at risk in such short-run efforts. However, it was also due to another 1970s legacy—the loss of faith in short-term economic stabilization. The 1970s had seemed to show that such stabilization could not work; it was too vulnerable to the whimsy of political disagreement and to unpredictable natural-resource shocks. Too often, presidents had been forced into humiliating reversals by failed forecasts.

Still, there persisted a belief that economic problems could be managed over the long haul, that stability could be re-created and that the prospects for growth could be fostered. Such ingenuity, creativity, and optimism could rescue a dream of prosperity. Therein policymakers might discover a long-term solution to unemployment—or the pathway to inequality and environmental ruin.

*University of California, Santa Barbara*

## Notes

1. From the cover of the paperback version of Alan S. Blinder, *Hard Heads, Soft Hearts: Tough-Minded Economics for a Just Society* (Reading, Mass., 1987).

2. David Wessel, "Central Bankers Say: Look Elsewhere on Jobs," *Wall Street Journal*, 29 August 1994, 1.

3. David Wessel, "Blinder Denies There's a Rift with Fed Chair," *Wall Street Journal*, 9 September 1994, A2.

4. George Graham, "Rift at the Top of Fed Is Denied," *Financial Times*, 9 September 1994, 5.

5. *Wall Street Journal*, 13 September 1994.

6. Robert J. Samuelson, "Economic Amnesia: Alan Blinder Forgets the Dangers of Inflation," *Newsweek*, 12 September 1994, 52

7. The main intellectual challenge came from the monetarists who seemed in some respects to be triumphant at the end of the decade. Their triumph, however, proved to be short-lived, and with that hindsight and in the interests of brevity I have included little here about the monetarists. For a Keynesian retrospective critique of the monetarists, see Blinder, *Hard Heads, Soft Hearts*, chap. 3; for a treatment of the monetarists as a political movement, see John T. Woolley, "Monetarists and the Politics of Monetary Policy," *Annals of the American Academy of Political and Social Science* 459 (January 1982): 148–60.

8. Judging from public opinion polls, very few worried about the economy even in early 1971, when Gallup polls reported that 11 percent thought inflation was the most important problem and 17 percent thought that unemployment was the most important problem.

9. Herbert Stein, *Presidential Economics: The Making of Economic Policy from Roosevelt to Clinton* (Washington, D.C., 1994), 134.

10. Retrospective characterizations of economists' consensus about that time and its subsequent dissolution include: James Tobin, "Stabilization Policy Ten Years After," *Brookings Papers on Economic Activity* 1:1980, 19–71; Herbert Stein, *Presidential Economics*; N. Gregory Mankiw, "A Quick Refresher Course in Macroeconomics," *Journal of Economic Literature* 28 (December 1990): 1645–60; George L. Perry, "Inflation in Theory and Practice," *Brookings Papers on Economic Activity*, 1:1980, 207–41, and especially the interesting comments on pp. 243–60; John Cassidy, "The Decline of Economics," *The New Yorker*, 2 December 1996, 50ff.

11. U.S. Council of Economic Advisors, *Economic Report of the President* (Washington, D.C., 1969); The Okun quotes are from Erwin C. Hargrove and Samuel A. Morley, *The President and the Council of Economic Advisors: Interviews with CEA Chairmen* (Boulder, 1984), 308.

12. Hargrove and Morley, *President and the Council*, 372.

13. By this, Nixon meant to signal his endorsement of the idea of a "full employment" budget, in which current deficits would be permitted if the budget would have been in balance at "full employment." Rowland Evans Jr. and Robert D. Novak, *Nixon in the White House: The Frustration of Power* (New York, 1971), 372.

14. H. R. Haldeman, *The Haldeman Diaries: Inside the Nixon White House* (multimedia edition, Santa Monica, 1994); on SST, see entries for 17 and 23 September 1969; on Penn Central, see entries for 4 and 19 June 1970. Also on the SST, see Evans and Novak, *Nixon in the White House*, 52–53, 376, 410. Also on the Penn Central, see Arthur F. Burns, *Reflections of an Economic Policy-Maker: Speeches and Congressional Statement: 1969–1978* (Washington, D.C., 1978), 110–11; Joseph R. Daughen and Peter Binzen, *The Wreck of the Penn Central* (Boston, 1971).

15. Wyatt C. Wells, *Economist in an Uncertain World: Arthur Burns and the Federal Reserve, 1970–78* (New York, 1994).

16. Lloyd Ulman and Robert J. Flanagan, *Wage Restraint: A Study of Incomes Policies in Western Europe* (Berkeley and Los Angeles, 1971); "A History of Incomes Policy," *The Economist*, 29 March 1975, 92–93; Anne Romanis Braun, "The Role of Incomes Policy in Industrial Countries Since World War II," *International Monetary Fund Staff Papers* 22 (March 1975): 1–36; see especially chart 1, p. 11. For contemporary views inside the government, see Memo, Ghiardi to Partee, "Prices and Incomes Policy Experience in Some Other Nations," 16 April 1970, Box B-59, File, "Incomes Policy, 1970," Arthur Burns Papers, Gerald R. Ford Library; and Memo Wernick and Zeisel to Partee, "A Case for Wage-Price Intervention," 17 April 1970, in ibid.

17. Tobin, "Stabilization Policy", 65.

18. Evans and Novak, *Nixon in the White House*, 184; James L. Cochrane, "The Johnson Administration: Moral Suasion Goes to War," in Craufurd D. Goodwin, ed., *Exhortation and Controls: The Search for a Wage-Price Policy, 1945-71* (Washington, D.C., 1975).

19. *The Haldeman Diaries*, entry for 25 March 1969.

20. Evans and Novak, *Nixon in the White House*, 185.

21. William Safire, *Before the Fall: An Inside View of the Pre-Watergate White House* (New York, 1975), 509.

22. Last utilized in the Korean War. Economist James Tobin later stated that "when the controls were removed [following the Korean War], prices and price expectations were stable, with unemployment at 3 percent." James Tobin, "Stabilization Policy", 65.

23. Memo, McCracken to President, 12 June 1971, McCracken Papers, Box 42, University of Michigan.

24. "Statement before the Joint Economic Committee of the U.S. Congress, July 23, 1971," reproduced in Burns, *Reflections*, 117-27. The quotation, which received front-page coverage in major newspapers, is on p. 118.

25. *New York Times*, 10 August 1971, 21.

26. These tensions are described in some detail in Wells, *Economist*; Donald F. Kettl, *Leadership at the Fed* (New Haven, 1986); Safire, *Before the Fall*; John T. Woolley, *Monetary Politics: The Federal Reserve and the Politics of Monetary Policy* (New York, 1984).

27. Neil de Marchi, "The First Nixon Administration: Prelude to Controls," in *Exhortation and Controls*, 317.

28. Herbert Stein, *Presidential Economics*, 159-61; the Davis-Bacon Act required the government to pay "prevailing wages" on government construction contracts. See also de Marchi, "The First Nixon Administration," 322-23.

29. *New York Times*, 24 February 1971, 1.

30. *New York Times*, 8 April 1971, 28.

31. The authority had originally been granted in August 1970, partly with an intent to put the president in the embarrassing position of having to explain why he was choosing not to use his power; de Marchi, "First Nixon Administration," 325; *New York Times*, 19 May 1971, 17.

32. de Marchi, "First Nixon Administration," 338-40.

33. Reported in Paul Peretz, *The Political Economy of Inflation in the United States* (Chicago, 1983), 117.

34. Ibid., 119, *New York Times*, 15 July 1971, 13; *The Gallup Poll: Public Opinion 1971* (Wilmington, Del., 1972). Public opinion as measured in Gallup polls was amazingly stable throughout the 1970s at about 50 percent support for "having the government bring back wage and price controls." In nine polls between 1974 and 1981, the mean approval was 50.3 percent with a standard deviation of 3.8 percent.

35. Stein, *Presidential Economics*, 193.

36. In a 1976 survey of a national sample of economists, the rate of agreement on this issue was second highest of all questions put to the economists—72 percent disagreeing with controls. In a 1990 followup survey with virtually an identical question, 74 percent disagreed with wage and price controls. J. R. Kearl, Clayne L. Pope, Gordon C. Whiting, and Larry T. Wimmer, "A Confusion of Economists?" *American Economic Review Papers and Proceedings* 69 (May 1979): 28-37; and Richard M. Alston, J. R. Kearl, and Michael B. Vaughan, "Is There a Consensus Among Economists in the 1990's?" *American Economic Review: Papers and Proceedings* 82 (May 1992): 203-9.

37. In June 1973, to cope with emergent inflation in Phase III, President Nixon was forced to declare another price freeze, this time for only sixty days. OMB Director George Shultz observed that "everybody thinks Phase III was a failure." *Congressional Quarterly Almanac, 1973*, 202.

38. "As the bulk of the economy entered Phase IV [on] Aug. 18, prices started rising immediately." *Congressional Quarterly Almanac, 1974*, 203.

39. Report, "Inflation," 5/10/79, File BE4-2, 5/1/79-5/31/79, Box BE-19, WHCF-Subject Files, Jimmy Carter Library.

40. Safire, *Before the Fall*, 102.

41. Craufurd D. Goodwin, "A Report of the Conference," in *Exhortation and Controls*, ed. Goodwin, 385-98.

42. Dale E. Hathaway, "Food Prices and Inflation, *Brookings Papers on Economic Activity*, 1:1974, pp. 63-174.

43. James. L. Pierce and Jared J. Enzler, "The Effects of External Inflationary Shocks," *Brookings Papers on Economic Activity*, 1:1974, pp. 13-61.

44. Stephen M. Goldfeld, "The Demand for Money Revisited," *Brookings Papers on Economic Activity*, 3:1973, pp. 577-646.

45. Stein, *Presidential Economics*, 210-12.

46. John Robert Green, *The Presidency of Gerald R. Ford* (Lawrence, Kan., 1995), 71.

47. The energy price index (as opposed to the change in the index, which is plotted in Figure 2), hit its peak in September 1974 and began to fall after that point. The big increase in energy prices had started in September 1973.

48. Stein, *Presidential Economics*, 213.

49. Memo, Stein to President, 12 August 1974, File "Memoranda to the President, August 1974(1)," Box 76, CEA Papers, Gerald R. Ford Library (emphasis in original).

50. Memo, Burns to President, 12 August 1974, File "Memoranda to the President, August 1974(1)," Box 76, CEA Papers, Gerald R. Ford Library.

51. Greene, *Gerald R. Ford*, 73; Memo, Greenspan to Ford, 26 November 1974, Folder BE5, 11/18/74-11/30/24, Box 17, WHCF BE5, Gerald R. Ford Library.

52. Blinder concluded that the shocks in food, energy, and from price decontrol can account for almost all the acceleration and deceleration of inflation in the 1973-75 period. Alan S. Blinder, "The Anatomy of Double-Digit Inflation in the 1970s," in Robert E. Hall, ed., *Inflation: Causes and Effects* (Chicago, 1982).

53. Inter alia, Memo, Gramley to Board of Governors, 8 December 1975, File "Gramley, Lyle (12) May-December 1975, Box C8, Arthur Burns Papers, Gerald R. Ford Library; Wells, *Economist*, chap. 6; Kettl, *Leadership at the Fed*, 133-37.

54. Useful accounts of these struggles are in Kettl, *Leadership at the Fed*, chap. 6, and Woolley, *Monetary Politics*, chap. 7.

55. Jimmy Carter, *Keeping Faith* (New York, 1982), 76.

56. These included restraining federal pay raises; adopting further budgetary restraint; require by executive order that federal regulations be cost-effective; and increase sales of lumber from the national forests.

57. Anthony S. Campagna, *Economic Policy in the Carter Administration* (Westport, Conn., 1995).

58. Hargrove and Morley, *The President and the Council*, 480.

59. Carter called it a "turning point," referring to "a major fiscal and political problem brought about by a resurgent economy and the rapidly building pressures of inflation." *Keeping Faith*, 77.

60. Ibid., 77; Burton I. Kaufman, *The Presidency of James Earl Carter* (Lawrence, Kan., 1993), 75-76, 99-100.

61. Carter himself observed, "The obvious inconsistency in my policy during this rapid transition from stimulating the economy to an overall battle against inflation was to plague me for a long time." *Keeping Faith*, 78. Schultze recalled that "there were a lot of people who really didn't like [the rebate proposal] but who had taken a political position on it to please Carter. Then the first thing he did was suddenly to reverse course." In Hargrove and Morley, *President and the Council*, 481.

62. Hargrove and Morley, *President and the Council*, 479.

63. Memo, Marshall to Schultze et al., 16 March 1979, File EX BE 4-2, 3/1/79-3/31/79, Box BE-19, WHCF—Subject Files, Jimmy Carter Library.

64. Indeed, the Council on Wage and Price Stability recommended its own dissolution. *Congressional Quarterly Almanac, 1980,* 272.

65. For a monetarist, the rapid money growth looked disturbingly inflationary; for Keynesians like Schultze, the increasing interest rates, in time of economic slack, looked disturbingly restrictive. The Fed explained that keeping money growth within the target ranges would have required increases in interest rates that "could have proved destructive to the smooth functioning of financial markets and might eventually have brought serious injury to our economy." Quoted in Richard W. Lang, "The Federal Open Market Committee in 1977," *Federal Reserve Bank of St. Louis Review*, March 1978, 13. Despite public wrangling with the Fed, Carter's economists projected in late 1977 that future monetary policy would be "highly expansionary." Memo, Gramley to EPG, 7 December 1977, File "Economic and Budgetary Outlook 1979-81," Box 191, WHCF, Jimmy Carter Library.

66. Steven H. Axilrod, "U.S. Monetary Policy in Recent Years: An Overview," *Federal Reserve Bulletin* 71 (January 1985): 15.

67. In mid-1978, Charles Schultze wrote that Miller was under pressure from board members, but that "he [Miller], himself, is very sensitive to the danger of overdoing monetary restraint." Memo, Schultze to President, 27 June 1978, File 6/28/78 [1], Box 93, Office of Staff Secretary, Jimmy Carter Library.

68. Schultze's account is available in Hargrove and Morley, *The President and the Council*, 485-86. Carter's note to Schultze, calling his action "unnecessary and improper," is written on Memo, Schultze to President, 11 April 1979, WHCF, FI-27, CF-F17 1/20/77-1/20/81, Jimmy Carter Presidential Library. Schultze and Treasury Secretary W. Michael Blumenthal had clearly informed the president of their concerns and had his approval to urge the board to tighten credit.

69. William R. Neikirk, *Volcker: Portrait of the Money Man* (New York, 1987).

70. Axilrod, "U.S. Monetary Policy," 17-18.

71. Hargrove and Morley, *The President and the Council*, 494.

72. *Congressional Quarterly Almanac, 1980,* 304, 272.

73. Paul Craig Roberts, *The Supply-Side Revolution* (Cambridge, Mass., 1984).

74. Using data starting in 1978, Tims et al. show that the normative content (i.e., positive or negative evaluation) of Associated Press wire stories dealing with the economy became extremely negative in 1979-80 and had a powerful negative impact on consumer sentiment. See A. R. Tims, D. P. Fan, and J. R Freeman, "The Cultivation of Consumer Confidence: A Longitudinal Analysis of News Media Influence on Consumer Sentiment," *Advances in Consumer Research* 16 (1989): 758-70; see also Douglas A. Hibbs Jr., "Public Concern about Inflation and Unemployment in the United States: Trends, Correlates, and Political Implications," in Robert E. Hall, ed., *Inflation: Causes and Effects* (Chicago, 1982).

75. My analysis of the data from Kernell dealing with mentions of unemployment and inflation in the Economic Report of the President from 1962 to 1992 shows a powerful time-trend effect on the relative mentions of inflation and unemployment that swamps all other effects, including the effects of partisanship and objective economic conditions identified by Kernell. (Results available from author upon request.) Samuel Kernell, *Going Public: New Strategies of Presidential Leadership*, 2d ed. (Washington, D.C., 1993), 211-13.

76. See Roberts, *The Supply-Side Revolution*, 60-64.

BALLARD C. CAMPBELL

# Tax Revolts and Political Change

The adoption of Proposition 13 in 1978 sent shock waves throughout the American polity. California's attack on property taxes was not the first fiscal limitation adopted in the 1970s, but it carried clear national implications that the earlier measures lacked. By successfully challenging the political establishment, the initiative drive in the Golden State energized campaigns elsewhere to restrict taxes. The echo of Proposition 13 reverberated in Massachusetts, whose voters approved a cap on property taxes (Proposition 2 1/2) in 1980. Citizens on the nation's two coasts had signaled thumbs down on fiscal affairs in their states.

Propositions 13 and 2 1/2 were the most influential of the state-based tax rebellions of the 1970s and early 1980s. Twenty-one states between 1978 and 1983 imposed limitations on local finances, including property tax levies, and sixteen states adopted restrictions on state finances. Ten states linked the growth of personal income taxes to changes in prices or income. In all, thirty states enacted fiscal limitation measures of some kind in these years, which added to restrictions adopted earlier in the 1970s in a dozen states. Some of these actions amended state constitutions, as in the instance of California's Proposition 13. Other limitations took form as statutes, enacted by state lawmakers or adopted through voter initiatives, as occurred with Proposition 2 1/2 in Massachusetts.[1] The antitax fever spread to federal finances, a contagion manifested in twenty-eight state resolutions between 1975 and 1979 that called for a balanced-budget amendment to the Constitution.[2]

Propositions 13 and 2 1/2 won approval in wealthy, relatively liberal states and became law by referenda votes, circumstances that accentuated their impact. Both measures placed more severe limitations on tax collections than the two dozen other restrictions that voters approved in the late 1970s. But the common theme underlying the support for all the antitax propositions was a general discontent with politics as usual. Although the substance of this dissatisfaction was amorphous, public officials sensed the frustration and modified their approach to numerous issues. Manifestations of these readjustments are visible in the Reagan tax cuts of 1981, the chorus of pledges for "no new taxes," and the increased defensiveness of liberals. The tax revolt had unleashed dynamics that contributed to the polity's rightward shift in the late 1970s and afterward.

The tax battles of the late 1970s raise intriguing questions about causes and effects. A glance at the history of the United States demonstrates that tax revolts are hardly new, with major protests registered in the 1780s, 1840s, 1870s, and 1930s. Analysis of these earlier episodes identifies ingredients that were common to most of the antitax movements. This record indicates that each prior revolt occurred in conjunction with a major economic depression. Each of these downturns triggered a state fiscal crisis, to which the polity responded with various relief and control measures. These remedies and other policy changes that flowed from the crisis left a discernible imprint on the style of governance for the next generation or two. The malady of the 1970s, however, was not a depression of the classic variety, but "stagflation," which combined elevated unemployment with inflation. Yet the political effect of this mixture was analogous to the reactions to prior depressions.

Figure 1 sketches elements in this sequence of events, grounded on three principles of historical causation. The first postulate holds that cause necessarily and invariably precedes effect. Establishing the chronological relationship of pertinent events is, therefore, a prerequisite for locating historical causation. The second principle rests on the logic of replication. This notion holds that confidence in drawing causal inferences between types of events increases with the frequency of association between a specific class of stimuli and similar outcomes. Economic cycles fall into this category of replicated phenomena. The third postulate states that unanticipated shocks periodically destabilize a polity's equilibrium and that the most severe intrusions can trigger shifts in the trajectory of governance. Economic depressions, wars, and major political crises contain this level of potency.

The flow of events depicted in Figure 1 begins with the concept of political equilibrium. During this phase of a polity's history, political relationships tend to remain stable, the corpus of public rules are relatively fixed, and routine rather than crises pervades the cadence of politics. A

Figure 1. Economic Disturbances, Tax Revolts, and Political Change

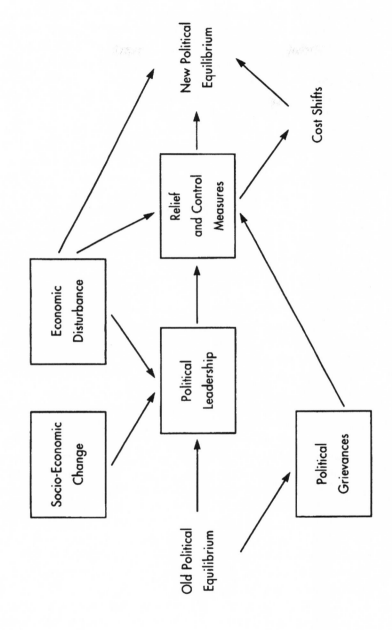

polity never remains completely at rest, of course, for it is always mutating, in response to socioeconomic and other factors. Despite the consensus and disinterest that usually attends these gradual changes, political griev-ances inevitability arise. During the polity's equilibrium phase, the domi-nant leadership usually can check this dissension. Periodically, however, a severe dislocation erodes the moorings of the political establishment and weakens its hold over the direction of governance.

Major economic depressions have the capacity to destabilize conven-tional politics. These dislocations are normally characterized by various combinations of decreasing production and trade, abrupt price changes, increases in unemployment, greater incidence of bankruptcy and personal indebtedness, and outbreaks of civil disorders and popular protests. The stagflation of the 1970s did not mirror all the maladies of earlier depres-sions, yet both kinds of disturbances disrupted customary economic rela-tionships. In both cases, distress and anxiety grew, thus fueling challenges to the political status quo. Failure of the political establishment to respond adequately to these complaints can trigger significant shifts in patterns of governance.

American history has recorded five major peacetime fiscal crises, each of which occurred in the context of severe economic disturbance. The depressions of the 1780s, 1830s–40s, 1870s, 1930s, and the stagflation of 1970s were pivotal factors in igniting movements to reform public finance. I have labeled these historical sequences "tax revolts." During each depres-sion and ensuing crisis, the polity responded with measures designed to vitiate immediate personal hardships and to reform structural conditions that had contributed to state fiscal difficulties (see Relief and Control Measures in Fig. 1).

American federalism affected the flow of these events. Between the 1780s and the 1930s, state and local government relied heavily on levies based on the value of land, improvements to it, and personal property. Property taxes became lightning rods for protest during depressions, partly because their heaviest burden fell on farmers and urban-suburban home owners. The assessment of property values, the adoption of tax rates, and revenue collections were done locally, which produced variations between places and groups and elevated perceptions of unfair taxation. Property taxes were also inelastic, which meant that incomes tended to drop faster than tax obligations during hard times. Tax delinquency rose during these periods; severe downturns caused widespread losses of homes, farms, and businesses. Given the gravity of such misfortune, hard times invariably generated demands for relief and reform of property taxes. These petitions usually targeted state governments, which set policy on property rights and the tax authority of local government.

Each depression left a residue of measures designed to ease tax obligations. Commonly these actions suspended penalties for tax delinquency and placed limits on the fiscal prerogatives of government. Legislative responses to these demands varied among the states, depending upon local factors such as the severity of the economic disturbance, the condition of state and local finance, and the behavior of the political establishment. Figure 1 does not depict these variations, which are inherent in the noncentralized structure of American politics. Generally speaking, however, tax revolts slowed local tax collections in the short run. In the longer run, fiscal crises tended to shift public costs between levels of government, between types of revenue devices, between specific places and communities, and between particular economic groups. This redistribution of the costs of government was part of a constellation of policy shifts that followed in the wake of each depression/fiscal crises. The initial manifestation of this historical cycle was local, but its eventual impact was national and intergovernmental. Viewed in the fullest perspective of history, the tax revolts were instrumental in triggering new directions in governance.[3]

The new American republic began the postwar years with a severe economic depression. A decline in commercial activity became apparent in 1783 and deepened over the next three years. Signs of the distress were visible in reduced imports, falling commodity prices and wages, stagnation in ship building and other industries, and widespread indebtedness.[4] The lack of specie, which tended to flow to Britain to pay for imports that flooded the country after the Revolution, was a prime symptom if not cause of the downturn. A chain of private indebtedness emerged, beginning with farmers and artisans scattered throughout the countryside and extending to local merchants, importers in the commercial cities, and London merchant houses. Desperate retailers inundated county courts with suits to collect debts between 1783 and 1786; prisons bulged with propertyless farmers unable to pay their obligations.[5] Although the middle states appeared to weather the storm better than New England and the South, John Fiske concluded that "the whole country was in some measure pauperized."[6]

Congress helped to turn this private dilemma into a national fiscal crisis by insisting that the states fund the public debt. Repeatedly between October 1781 and August 1786, Congress requisitioned the states, demanding much of the payment in specie.[7] State lawmakers, many of whom were firmly committed to the payment of public debts, both state and national, complied with congressional requests. They reinforced these tax levies with stiff enforcement provisions that threatened delinquent citizens and tax collectors with property seizure and debtor's prison. But the population labored under a staggering financial burden. Private and public debt in New Hampshire equaled half of a year's salary for all its adult men in 1787; debtor cases in western Massachusetts counties approached one-third of the adult male population.[8] Communities throughout New England and other states petitioned legislators for relief, recommending the issuance of paper money, stay laws that delayed tax collections, and other remedies.[9]

Responses varied, but all states adopted measures to cope with the crisis. Six commonwealths issued paper money, and others came close to overcoming the opposition of conservatives such as James Madison of Virginia, who maneuvered to avert the "mischief." New York turned to import and reimport duties. Conservatives in Massachusetts, New Hampshire, and Maryland defeated demands for currency inflation, outcomes that provoked numerous protests, manifested initially as petitions and county conventions, and then as tax boycotts, armed attacks on court proceedings, and arson. Civil disorders erupted in most states in 1785 and 1786, highlighted by Shays's Rebellion in Massachusetts. Armed insurrection in the winter of 1786–87 pushed the tax rebellion to the brink of "anarchy."[10]

Nationalists parlayed the tax revolt into a successful counter-rebellion. They denounced tax avoidance as moral sloth, lamented the distribution of paper currency, and charged that state import duties strangled commerce. The breakdown of law and order was beyond acceptance, a sentiment shared by delegates who met Philadelphia in 1787.[11] The Constitution that they wrote to tame the "wicked projects" in the commonwealths denied authority to the states to print paper money, impose tariffs, emit bills of credit, and impair the obligation of contracts. The first power the Constitution granted to Congress was authority to tax, which was coupled with the power to pay debts, borrow, coin money, and punish counterfeiters. To ensure compliance, the United States was empowered to exercise coercive force, through the maintenance of an army and navy and by permitting Congress to call out the militia to "suppress Insurrections." The fiscal crisis of the 1780s had triggered a decisive shift of power and financial prerogative away from the states toward the central government.

The Panic of 1837 burst a bubble of economic expansion that had grown since the 1820s. Five years of depression followed, as commodity prices and wages fell, northern factories closed, and banks failed in droves.[12] The commercial collapse threatened the financial integrity of state governments, many of which had borrowed heavily to finance the construction of transportation projects. Faced with contracting revenues, nine states defaulted on loan payments, several repudiated their debt, and the value of state bonds plummeted.[13] Reaction to the predicament swept Whigs from office in numerous states, inaugurated a wave of belt tightening in state and local governments' spending, and produced new tax levies to meet debt obligations. In New York, whose comptroller claimed the crisis had "pressed the state to the very brink of dishonor and bankruptcy," state lawmakers suspended work on improvements to the Erie canal and adopted a general state property tax, with half of the proceeds earmarked for the canal fund.[14] Demands on state legislatures for relief included proposals to abolish imprisonment for debt, regulate banking practices and the issuance of paper notes, and adoption of stay and bankruptcy laws.

The depression and fiscal crisis set the stage for a tax revolt, which took form chiefly as a movement to adopt constitutional limitations on state finance. Between 1840 and 1855, nineteen states amended their charters to restrict or prohibit state borrowing and to prohibit state investment in public works and private corporations. New York's constitution of 1846 severely limited the amount, purpose, and repayment schedule for state loans, and required electoral approval of general bond issues. The new charter charged the legislature with restricting municipal taxation and debt, a directive placed in other constitutions.[15] The drive to curtail state financial prerogatives and a heightened mood of fiscal austerity in Congress contributed to a shift of responsibility for public works away from state and national government to municipalities and local property taxes.

Two generations later the failure of the investment firm of Jay Cooke and Company sparked a financial panic that spiraled into a prolonged depression (1873-78). A composite indicator of business conditions measured a 32 percent decline from the onset to the trough of the slowdown; railroad stock prices fell nearly 60 percent. Estimates of joblessness among nonagricultural workers reached as high as 16 percent and averaged 10.7 percent between 1874 and 1878.[16] Whatever the actual number of jobless, distress was widespread. Private relief soared during the middle years of the decade; "tramps" who wandered from community to community in search of work and welfare multiplied.[17] Because the volume of manufacturing and agricultural production increased during the decade, the depression's sharpest sting was manifested as a decline in prices, which induced employers to cut wages, squeezed farmers' income, and eroded property values.[18] The collapse of real estate values triggered waves of bank and savings and loan failures across the country.[19]

The business slump threw public finance into turmoil. Constitutional restrictions placed on state fiscal prerogatives in prior decades had diverted funding of public improvements to municipalities, which had increased their indebtedness substantially between 1866 and the mid-1870s. The depression punctured the boom in private and public building, causing a drop in property valuations, bank failures, and sharp reductions in property tax levies.[20] The result was widespread fiscal distress. North Carolina repudiated its debt, Houston and other cities verged on bankruptcy, and municipal bond defaults peaked in Illinois.[21] Mayors and governors made retrenchment the order of the day.

Middle-class home owners, who bore the brunt of urban property taxes and who blamed unscrupulous politicians for unnecessary spending, pushed for new fiscal discipline.[22] Additional restrictions were implanted in twenty-two state constitutions between 1874 and 1879. The most common reform prohibited states and municipalities from lending credit to private firms or holding stock in them, and limited public indebtedness, sometimes drastically. Several states imposed tax limitations on state government and localities. The movement to cap local debt swept through the South as well as the North, and retained vitality after the immediate crisis had waned. By 1918 twenty-eight state constitutions had restricted urban indebtedness.[23] Lawmakers elsewhere enacted statutory controls on local finance. A stream of exemptions to these restrictions commenced soon after their enactment, yet the political impact of the dislocations of the 1870s and mid-1880s created a web of new fiscal constraints. The result of these actions shifted greater fiscal reliance to state governments, whose expenditures increased in the last decades of the nineteenth century. An analogous expansion of the national government's fiscal role occurred in the Progressive Era.

The Great Depression plunged the polity into a new fiscal crisis. Between 1929 and 1932 real GNP declined 30 percent, disposable personal income dropped 45 percent (in nominal dollars), the housing and automobile industries came to a standstill, and corporate earnings sank. Blue-collar workers endured record unemployment, the middle class lost much of their savings, and banks and county tax collectors dispossessed thousands of farmers of their land. These private struggles were mirrored in the public sector, whose revenues shriveled as commercial activity contracted. Although state and local receipts dropped less precipitously than national revenue, subnational governments faced a unique fiscal dilemma. Their tax receipts, especially from property, contracted at the very time that the depression magnified the financial burden on local governments, the level historically responsible for providing income assistance.[24] The crisis was exacerbated by widespread tax delinquencies, stay laws that delayed tax collection, and bankers' reluctance to extend credit to cities tottering on bankruptcy.

State governments extended only minimal aid to localities during the Hoover phase of the depression, in part because they were captives of their tax history. State revenue capacity remained truncated and the accumulation of constitutional restrictions impeded state borrowing and taxing. Long-standing ideological and partisan traditions reinforced these structural constraints. Tax rebellions that had sprouted around the country, especially among urban home owners who demanded property tax relief, reminded state legislators of this small-budget tradition. More states adopted new limitations on property taxes in 1932–33, when the depression reached bottom, than provided financial assistance for the unemployed.[25]

The partisan realignment in Congress and the presidency eased the fiscal crisis in the states. Taking advantage of the national government's unrestricted capacity to borrow, New Deal Democrats placed the lion's share of relief and recovery costs on Washington during the mid-1930s. The contributory requirements of New Deal grant programs, pressure from federal administrators, and improving economic conditions stimulated a record number of state new tax adoptions, such as levies on consumer purchases, during the latter 1930s. As a result, the states and the federal government assumed a larger share of public costs, while reliance on local property taxes dropped noticeably.[26] These intergovernmental fiscal shifts placed new reliance on general sales and Social Security payroll taxes, developments that added regressivity to the nation's financial scheme.

Economic troubles returned to America in the 1970s. Unlike the Great Depression, the new hardship coupled an elevation in unemployment with rising prices. In the 1970s the standard for gauging economic progress was the 1950s and 1960s, years of unparalleled economic growth, broad prosperity, and negligible inflation (see Table 1). The nation's economic health began to slip in the late 1960s and early 1970s, dipped further during the recession of 1974–75 (the most severe since the 1930s), and ended the decade with a mixture of persistent unemployment and unprecedented peacetime inflation. The stagflation rate (or "misery index") climbed from a yearly average of 6.4 percent

during the good-time years (1953-65) to 8.6 percent during the Vietnam War era (1966-72), when inflation began to accelerate, and then
hit double digits in the mid-1970s as both joblessness and price increases rose. The 1974-75 recession surprised economists, who expected
prices to decline when unemployment rose.[27] This perplexing situation,
which lowered corporate profits, prompted businesses to adopt rigor-
ous cost-cutting and anti-union strategies, as well as a crusade to reduce
governmental regulations. By the end of the 1970s business had emerged
as an energetic opponent of taxation.[28]

Table 1. Stagflation, 1946-1989

| Period | N Years | Unemployment % | CPI % | Stagflation Index % |
|--------|---------|----------------|-------|---------------------|
| 1946-1952 | 7 | 4.2 | 5.9 | 10.0 |
| 1953-1965 | 13 | 5.1 | 1.3 | 6.4 |
| 1966-1972 | 7 | 4.4 | 4.1 | 8.6 |
| 1973-1977 | 5 | 6.7 | 7.7 | 14.5 |
| 1978-1980 | 3 | 6.3 | 10.8 | 17.2 |
| 1981-1983 | 3 | 8.9 | 6.6 | 15.5 |
| 1984-1989 | 6 | 6.4 | 3.7 | 10.2 |

Sources: Unemployment (rate of unemployment, civilian labor force). 1946-1969: *Historical Statistics of the United States* series D86; 1970-*Statistical Abstract of the United States* (various
years). Consumer Price Index (CPI). 1946-1950: *Historical Statistics* series E 135; 1950-
1972: *Statistical Abstract, 1972* Table 558; 1972-1989: *Statistical Abstract* (various years).

Stagflation receded somewhat in 1976 and 1977, before trending upward again in 1978. The index crested at 20.6 percent in
1980, three and a half times higher than the average during the
1950s. Inflation was the component that was most responsible for
this surge. The Consumer Price Index increased by 13.5 percent in
1980, after climbing to 18 percent early in the year. Unlike high unemployment, which eventually declines, inflation has a cumulative characteristic. Even when the rate of inflation decreased, prices did not
return to former levels. Between 1966 and 1978 the price of consumer
goods and services on average doubled. Fuel tripled, medical care increased 124 percent, and food prices nearly doubled between 1973 and

1980. Mortgage rates in 1979 were twice their 1965 level and they rose higher in 1980. These price hikes ended the country's history of cheap food and gasoline and reversed the postwar pattern of affordable housing. Prices on the stock market, on the other hand, languished, recording four losing years between 1973 and 1981. These events set the stage for President Jimmy Carter's "crisis of confidence" speech in the summer of 1979, when he implied that inflation was the cause of the "widespread national malaise."

Modest price increases usually are tolerable and perhaps desirable in a growing economy. Only when price increases accelerate sharply or persist is inflation viewed as harmful. Modest levels of unemployment, by comparison, do not aggregate into depression. Depression and inflation both affect various strata of the economy. But joblessness tends to concentrate among lower-income workers, while inflation readjusts the nominal basis of most pocketbooks and causes the greatest distress among middle- and upper-middle income earners.[29] Rapid price increases can be threatening to individuals on fixed incomes, such as retirees. Small businesses suffer more than large corporations, which have access to more sources of credit and wider profit margins, although both kinds of firms saw inflation eat into earnings during the 1970s. The budgets of low-income families are more sensitive to price hikes on basic consumer items such as food, shelter, and fuel than are upper-income families, yet inflation pushed individuals at most income levels into higher tax brackets. The value of assets such as bonds, whose ownership is concentrated among the wealthy, eroded during periods of high inflation. Still, identifying groups most harmed by rising prices is problematic. Arguably, the most politically potent effect of the inflation in the 1970s was widespread perception of its random unfairness and the prospective that it would continue and even worsen. The unchecked price increases of the 1970s, Theodore White observed, produced "a contagion of fear."[30]

Inflation alone did not cause the tax revolt of the 1970s. Political change usually flows from the fortuitous interaction of several factors. The contribution of economic conditions to this mix can be likened to the storm surge of a hurricane, which raised the surface on which political eddies swirled. Stagflation interacted and magnified the effect of three trends that grew in the 1970s: a backlash against the Great Society, the rise in taxation, and a stream of "bad news." The adoption of rights-based policy in the 1960s, epitomized by compensatory programs for blacks and women, produced widening resentments, especially among lower-income white males. Members of the business community complained about the costs of environmental standards and other regulations. Hostility to the perceived favoritism of Great Society policy overlapped with animosity toward the expansion of welfare and judicial liberalism concerning crime and privacy. Riots in the black urban ghettos and the stagnation of income among most families after 1973 reinforced the growing perception that liberalism undermined traditional values and hurt the middle and working classes.[31]

Complaints about the cost of government comprised a second irritant that grew during the 1970s. Real (constant dollar) public-sector expenditures doubled between 1960 and 1980, while government's revenue collection grew over 50 percent in per capita constant dollars between 1967 and 1980.[32] The effective rate of federal taxation on middle- and upper-middle-class families increased during these years. The amount of state and local revenues rose faster, consuming 10.4 percent of personal income in 1965 and 12.7 percent in 1978. Although the national average of property tax collections as a percentage of income was stable between 1967 and the late 1970s, inflation and local factors in some states pushed property taxes up significantly, often in seemingly random patterns across communities and classes of real estate. Reliance on property taxes to fund state and local services varied considerably from state to state. California and Massachusetts depended heavily on taxes based on the value of real estate.[33]

Resentment about taxes also appeared to be linked to the confidence that citizens had in officials. The University of Michigan's measure of the "trust in government" registered substantial support for civic activity from 1958 through 1964. The trust indicator began a sharp decline over the next ten years, and it continued to drift downward through the remainder of the 1970s.[34] Harris polls recorded that confidence in government fell to its lowest mark in 1978. Other surveys showed an increase of antigovernment attitudes after 1964; support for the statement that government was "too powerful" peaked in the late 1970s.[35] While it remains unclear what lay behind these opinions, surveys suggest that the public had soured more on the way politics was conducted than on the generic functions of government. The polls disclosed that citizens continued to support public intervention as a tactic of addressing numerous problems in society. When given a choice between cutting taxes or retaining benefits, most people choose benefits.[36]

The survey data suggest that the decline in trust was not driven by an across-the-board antipathy toward government, but rather was tied to three specific grievances: the rise in stagflation, a perception that government was wasteful and inefficient, and a succession of "bad news." Negative events of the latter sort in the late 1960s and early 1970s included urban riots, protests against the war in Vietnam, and the Watergate scandal, which culminated in the president's resignation. The confidence indicator began its nosedive as these stories unfolded. New York City's flirtation with bankruptcy, the accident at the Three Mile Island Nuclear plant, and Iran's seizure of American hostages kept the bad news coming in the late 1970s. Students of public opinion suggest that these events reinforced the public's deepening skepticism about the ability of politicians to solve the nation's problems.[37]

Anger over governmental inefficacy, rights-based liberalism, and stagflation prepared the soil from which tax revolts sprouted. A growing tax burden in some states added a volatile ingredient to this mixture. High tax levels, nonetheless, did not automatically spark tax rebellion. New York, Vermont, Minnesota, and Wisconsin did not adopt fiscal limitations despite tax loads in excess of the national average (see "Tax Burden, 1978" in Table 2, panel A). Nor did the belief of voters that taxes were too high or that government was wasteful and inefficient lead directly to a successful antitax drive.[38] The roots of the tax revolt appeared to be entangled in a complex web of local political circumstances that varied from state to state. Three factors were instrumental in explaining the adoption of antitax measures in the states between 1978 and 1982: the strength of partisan organization, the availability of the voter initiatives, and a state's tax history.

Partisan history and culture had a bearing on how states had managed their treasury. David Mayhew found that states with histories of strong partisan organizations tended to have smaller public economies (low per capita taxation and expenditure) than did states with traditions of individualistic politics.[39] Weak-party states, one can predict, made good candidates for tax revolts because they lacked entrenched organizations that maintained an interest in deflecting grassroots challenges to the political establishment. Strong-party states, on the other hand, possessed organizations with both the motivation and potential capacity to block the crusades of political outsiders. Citizen access to policy making via ballot initiatives (available in twenty-three commonwealths) further increased the

Table 2. State-Local Finances, 1967-1988.

A. Percent of State-Local Revenue Collected by State Government[a]

| State | FY 1967 | FY 1977 | FY 1988 | Exhibit: Tax Burden, 1978[b] |
|---|---|---|---|---|
| U.S. (mean) | 50 | 54 | 55 | 12.75 % |
| California | 42 | 49 | 55 | 15.8 |
| Massachusetts | 47 | 51 | 66 | 15.1 |
| New York | 46 | 46 | 47 | 17.2 |
| Illinois | 43 | 52 | 51 | 11.8 |
| New Hampshire | 42 | 43 | 45 | 10.5 |
| Oregon | 50 | 51 | 50 | 12.8 |
| Texas | 50 | 54 | 48 | 10.5 |
| Virginia | 58 | 59 | 59 | 11.0 |

B. Percent of State-Local Revenue derived from Local Property Taxes[a]

| State | FY 1967 | FY 1977 | FY 1988 | Tax Burden, 1988[b] |
|---|---|---|---|---|
| U.S. (mean) | 33 | 27 | 21 | 11.6 |
| California | 40 | 33 | 17 | 11.2 |
| Massachusetts | 45 | 42 | 25 | 11.4 |
| New York | 33 | 29 | 23 | 16.4 |
| Illinois | 41 | 31 | 26 | 10.9 |
| New Hampshire | 50 | 47 | 45 | 8.4 |
| Oregon | 36 | 33 | 31 | 11.7 |
| Texas | 35 | 27 | 27 | 10.8 |
| Virginia | 23 | 22 | 21 | 10.4 |

a. State-local own general revenue.
b. State-local tax revenue as a percentage of personal income.

Sources: U.S. Census Bureau, Historical Statistics on Governmental Finances and Employment, vol.6 of 1977 Census of Governments (Washington, D.C., 1979), table 18; Advisory Commission on Intergovernmental Relations, Significant Features of Fiscal Federalism, 1988, vol. 2 Revenues and Expenditures (Washington, D.C., 1990), state tables, for 1988 data, Table 77 for State and Local Tax Revenue as a percentage of personal income.

opportunity for successful grassroots policy campaigns. Finally, heavy reliance on local property taxes elevated the potential for a tax backlash, especially if a state's overall tax burden was high and its legislature had failed to confront the problem. These three criteria made California and Massachusetts prime candidates for tax revolts.

Table 3.  Fiscal Limitations, Party Types, and Initiative
         Accessibility in the States, 1978-1983

|              | Initiatives | |
|--------------|-----------|-----------|
|              | None      | Have      |
| Party Type   |           |           |
| Strong       | 16        | 4         |
|              | Limits: 9 | Limits: 2 |
| Weak         | 11        | 19        |
|              | Limits: 4 | Limits: 13 |

Sources. Fiscal limitations: see note 1.  Party types: David R. Mayhew, *Placing Parties in American Politics* (Princeton, NJ: 1986), table 7.1. States coded 1 were classified as weak party.  Initiatives: David B. Magleby, *Direct Legislation: Voting on Ballot Propositions in the United States* (Baltimore: 1984), table 3.1.

Classifying the states by the strength of traditional partisan organization and the availability of voter initiatives roughs out two key parameters of fiscal limitations adopted in the states (see Table 3). The largest number of tax and expenditure caps occurred in states with weak-party traditions and initiatives. This set includes California, Massachusetts, Arizona, Idaho, Michigan, and Nevada, the states in which voters imposed limits on local property taxes.[40] This category also contains states whose legislatures enacted limitations, sometimes after an unsuccessful initiative, as occurred in Oregon. States that possessed strong party organizations and did not offer initiatives also enacted a fair number of fiscal limitations, although only three of the nine states in this group restricted property taxes.[41] Most of the weak-party states that avoided tax revolt adoptions had reduced their property tax burden before 1978; Kansas, Minnesota, North Carolina, and Wisconsin fall into this group (none possessed the initiative). The general tax-burden index (state-local tax revenue as a proportion of personal income) showed a modest relationship to categories of states classified on the basis of the Mayhew party-strength index and fiscal limitation adoptions.[42] But this relationship obscures a potent factor that bore on state tax politics: whether officials had enacted property tax reform. Here leaders in California and Massachusetts had put themselves at risk.

California possessed the preconditions for a tax rebellion. The state lacked a strong party tradition, allowed citizens to set policy via initiatives, and had a rising tax burden since the mid-1960s. California's state-local tax load increased from 12 percent of personal income in 1965 to 15.8 percent in 1978; the property tax burden as a percentage of income was higher in 1977 (6.5 percent) than in 1967 (6.2 percent), although it had peaked at 7.2 percent in 1972. Some critics pointed to strikes by public employees as the cause of expenditure increases. Unlike most other states, moreover, local government in California bore part of the cost of welfare, an arrangement that increased the local visibility of this unpopular program. The combination of activist government and rising expenditures fed discontents in southern California, long a hotbed of political conservatism and home to prior antigovernment drives. Still, these elements had not self-ignited into a successful tax rebellion before 1978. Prior attempts to cap taxes through the ballot box had failed, including a push by Governor Ronald Reagan for Proposition 1 (1973), which would have held state revenues to a percentage of state income.[43]

The tax revolt in California materialized as a special-interest movement that capitalized on a burst of inflation-driven property tax increases. With recovery from the 1974–75 recession, the California housing market boomed; housing prices soared and homes turned over frequently. At the same time, property taxes doubled and tripled, in part because of a statutory requirement that assessments be undertaken periodically and reflect a uniform proportion of market value. The tax sting cut two ways. First, property taxes rose faster than incomes, and second, anomalous disparities in tax obligations developed among neighbors. The state legislature had considered but failed to remedy the problem in 1977, which created an opportunity for Howard Jarvis. A retired manufacturer and political gadfly, who had mounted previous antitax campaigns, Jarvis hooked up with Paul Gann, another longtime antitaxer, secured the required number of signatures to put Proposition 13 on the ballot, and barnstormed the state for the measure on a shoestring.

Proposition 13 rolled property assessments back to the 1975 level, limited future assessment increases to 2 percent a year (unless the property was sold), and limited the total tax to one percent of a property's full cash value. Promising a substantial cut in local funds and facing the opposition of the state's political establishment, the proposal appeared doomed as the June election approached. Two last-minute developments turned the tide. First, several weeks before the referendum the Los Angeles assessor's office released the 1978 assessments, which tripled the values of some homes and promised higher taxes for most people in the region. And second, the state's director of finance announced a highly optimistic prediction of a state revenue surplus. Proposition 13 won by a 65–35 margin. Predictably, home owners and upper-income groups cast lopsided votes for Proposition 13, but polls documented support among most voter groups. Half of self-identified liberals and nearly half of renters surveyed said yes to Thirteen. The self-interest of middle-class home owners coupled with festering antagonisms toward politics in general among diverse groups in California appeared to account for passage of the initiative.

The thunderclap from California rolled east, energizing antitax campaigns elsewhere, including in the Bay State. Components for a tax revolt had been building for years in Massachusetts. The state maintained a generous public economy, including liberal welfare benefits, and it depended heavily on local property taxes to fund public services. Only New Hampshire, a low-tax state that possessed neither a personal income nor a general sales tax, surpassed the Bay's State's reliance on local property taxes. Together its state and local levies gave Massachusetts one of the highest tax burdens in the nation; and the rate of its increase since the middle 1960s surpassed the regional and national averages. Bay State policymakers did little to reverse these trends, even as the tax system came under greater pressure from inflation and a 1974 judicial mandate to assess properties at full market value. Governor Michael Dukakis and state legislators provided additional local aid in 1977, but the measure neglected to couple the grants with a mandatory reduction of local property taxes.[44]

Proposition 13 reset the political stage in Massachusetts. Dukakis lost the Democratic primary in 1978 to Edward J. King, an advocate of tax cuts and supply-side economics. Citizens for Limited Taxation (CLT), organized in 1973, took its tax-cap proposal to the voters after the legislature rejected it by a lopsided vote. CLT's Proposition 2 1/2, which capped the property tax levy at 2 1/2 percent of the assessed property value and limited annual increases in a community's total property tax collection to 2 1/2 percent over the prior year, came before voters in 1980 on the same ballot that pitted Ronald Reagan against Jimmy Carter.

Polls indicated that most Bay Staters opposed cutting public services, but they saw property taxes as too high and government as wasteful and inefficient, especially at the state level. Although Proposition 2 1/2 was directed at local property taxes and thus placed local services in greatest jeopardy of funding cuts, the measure offered the public a vehicle to register complaints about the management of government in general. Barbara Anderson, CLT's executive director, who made up in energy what her organization lacked in funds, seized on this discontent by urging voters to send the legislature a "message." Two last-minute developments worked in CLT's favor. The High Tech Council, a collective of Bay State businesses, came to the rescue of the CLT's empty treasury, and a month before the referendum the state Department of Revenue began the release of the property tax bills, which contained substantial increases. In November, Reagan carried Massachusetts with less than 42 percent of the vote, but Proposition 2 1/2 attracted 59 percent. More than 40 percent of self-identified "liberals" supported the measure, as did the majority of voters in 80 percent of the state's town and cities. Among these communities were most of the state's older industrial (and poorer) cities, which faced large revenue reductions under Proposition 2 1/2.

Weak parties and the availability of the initiative created structural opportunities for grassroots tax rebellions in Massachusetts and California. New York and Illinois, by comparison, deflected the full force of populist challenges to fiscal policy, largely because of the strength of their party systems and the absence of the voter initiative. New York had the highest state-local tax burden in the nation in the 1970s, a record due in part to the legacy of Republican governor Nelson Rockefeller (1959–73). But fiscal expansion in the Empire State had peaked by mid-decade, when the story of New York City's close brush with bankruptcy captured national attention. Thereafter party leaders in New York followed a more cautious fiscal course and negotiated reductions in taxes.[45] Illinois had a long history as a low tax state, a record it maintained in the 1970s. The state's overall tax burden ranked near the bottom among industrial states and it had reduced dependence on property tax revenues between 1967 and 1977 (see Table 2). The powerful Chicago Democratic organization, headed by Mayor Richard J. Daley until his death in 1976, kept a tight grip over city politics throughout the 1970s, and had brokered fiscal understandings with state officials, including Republican governors. Notwithstanding this tradition of frugality, the National Tax Limitation Committee targeted Illinois for a tax-cap campaign. The House adopted a constitutional amendment that limited state and local levies, but the measure died in the Senate, partially on the urging of Republican Governor James Thompson. The governor supported a more controlled downsizing of government, which he argued "should learn to do more with less." Notwithstanding a tax increase in 1983 to repair fiscal damage from the recession of 1981-82, Illinois's tax burden dropped during the Thompson era (1977-91).[46]

Despite their political and structural differences, Illinois, New York, Massachusetts, and California all reduced their overall tax burdens and their dependence on property taxes after 1978 (see Table 2). Party organization appeared to influence how these cuts were executed. One study found that California's tax structure became more regressive between the late 1970s and 1991, while in New York, where Democrats acted as advocates of low-income voters, levies became less regressive.[47] To the extent that fiscal policy in the late 1970s and 1980s shifted the costs of government away from taxes on home owners to flat-rate levies, such as state taxes on consumer purchases and individual incomes, the tax revolt increased the regressivity of subnational finance. Propositions 13 and 2 1/2 forced substantial reductions in property taxes: California's property tax fell from 6.5 percent of personal income in 1977 to 3.1 percent in 1988; the drop in Massachusetts went from 7.4 to 3.6 percent. Dependence on property taxes (as a proportion of total state and local revenue) dropped markedly in each state, epitomizing an ongoing national trend (see Table 2, panel B). Property taxes equaled 3.3 percent of the GNP in 1976 and 2.8 percent in 1990.

Many home owners benefited from tax-cap actions, but some communities suffered substantial revenue losses. This occurred in California and Massachusetts, where the tax caps mandated revenue rollbacks. Assessing how the new constraints affected public services and the quality of governance is problematic, because effects varied between communities, and they unfolded over the years and interacted with changing conditions. But several short-run consequences appear to be evident in California and Massachusetts. Expenditure reductions for education, general government, and other services occurred in both states in the years immediately following the tax caps. Proposition 2 1/2 had the heaviest impact on cities, the poorest communities in the Bay State; not only did their revenue collections drop, but urban centers trailed suburbs and rural areas in attempting "override" referenda that could authorize additional taxation.[48] Proposition 13 also produced new inequities, both among communities, and among recent home buyers compared to individuals who purchased property before 1978.[49]

Propositions 13 and 2 1/2 forced communities in California and Massachusetts to adjust to the new revenue scarcity. Most localities increased user fees and adopted administrative efficiencies, including the privatization of services. Hiring private contractors not only lowered direct costs (e.g., by reducing fringe benefits), but in effect pressured public employee unions to temper wage demands with the implied threat of further privatization. Proposition 2 1/2 induced communities in Massachusetts to implement regular reassessments of property at full market value. Legislative amendment to the tax cap muffled some of its severity. Massachusetts lawmakers reduced the vote margin needed to approve "overrides" of the tax limitation, allowed capital expenditures to be excluded from the cap, and placed certain functions (e.g., water and sewer services in Boston metropolitan region) outside the radius of Proposition 2 1/2. Actions in California allowed communities to fund facilities with bonds outside the limits of Proposition 13 and permitted older residents to purchase another home within their county without giving up their existing property assessment. Proposition 98 (1988) earmarked a healthy percentage of state revenues for education.

The most significant response to local revenue loss in the 1980s was increased state financial aid. California and Massachusetts doubled their dollar contributions to local budgets in the ten years after 1978, actions that expanded the fiscal presence of each state (see Table 2, panel A). This intergovernmental cost shift brought with it increased risk from business cycles. During the recession of 1981–83, which confronted states with deficits, lawmakers adopted a battery of new taxes to comply with balanced-budget requirements. But legislators displayed an antitax mood in the next economic downturn (1990–91), which reduced revenue collections and pushed numerous states into another fiscal crisis. Bitter partisan battles erupted in California and Massachusetts over budgets that eventually cut local aid substantially.[50] The contraction of state grants in California helps to explain why officials in Orange County invested a pool of funds managed for 186 jurisdictions plus billions of borrowed money in highly risky securities. Late in 1994, after four years of recession in California and the collapse of bond prices, Orange County declared bankruptcy and began laying off employees. Mounting stress on state finances encouraged other questionable fiscal decisions, such as reliance on lotteries and casinos to raise public monies. States that tapped streams of gambling receipts increased the regressivity of their revenue systems.

California's Proposition 13, Sears and Citron observed, "rearranged the political agenda at all levels of government."[51] One can add that grassroots attacks on taxes and spending among the states were instrumental in fueling demands for greater restraint on numerous aspects of civic activity. These local frustrations drifted into national politics, as they usually do in America's federal polity. Ronald Reagan's 1980 presidential victory and the massive tax cut in the following year rode the wave of antitax fever. The 1981 budgeting decisions in Washington had substantial cost-shifting implications for income groups, intergovernmental programs, and age cohorts. The Reagan administration's fiscal policies helped to institutionalize a restrained polity, whose defining attributes were a hesitancy to expand the public sector, deregulation of business, slowed enforcement of nondiscrimination law, reduced rates of spending increases, and increased opposition to (for some, "no") new taxes. Market-oriented thinking gained wider acceptance, while Keynesian macroeconomics lost credence. Although the civic edifice underwent incremental rather than wholesale contraction, policy innovation clearly slowed. Stasis had become the order of the day, as the polity settled into a new equilibrium.[52]

The economic dislocations of the 1970s were a primary cause of this shift to the right. The long view of history suggests that the evolution from the liberalism of the 1960s to the comparative austerity of the 1980s repeats a pattern that occurred roughly every two generations. In these sequences, economic stress ignited fiscal crises, which in turn interacted with other factors to trigger a transition to a new stage of governance. At least five such cycles have undermined extant political equilibria since the American Revolution. The first of these transformations was rooted in the tax revolt of the 1780s. The adoption of the Constitution of the United States resolved the immediate fiscal crisis of that decade and helped to inaugurate a policy period that can be labeled the era of civic mercantilism (1790s–1830s).[53] The Depression of the 1830s and 1840s discredited this regime and sparked a shift toward an era of political egalitarianism, in which state and federal intervention into the economy slowed and dual federalism became accentuated. The Civil War occasioned marked deviations from this course, but most aspects of this expansion were short-lived.

The economic problems of the 1870s were serious, although not catastrophic. Nonetheless, this slump in commerce appears linked by timing and policy reverberations to the formation of a new policy stage that I call the transitional polity (1880s–1920s). Its signature was increased activism and policy innovation at all levels of government, but especially among the states. The depression of the 1890s and the crystallization of reform sentiment during the height of the progressive period (1907–15) accelerated these lines of change. The Great Depression provided the critical dynamic in the formation of the next political stage, the modern liberal state (1930s-early 1970s), whose dimensions evolved during World War II and from Great Society programs.

Complaints about modern liberalism grew more numerous and insistent during the 1970s. Critics charged that political elites displayed favoritism toward special interests, expanded unfair entitlement programs, placed crippling regulations on business, and imposed unsustainable costs on taxpayers and the economy. The airing of these grievances prepared the ground for the antitax crusades, whose appeal grew as economic conditions deteriorated after 1973. By challenging the political establishment and its policy foundations, the tax revolt created opportunities for conservatives, whose coalition strength came to rival the factions of liberalism. This reconfiguration of political alliances caused the polity to gravitate toward a new political equilibrium in which restraints on government increased and the expansion of liberalism was stalemated.

*Northeastern University*

## Notes

1. Advisory Commission on Intergovernmental Relations, *Significant Features of Fiscal Federalism, 1984* (Washington, D.C., 1985), tables 93, 94; Sherry Tvedt, "Enough Is Enough: The Origins of Proposition 2 1/2" (M.A. thesis, Massachusetts Institute of Technology 1981), 19–20; Robert Kuttner, *Revolt of the Haves: Tax Rebellions and Hard Times* (New York, 1980). State indexing laws: Advisory Commission on Intergovernmental Relations, *Significant Features of Fiscal Federalism, 1982–1983* (Washington, D.C., 1984), table 67.

2. *Washington Post*, 2 February 1979. The push for a balanced-budget amendment stalled at thirty-two states in the mid-1980s. *New York Times*, 19 March 1985.

3. This article cannot discuss all aspects of the model. I will review its general contours, noting changes in fiscal policy in four major crises prior to the 1970s.

4. Curtis Nettels, *The Emergence of a National Economy, 1775–1815* (New York, 1962), chap. 3; Richard B. Morris, *The Forging of the Union, 1781–1789* (New York, 1987), chap. 6; John H. Flannagan, "Trying Times: Depression in New Hampshire, 1781–1789" (Ph.D. dissertation, Georgetown University, 1972); John J. McCusker and Russell R. Menard, *The Economy of British America, 1607–1789* (Chapel Hill, 1985), chap. 17.

5. Flannagan, "Depression in New Hampshire," 81–119; David P. Szatmary, *Shays's Rebellion: The Making of an Agrarian Insurrection* (Amherst, Mass., 1980), chap. 2.

6. John Fiske, *The Critical Period in American History, 1783–1789* (Boston, 1888), 166.

7. Rodger Brown, *Redeeming the Republic: Federalists, Taxation, and the Origins of the Constitution* (Baltimore, 1993).

8. Flanngan, "Trying Times," 248; Szatmary, *Shays's Rebellion*, 29.

9. Allan Nevins, *The American States During and After the Revolution, 1775–1789* (New York, 1924), 432–56, 529–33, 557–60; Nettels, *National Economy*, chap. 4.

10. Szatmary, *Shays's Rebellion*, chaps. 4, 5, and 124-26; Nettels, *National Economy*, 83-88; Brown, *Redeeming the Republic*, 104-20; Edward C. Papenfuse, "The Legislative Response to a Costly War: Fiscal Policy and Factional Politics in Maryland, 1777-1789," in R. Hoffman and P. Albert, eds., *Sovereign States in an Age of Uncertainty* (Charlottesville, Va., 1981), 134-56; Morris, *Forging of the Union*, 266; and Fisk, *Critical Period*, chap. 4, "Drifting Toward Anarchy."

11. Scholars who saw conservative reaction to state actions as central to the movement for a stronger national government include Nevins, *The American States*, 570; Nettels, *National Economy*, 89-92; Brown, *Redeeming the Republic*; Gordon S. Wood, *The Creation of the American Republic, 1776-1787* (New York, 1969), chaps. 10, 11, esp. p. 465.

12. Samuel Rezneck, "The Social History of an American Depression, 1837-43," *American Historical Review* (1935): 662-87; Robert A. Margo, "Wages and Prices during the Antebellum Period: A Survey of New Evidence," in R. Gallman and J. Wallis, eds., *American Economic Growth and Standards of Living Before the Civil War* (Chicago, 1992); Michael F. Holt, "The Election of 1840, Voter Mobilization, and the Emergence of the Second Party System," in W. Cooper, M. Holt, and J. McCardell, eds., *A Master's Due* (Baton Rouge, La., 1985), esp. 35.

13. B. U. Ratchford, *American State Debts* (Durham, N.C., 1941), 79-105; Edward C. Kirkland, *Men, Cities, and Transportation* (Cambridge, Mass., 1948), 1:132-34.

14. Don C. Sowers, *The Financial History of New York State: From 1789 to 1912* (New York, 1914), 70; L. Ray Gunn, *The Decline of Authority: Public Economic Policy and Political Development in New York, 1800-1860* (Ithaca, N.Y., 1988), chap. 5.

15. Carter Goodrich, "The Revulsion Against Internal Improvements," *Journal of Economic History* (1950): esp. 156-57; Ratchford, *American State Debts*, 121-22.

16. Samuel Rezneck, "Distress, Relief, and Discontent in the United States During the Depression of 1873-78," *Journal of Political Economy* (1950): 498, 501; Ernest L. Bogart and C. M. Thompson, *The Industrial State, 1870-1893* (Springfield, Ill., 1920), 438; Paul Kleppner, *The Third Electoral System, 1853-1892: Parties, Voters, and Political Cultures* (Chapel Hill, N.C., 1979), 122.

17. For example, Alexander Keyssar, *Out of Work: The First Century of Unemployment in Massachusetts* (Cambridge, Mass., 1986), 133-35.

18 O. V. Wells, "Depression of 1873-79," *Agricultural History* (1937): 240-47; Milton Friedman and A. J. Schwartz, *A Monetary History of the United States, 1867-1960* (Princeton, 1963), 34-44.

19. Albert B. Hart, *Commonwealth History of Massachusetts*, vol. 5 (New York, 1930, 1966 ed.), 352; Bogart and Thompson, *Industrial State*, 289; Carl B. Swisher, *Motivation and Political Technique in the California Constitutional Convention, 1878-79* (Claremont, Calif., 1930), 9.

20. Charles J. Bullock, *Historical Sketch of the Finances and Fiscal Policy of Massachusetts from 1780 to 1905* (New York, 1907), 139 (appendix A); Charles P. Huse, *The Financial History of Boston, 1822-1909* (Cambridge, Mass., 1916), 206-11; Bogart and Thompson, *Industrial State*, 289, 302; Edmund T. Miller, *A Financial History of Texas* (Austin, 1916), 416-17 (table 14), 399; Swisher, *California Constitutional Convention*, 7-9.

21. Richard Sylla, "Long-Term Trends in State and Local Finance: Sources and Uses of Funds in North Carolina, 1800-1977," in S. Engerman and R. Gallman, eds., *Long-Term Factors in American Economic Growth* (Chicago, 1986), 842-43; Harold Platt, *City Building in the New South: The Growth of Public Services in Houston, Texas, 1830-1910* (Philadelphia, 1983), 51-63; Eric H. Monkkonen, *The Local State: Public Money and American Cities* (Stanford, Calif., 1995), 26, 68.

22. Clifton K. Yearley, *The Money Machines: The Breakdown and Reform of Governmental and Party Finance in the North, 1860-1920* (Albany, N.Y., 1970), esp. chap. 1; also Jon C. Teaford, *The Unheralded Triumph: City Government in America, 1870-1900* (Baltimore, 1984), 287-304; Swisher, *California Constitutional Convention*, 66-85.

23. Goodrich, "Revulsion Against Internal Improvements"; Horace Secrist, *An Economic Analysis of the Constitutional Restrictions upon Public Indebtedness in the United States* (Madison, Wis., 1914), 59–60, and appendixes I–III; Illinois Legislative Reference Bureau, "State and Local Finance," *Constitutional Convention Bulletins* (Springfield, 1920), 4:294–300.

24. The crisis of subnational finance in the 1930s is summarized in Ballard C. Campbell, *The Growth of American Government: Governance from the Cleveland Era to the Present* (Bloomington, Ind., 1995), 83–87, 178–81.

25. David T. Beito, *Taxpayers in Revolt: Tax Resistance During the Great Depression* (Chapel Hill, 1989), chap. 1, 141; James R. Adams, *Secret of the Tax Revolt* (San Diego, 1984), 277; James E. Hartley, S. Sheffrin, and J. D. Vasche, "Reform During Crises: The Transformation of California's Fiscal System During the Great Depression," *Journal of Economic History* (1996): 660–62; Harold Gorvine, "The New Deal in Massachusetts," in John Braeman, R. Bremner, and D. Brody, *The New Deal* (Columbus, Ohio, 1975), 2:13–20.

26. Campbell, *Growth of American Government*, 179–84.

27. In 1975 joblessness rose to 8.5 percent, but the CPI dropped only to 9.1 percent, down from 11.0 percent in the previous year. The 1975 stagflation rate of 17.6 was exceeded only by 1980 (20.6) and 1981 (17.9).

28. David Vogel, *Fluctuating Fortunes: The Political Power of Business in America* (New York, 1990), esp. chaps. 6 and 7; Thomas Ferguson and Joel Rodgers, *Right Turn: The Decline of the Democrats and the Future of American Politics* (New York, 1986), chap. 3; David M. Gordon, *Fat and Mean: The Corporate Squeeze of Working Americans and the Myth of Managerial "Downsizing"* (New York, 1996), 69, 81, 262, and chap. 8.

29. Douglas A. Hibbs Jr., *The American Political Economy: Macroeconomics and Electoral Politics* (Cambridge, Mass., 1987), 138–41; D. Roderick Kiewiet, "Policy-Oriented Voting in Response to Economic Issues," *American Political Science Review* 75 (1981): 448–59.

30. George Wilson, *Inflation: Causes, Consequences, and Cures* (Bloomington, Ind., 1982), chap. 6; Kuttner, *Revolt of the Haves*, 201–8; George G. Kaufman, "Inflation, Proposition 13 Fever, and Suggested Relief," in Kaufman and K. Rosen, eds., *The Property Tax Revolt: The Case of Proposition 13* (Cambridge, Mass., 1981), 215–17. See the index of consumer confidence in Harold W. Stanley and R. Niemi, *Vital Statistics on American Politics* (Washington, D.C., 1995), 400. White quoted in Joseph Nocera, *A Piece of the Action: How the Middle Class Joined the Moneyed Class* (New York, 1994), 178.

31. Thomas B. Edsall, *Chain Reaction: The Impact of Race, Rights, and Taxes on American Politics* (New York, 1992); Michael A. Bernstein and D. Adler, eds., *Understanding American Economic Decline* (New York, 1994).

32. Campbell, *Growth of American Government*, 113, 182.

33. Advisory Commission on Intergovernmental Relations, *Intergovernmental Perspective* 7 (Fall 1981): 27; Lawrence Mishel, J. Bernstein, and J. Schmitt, *The State of Working America, 1996–1997* (Washington, D.C., 1996), 96–97; ACIR, *Significant Features of Fiscal Federalism, 1984* (Washington, D.C., 1985), table 36; ACIR, *Significant Features of Fiscal Federalism, 1976–77* (Washington, D.C., 1977), table 76; ACIR, *Significant Features of Fiscal Federalism, 1990* (Washington, D.C., 1992), table 82.

34. Warren E. Miller and Santa A. Traugott, *American National Election Studies Data Sourcebook* (Cambridge, Mass., 1989), 272, 274.

35. *New York Times*, 11 November 1989; Linda L. M. and Stephen E. Bennett, *Living with Leviathan: Americans Coming to Terms with Big Government* (Lawrence, Kan., 1990), 27–34.

36. Bennett, *Leviathan*, 87; David O. Sears and Jack Citrin, *Tax Revolt: Something for Nothing in California* (Cambridge, Mass., 1982), 47–70, 231; Ferguson, *Right Turn*, 18–19; Campbell, *Growth of American Government*, 234.

37. Seymour M. Lipset and William Schneider, *The Confidence Gap: Business, Labor, and Government in the Public Mind* (New York, 1983), 151–59; Kuttner, *Revolt of the Haves*, 8, 18, 331;

Bennett, *Leviathan*, 81; Benjamin Page and Robert Shapiro, "Changes in Americans' Policy Preferences," *Political Science Quarterly* (1982): 38; Hibbs, *American Political Economy*, 128-33.

38. David Lowery and Lee Sigelman, "Understanding the Tax Revolt: Eight Explanations," *American Political Science Review* (1981): 963-74; David Broder, "The Puzzlement of Taxation," *Boston Globe*, 29 February 1979. Also Sears and Citrin, *Tax Revolt*, 208-15, 230-31; Kuttner, *Revolt of the Haves*, 164; Jack Citrin, Introduction, in Terry Schwadron, ed., *California and the American Tax Revolt* (Berkeley and Los Angeles, 1984), 16-17.

39. David R. Mayhew, *Placing Parties in American Politics* (Princeton, 1986), chap. 10. Mayhew found that strong partisan traditions were consistently related to small public economics between 1953 and 1980, although the relationship diminished to near zero over time.

40. Nevada voters passed a Proposition 13 clone as a constitutional initiative in 1978, but they rejected it in 1980 on the required second referendum. In the intervening year the legislature adopted a tax-reform and expenditure-limit measure.

41. Moreover, states in the traditional party/no initiative category that enacted limitation measures had lower readings on the Mayhew Traditional Party Organization scale than did the states that avoided cap laws. The three states that adopted property-levy limitations were Indiana, Louisiana, and New Mexico.

42. The median "tax burden" (state-local tax revenue as a percentage of personal income) among strong-party states where limitations were adopted was 11.6 percent and 12.2 percent where they were not. Among the weak-party states, the median tax burden among states that adopted limitations was 12.7 percent and 11.6 percent among states that did not. The tax burden among the six states where voters initiated property tax limitations (California et al.) was 12.9 percent.

The median percentage reduction in revenue dependence on local property taxes between FY 67 and FY 77 was -22 percent for all fifty states, but only -11.5 percent for the six Proposition 13-type states (California et al.), signifying that latter group had lagged in reforming property taxes.

43. Kuttner, *Revolt of the Haves*, chaps. 1-6; Sears and Citrin, *Tax Revolt*; Kaufman, "Inflation," 217-19; Winston W. Couch, J. Bollens, and S. Scott, *California Government and Politics* (Englewood Cliffs, N.J., 1981), esp. 234-35, 276-77; Adams, *Secret of the Tax Revolt*, chap. 6.

44. On proposition 2 1/2: Kuttner, *Revolt of the Haves*, 162-63, chap. 8; Tevdt, "Enough Is Enough"; Adams, *Secret of the Tax Revolt*, chap. 12; Lawrence Susskind and Cynthia Horan, "Proposition 2 1/2: The Response to Tax Restrictions in Massachusetts," *Proceedings* of the *Academy of Political Science* (1983), 57-71; Dennis Hale, "Massachusetts: William F. Weld and the End of Business as Usual," in Thad L. Beyle, ed., *Governors and Hard Times* (Washington, D.C., 1992).

45. Diana Dwyre, M. O'Gorman, J. Stonecash, and R. Young, "Disorganized Politics and the Have-Nots: Politics and Taxes in New York and California," *Polity* (1994): 29-32, 35-37; Adams, *Secrets of the Tax Revolt*, chap. 5.

46. Bennett S. Stark, "The Political Economy of State Public Finance: A Model of the Determinants of Revenue Policy: the Illinois Case, 1850-1970" (Ph.D. dissertation, University of Wisconsin, Madison, 1982); Samuel K. Gove and Louis H. Masotti, eds., *After Daley: Chicago Politics in Transition* (Urbana, Ill. 1981), esp. chapters by Gove and Milton Rakove; Kuttner, *Revolt of the Haves*, 300-301; *New York Times*, 8 March 1979; Joan A. Parker, *The Illinois Tax Increase of 1983: Summit and Resolution* (Springfield, Ill., 1984), 10-12.

47. Dwyre, "Disorganized Politics," 44-46. George Break, "Proposition 13's Tenth Birthday," in Frederick D. Stocker, ed., *Proposition 13: A Ten-Year Retrospective* (Cambridge, Mass., 1991), 191-93, discounted a major shift toward regressivity in California.

48. Suskind, "Proposition 2 1/2," 160-63; Division of Local Services, Massachusetts Department of Revenue, *City and Town* (November 1994), 4, and (December 1993), 6.

49. Rodney T. Smith, "Local Fiscal Arrangements, Home Rule, and California's Fiscal Constitution After Proposition 13," in Stocker, *Proposition 13*, 79–80; Arthur O'Sullivan, Terri A. Sexton, and Steven M. Sheffrin, *Property Taxes and Tax Revolts: The Legacy of Proposition 13* (New York, 1995), 115, 137; Schwadron, *California and the American Tax Revolt*, 80.

50. See the essays by Richard W. Gable on California and Dennis Hall on Massachusetts in Beyle, *Governors and Hard Times*, and the chapters by Jeffrey I. Chapman on California and Bruce Wallin on Massachusetts in Steven D. Gold, ed., *The Fiscal Crisis of the States* (Washington, D.C., 1995).

51. Sears and Citrin, *Tax Revolt*, 41.

52. Campbell, *The Growth of American Government*, chap. 10.

53. Campbell, *The Growth of American Government*, 2–5, and *Federalism and Public Performance: Perspectives on American Political Development* (forthcoming) develops this typology.

# Contributors

BALLARD C. CAMPBELL is professor of history at Northeastern University in Boston. He is the author of *The Growth of American Government: Governance from the Cleveland Era to the Present* (1995) and *Federalism and Public Performance* (forthcoming).

JOSEPH HINCHLIFFE is a doctoral candidate in political science at the University of Illinois at Urbana-Champaign. His dissertation research is on public opinion and bureaucratic policymaking.

J. DAVID HOEVELER is professor of history at the University of Wisconsin – Milwaukee. His most recent book is *The Postmodernist Turn: American Thought and Culture in the 1970s*.

SIDNEY M. MILKIS is professor and chair of the Department of Politics at Brandeis University. He is the author of *The President and the Parties: The Transformation of the American Party System Since the New Deal*, and coauthor of *The Politics of Regulatory Change: A Tale of Two Cities*, and *The American Presidency: Origins and Development*.

ALICE O'CONNOR is assistant professor of history at the University of California, Santa Barbara. She has written about urban and social welfare policy, and is completing a book on the poor in social science and federal government policy since the 1920s.

PAUL J. QUIRK is a professor in the Department of Political Science and the Institute of Government and Public Affairs at the University of Illinois at Urbana-Champaign. He has published widely on the presidency and public policymaking in U.S. national government.

DAVID BRIAN ROBERTSON is associate professor of political science at the University of Missouri, St. Louis. He has recently completed a manuscript titled *Capital, Labor and State: The Battle for American Labor Market Policy from the Civil War to the New Deal*.

JOHN T. WOOLLEY is professor of political science at the University of California, Santa Barbara. He is currently completing manuscripts on the politics of monetary policy and on the place of values in environmental restoration.